"It's true, as we are often reminded by cynics of the sport, that baseball is a business – and every day when free agency is rampant and players go to the highest bidder, the business of baseball cannot be denied. But if that's the beginning and the end of one's understanding of the world's greatest game, it reveals an elementary ignorance of something so uniquely American that our national experience cannot be understood independent of it…but what we cherish about the game, its beauty, poetry, and nuances, are, in the end, what separates the business of baseball from the game of baseball.

"We may be indifferent to the first reality but we hold to the second as surely as we cling to any fundamental essential in the American character; for it defines us and elevates us to a level higher than what is otherwise the commonplace of our existence."

— George Mitrovich, *Elysian Fields Quarterly: The Baseball Review*, Volume 22, Number 1, 2005

"His versatility was exceeded only by his passion; and, lucky for us one of those passions was baseball. In reading George's Baseball Notes you could be sure of one thing – George was often wrong but never in doubt and he provided a daily source of information, insight, and informed opinion. We miss him and his Baseball Notes very much."

—Larry Lucchino, Boston Red Sox President/CEO Emeritus

George Mitrovich's Baseball Notes

The Informed Opinions of an Elegant Gentleman

by
George Mitrovich

edited by
Tim Peeler

Redhawk Publications
The Catawba Valley Community College Press
2550 US Hwy 70 SE
Hickory NC 28602

ISBN: 978-1-952485-84-8
Library of Congress Control Number: 2022943216

Printed in the United States of America

First Printing

Table of Contents

Tributes

My Friend George Mitrovich

"DC" Boomed the voice on the other end of the telephone…."I need you in Chicago. Dr. Charles can't make it, you will be terrific!!!" Well let's face it, we both knew that I wasn't an adequate substitute for the great Dr. Charles Steinberg of the Boston Red Sox and yet George knew my response: "Of Course"….

"DC" Boomed the voice on the other end of the telephone… – "I need you in San Diego – All Star Game Luncheon – Peter Gammons had to cancel – You will be terrific!!!" And yet again, we both knew that I wasn't an adequate substitute for the great Peter Gammons and yet George also knew my response…

"Of Course"

"DC" ….long unusual pause…. "DC" ….this time with a low volume… "I want you to be a eulogist. The outcome is dire but I am resolute." And with that and a tear in my eye, we both knew my response.

I met George Mitrovich through the Great Fenway Park Writers Series. His ability to host, entertain, regale stories of his life and make everyone in the room feel included and important was uncanny. An elegant gentleman with a zest for life and for the people he met along the way, the likes of which we shall not soon see again. I thank him for his friendship, for the friends I met through him, and the friends of friends who are now also my friends. With great admiration, your friend, DC
—Donna Cohen, Great Fenway Park Writers Series

In tribute to our friend, George Mitrovich (1935-2019)

A man of surpassing intellect, opinions, passions and pursuits, including but hardly limited to the vagaries of politics, civics and, of course, baseball, George Mitrovich was an immutable force in San Diego's civic fabric for more than a half-century and perhaps longer.

Mr. Mitrovich died July 24, 2019, at age 83, days before he was to turn 84.

A native San Diegan, George was a proud graduate of Helix High, where he competed in baseball and basketball. He earned his undergraduate degree from Pasadena College, which later became Point Loma Nazarene University in San Diego. In 2007, the institution awarded him an honorary doctorate in Humane Letters.

Among countless civic-minded credentials, achievements and accolades, many self-proclaimed in his endearing style of talking about himself, George might have been most proud of his own lengthy career as a ballplayer.

Indeed, unwilling as he was to willingly yield to time's inexorable toll, he played and often served as a player/manager for several decades with the Marston Mets of the San Diego Adult Baseball League (SDABL), 45 and over division.

Let the record show: The Mets won league titles in 2004, 2010, 2012, and 2013.
Aside from baseball, which George rightly viewed as analogous to life itself, he was a whirlwind of interests and expertise on innumerable topics that freely entered his every-day conversations at the slightest provocation.

His was a world without limits on whatever he deemed intellectually stimulating and worthy of impassioned dialogue and further discussion, his sharp wit and high-pitched laugh never far behind.

George with Robert Kennedy.

A life-long Democrat who prided himself on his reasoned outlook and who valued respectful give-and-take with friends who might inexplicably hold opposing views, George earned his political stripes with several national figures, led by his role as press aide to the presidential campaign of 1968 of Senator Robert F. Kennedy.

He subsequently served as press secretary to Senator Charles E. Goodell (R-NY), whose son Roger went on to become NFL Commissioner; and Senator Harold E. Hughes, Democrat of Iowa. In addition, he worked for two members of the United States House of Representatives.

His close connections in Washington and elsewhere were legendary, extending from political to sports to literature and beyond. It seemed as if he knew everyone who was anyone, not only in San Diego but everywhere else his travels took him.

When our friend George said he "knew" someone, it was doubtless true, despite his forgivable tendency to drop more than a few names along the way.

Recently, he was fond of pointing out that two of the current Democratic presidential candidates, former Vice President Joe Biden and former Colorado governor John Hickenlooper, were personal friends of long standing. Indeed, they were.

Above all, he was a crusader for the enduring tenets of democracy, civility and kindness, given freely to friends and strangers alike. His self-selected slogan for the City Club, the San Diego-based forum he founded in 1975 that over the decades attracted hundreds, perhaps thousands of prominent speakers, was "Dedicated to the Dialogue of Democracy."

He also served as the driving force for three other similar non-profit public forums that he personally founded and hosted, in Denver (since 1985), the Great Washington D.C. Writers Series, and also the Great Fenway Park Writers Series in Boston, where he was designated as a national ambassador for the Boston Red Sox, World Series champions in 2018. The forum stands as the only on-going literary program ever sponsored by a professional sports team.

George also chaired the Red Sox's annual birthday tribute to Jackie Robinson. Over more than 40 years, he presented more than 2,000 public forums, an average of some 50 every year.

It was in his Red Sox role that he proudly showed off his diamond-laded 2018 World Series ring to dozens of Alaska Airlines flight attendants, who then were treated to a personal VIP walking tour, and even a game if schedules permitted, at fabled Fenway Park.

A United Methodist layman, he preached in some of America's leading churches, including Washington's National Cathedral and Highland Park United Methodist in Dallas.

In addition to public speaking, George wrote extensively for numerous major publications, including The New York Times, Boston Globe, Toronto Globe and Mail, Baltimore Sun, San Diego Union Tribune, Denver Post, and Los Angeles Times, as well as faith-based magazines.

His almost-daily Facebook posts, written under the unfettered title "Baseball Notes," drew a national following in the thousands, including many of the game's top executives and media hosts such as ESPN's Tony Kornheiser.

Throughout his life, George served on dozens of public boards and commissions that helped reshape San Diego, most notably as chairman of the Committee on Charter Reform, whose proposal for changing city government from council manager to mayor council was adopted by voters in 2004.

In addition, he chaired the Committee of 2000, a citizens group that successfully supported the building of Petco Park, the city's downtown ballpark. The measure passed with nearly 60 percent of the vote.

Despite medical issues that entered his recent years, George continued at his indefatigable pace, hardly slowing down until his final weeks and days.

As if offering up printed evidence of that life force could fully capture his essence, so familiar to his many friends for so many years, consider what George wrote about himself last year: "I am 83. I dare anyone, anyone, to tell me I'm too old to be running four public forums in four different American cities; too old to keep up with six emails; too old to write, on average, 1,500 words a day; too old to grocery shop and plan dinners most nights; too old to be as active as I am — which is mostly the same degree of activity I had twenty or forty years ago."

—John Freeman, San Diego, Author of Ted Talks: Uncle Teddy's Fond Memories, Crazy Stories and Heartfelt Reflections

George and daughter Carolyn on beach.

Preface

There is no doubt that George Mitrovich possessed radical empathy, a term occasionally used in the literary world to reference an author's unique and powerful ability to understand and to care about his or her characters. How else to explain the Mitrovich Moment, when some fortunate person or persons happened upon George Sherman Mitrovich during the course of his every day comings and goings. Ask the many flight attendants and pilots who watched Red Sox games from a luxury box during a stopover. Ask the foreign student who waited on us at breakfast in Boston about the personal tour of the US Senate that George arranged for her while we waited on our check. Ask the cab drivers and bell men, persons sitting in adjacent airline seats, people standing in lines with him most anywhere, whose stories he engaged with great interest, whose lives were as important to him as the writers, celebrities, sports stars, and politicians who spoke at the three public forums he managed. Ask the many many people who had their pictures made wearing George's Red Sox World Series rings, thereby joining the Fellowship of the World Series Ring. Ask me: a third level academic with a quixotic interest in baseball poetry who ended up speaking at a first rate writers' series and attending a Red Sox-Yankees game, the very game in which Alex Rodriguez returned from his steroid suspension.

For me, it began with the Baseball Notes. My publisher had sent a copy of my second book of baseball poems to George. He would occasionally use one of the poems as the Quote of the Day at the end of his notes. When one of his readers, the legendary sports broadcaster Dick Enberg responded favorably to the poems, George decided to bring me in for a reading at the Great Fenway Park Writers Series. That was in 2013. It was an ultimate Mitrovich Moment. I had the time of my life, got to meet Peter Gammons on the field before the game, watched and heard Dick Flavin recite an ode to the history of the Red Sox to a tour group atop the Green Monster, and met many fine people at the writers' series, in the press box, and in the Red Sox offices. George and I hit it off and continued to correspond via email and phone in the years that followed.

And now let me relate my really ultimate Mitrovich Moment, one that only George could or would have pulled off. The night before the luncheon where I would speak at the Hotel Commonwealth, I had given George a copy of my first book of baseball poems, Touching All the Bases, a volume that had been published thirteen years before. When I met him the next morning, after what had been a late night for me, he told me that he had read the entire book. Touching All the Bases contains an introduction that my father, a Lutheran minister, had written. In it he relates his enthusiasm for baseball that he traces back to his childhood on a rural farm in the Piedmont area of Western North Carolina. He speaks of how that enthusiasm lives on in my work and through the hopes he holds for my children and future generations. It is a very heartfelt piece, and when George introduced me that day, he did so by reading my dad's words in their entirety. It was like the scene in Field of Dreams where Ray Kinsella encounters his father in the cornfield stadium. Dad had died eight years before, and I had not thought of his introductory essay in a long time. But that day, it was as if he spoke it through George; it was as if that Rowan County farm boy who loved baseball so much that he would listen to games on the radio that the neighbors kept in their milk barn, was in the room. I was so emotional that it was all I could do to get up and read my poems. Thanks always—for that moment—George.

In early 2016 I was working on my third book of baseball poems, *Wild in the Strike Zone*, and began sending them to George to use in his Notes. He obliged not only by doing so, but with the kind of enthusiasm that a poet rarely gets to enjoy. He was my biggest cheerleader, if not indeed the Muse for the baseball poems that I continued to write each of the following years for his Baseball Notes. After George passed, I had first considered doing a collection of the poems that he chose to use for his Notes. But I think they belong here with the Notes, the man, and the voice that inspired them to be written.

George Mitrovich's *Baseball Notes* are a love letter to the game and to the people who were lucky enough to receive them almost daily via email, phone, or Facebook. They were a massive, early morning undertaking by a man who had endless intellectual curiosity and a passion for the game that he still played in an adult league, nearly to the end. Mitrovich was also passionate about civil discourse which he fostered in the three forums he was a part of: City Club in his home town of San Diego; the Denver Forum, and of course; The Great Fenway Park Writers Series in Boston, where he was the official ambassador for the Red Sox. His Baseball Notes reveal him to be a man of ideas and will, faith, and extraordinarily high standards. I would challenge anyone to find a bigger fan or a harsher critic of the teams he supported. As you will see, he had definite opinions about the game, how it should be played, and the importance of its place in American history. He loved the nuances and the rhythm of the game, as well as its unpredictable nature.

It is not likely that you will encounter another prose stylist more earnest about his topic. If you were fortunate enough to know George, you will hear his voice in these pages. Even if you did not know him.

You will hear it. You cannot "not" hear someone who is this present, and so much, still with us.
At the beginning of his last half year of NOTES, George lamented:

> "THIS IS MY EIGHTH YEAR OF DOING NOTES. In the past seven years, I've written more than 750,000 words, which equates to approximately 3,000 pages, or in book form would amount to six volumes of 500 pages of Baseball Notes.
>
> No publisher is publishing six volumes, unless it's a vanity press, and I lack the means to create my own publishing house. But, if I would if I could, because, as Tony Kornheiser says, 'Mitrovich's Baseball Notes are great.'"

I agree that a volume of that length with its thousands of potential permissions would be a nearly impossible undertaking. Nevertheless, here we are with this much abridged edition, a vessel that can barely contain his passion, his charisma, his belief, and his abundant zest for life.

Tim Peeler
July 2021

2016

BASEBALL NOTES – MONDAY, APRIL 4

SINCE I HAVE LONG RUED PITCH COUNTS, NORM CHAD'S COLUMN IN TODAY'S WASHINGTON POST CAUGHT MY EYE.

And, since I don't think I can improve upon it, nor am I inclined to try, as I am currently flying home from my weekend preaching/speaking assignment in St. Petersburg, Florida, I will just share Mr. Chad's brilliant insights, while asking a question:

Why is Norm Chad of the *Washington Post* so much smarter than the people in baseball ops at the Washington Nationals?

Ponder that as you read his well-documented column:

"Chicago Cubs ace Jake Arrieta pitched 229 regular season innings last year. Then a couple of his postseason starts were substandard; conventional wisdom says his arm was tired, so this season he will be limited to six or seven innings in many starts to stay fresh.

"Ooh — 229 innings!

"I'm surprised Arrieta didn't file a workman's comp claim at season's end.

"I'm confused — to be honest, this has become a perpetual state — in regard to the current trend toward 'pitch count' and 'innings limits.'

"The pitcher's mound has been 60 feet 6 inches away from home plate since 1893. Athletes today are bigger, stronger and faster than in generations past, because of human evolution, improved nutrition and superior training methods.

"So how come 50 years ago pitchers could start every fourth day and throw 250 innings a year and now they start every fifth day and seldom reach 200 innings?

"What I'm told is that we've discovered that one-inning relief pitchers can be more effective than tiring starters, plus we now know more about how to maintain pitchers' arm health better.

"Fiddlesticks.

"Uh, how come Cy Young — yeah, that Cy Young — threw at least 320 innings 15 straight seasons, until he was 38 years old? He was pitching doubleheaders, then going home and throwing a complete game on Wii baseball.

"Young finished his career with 7,356 innings in the books; at his current pace, the Washington Nationals' Stephen Strasburg would have to live until he was 137 to reach that total.

"So, you say, Cy Young was an anomaly, an overly ambitious uber-achiever whose only goal in life was to have an award named after him.

"Well, how about these fellas:

• Walter Johnson pitched at least 290 innings 11 straight seasons (1909-19). His arm was so worn out, in 1924 — at age 36 — he threw 277 innings, with a 2.72 ERA, 23-7 record and 1.12 WHIP.

• Grover Alexander pitched at least 300 innings the first seven seasons of his career (1911-17). His arm was so worn out, in 1927 — at age 40 — he threw 268 innings, with a 2.52 ERA, 21-10 record and 1.12 WHIP.

• Warren Spahn pitched at least 245 innings 17 straight seasons (1947-63). His arm was so worn out, in 1963 — at age 42 — he threw 259 innings, with a 2.60 ERA, 23-7 record and 1.12 WHIP.

• Don Sutton pitched at least 200 innings the first 15 seasons of his career (1966-80). His arm was so worn out, in 1982 — at age 37 — he threw 249 innings, with a 3.06 ERA, 17-9 record and 1.15 WHIP.

• Steve Carlton pitched at least 230 innings 13 straight seasons (1968-80). His arm was so worn out, in 1982 – at age 37 – he threw 295 innings, with a 3.10 ERA, 23-11 record and 1.15 WHIP.

"Ah, but nowadays starting pitchers are delicate flowers, opera divas speaking at a whisper until the curtain goes up. Pitch counts are treated with the gravity of electrocardiogram readings.

"Did Dostoyevsky have a word count?

"Did Rembrandt have a brushstroke count?

"Did Genghis Khan have a conquered-territory count?

"Trust me, being an MLB pitcher is not as difficult as, say, being a U.S. president. That's a seven-day-a-week job (minus an occasional round of golf).

"Do you see POTUSes on a bills limit or a vetoes limit? No. They're signing legislation, nominating justices, meeting prime ministers around the clock (minus an occasional round of golf).

"You're telling me a 21st-century pitcher can't pitch 250 innings? Heck, he only works half the year. And the half a year he's working, most of the time he's sitting in the bullpen spitting out sunflower seeds.

"I say: You pitch until your arm falls off! And that's just an expression — your arm is not going to fall off. But if it does, you've got another arm."

Good stuff. A hanging chad Norman Chad is not.

EIGHT SPORTS WRITERS & COLUMNISTS FOR THE SAN DIEGO UNION TRIBUNE went on-the-record today with their winners this '16 baseball season.

All eight picked the Giants in the NL West and the Cubs in the NL Central. Five of the eight picked the Metropolitans in the NL East.

In the AL West, four picked the Rangers, three the Astros, and one LAA. In the AL Central, seven picked KC and one the Indians. In the AL East, there was a four-way split between the Blue Jays and Red Sox.

As to the winner of the World Series, four picked San Francisco, two picked the Cubs, while the Rangers and Nationals got one vote each.

OH, THE RED SOX ARE SITTING PABLO SANDOVAL IN FAVOR OF TRAVIS SHAW AS THEIR THIRD BASEMAN, which prompted Tom Clavin, who wrote that wonderful book on the DiMaggio brothers, to send me the following email:

"Interesting about BoSox benching Sandoval in favor of Shaw, who you championed last season."

Yes I did, as well as Eduardo Rodriquez.

Both before the Red Sox saw the light.

QUOTE OF THE DAY:

“Billions of dollars were infused into baseball coffers. But when the rights fee become so large that cable carriers are unable to pass along the charges to subscribers, the electronic spigot is turned off. Such is the case with the Los Angeles Dodgers’ ill-advised grab for gold with Time Warner cable, in which some 70 percent of the team’s home market could not receive the new regional sports network’s games because area cable carriers were unwilling to charge $5 to subscribers to offset the fees TWC had demanded.” – “Baseball’s Game Changers” by George Castle (Lyons Press)

George with President Joe Biden.

BASEBALL NOTES – April 7, 2016

THE PADRES' GREATEST FEAR AT SEASON'S START WAS A BAD START.

Well, fear became reality last night as the Gas Lamp Gang opened with three straight losses to LAD: 15-0, 8-0, and 7-0. Thus was set a new MLB record: No team in the game's history had ever before opened a season by being scoreless in its first three games.

	R	H	E
Los Angeles Dodgers	30	34	1
San Diego Padres	0	13	3

What Padre fans saw last night at Petco is what Padre fans have seen too many times from Andrew Cashner, another woeful performance, allowing four runs to LAD in the top of the 1st, which effectively was the ball game.

The Padres are off to Denver and a three game weekend series with the Rockies.

Colorado is not the Dodgers, so hope is born anew.

THE PADRES PLAYED GAMES TWO AND THREE VS. LAD AT PETCO PARK in brown and yellow and in camouflage blue and white jerseys. So losing three straight was bad enough, but losing three straight in brown and test pattern blue tops compounded my misery.

I love Ron Fowler and the Brothers Seidlers, but the PCL Padre teams I grew up with wore red, white and blue, red and white, pin stripe blue and white, and one year black and orange. They never, ever wore brown and yellow.

Brown and yellow came into play because then owner Arnholt Smith, the convicted bank swindler, loved the color brown. Reason sufficient never to dress our boys in brown again.

I know uniforms; yes, I do.

I am friends with Peter Capolino at Mitchell & Ness in Philly and Jerry Cohen at Ebbets Field in Seattle, the two creative geniuses who started the whole authentic throwback jersey business.

I own more than 50 of their authentic minor and major league jerseys, jackets and hats, and I regularly promote both Ebbets Field and Mitchell & Ness because their work is absolutely superb; and I've looked at every minor and major league uniform ever worn by any team in any league in any year at any level of pro ball, and outside of the St. Louis Browns, brown has never been the color of choice – and, in the case of the Browns, they were smart enough to outline their brown jerseys, jackets and hats with orange.

I have argued, often, that in San Diego, the USA's most patriotic city, red, white and blue should be the colors of the home town Padres, not brown and yellow.

Okay, what about the unies the Padres wore Opening Game, white and blue with yellow trim? Nice, if you like UCLA or Cal Berkeley; but still, why not red, white and blue?

(In the photos below you see Ms. Ashley Duck, in four Ebbets Field vintage PCL Padres retro jerseys. You do not see brown.)

I have lost this argument (you think?); so this is it, the end of my uniform rant.

Just play ball. And, in the Padres case, win one or two and score some runs at Coors.

Projected weather for the series: 49, Friday; 42 Saturday, and 44 Sunday, with clouds and some sun.

THE STORY IN COLORADO IS TULO'S SUCCESSOR AT SHORT, TREVOR STORY.

Three games into 2016 Trevor has four HRs and seven RBIs, as the Rockies won two of three from the D-Backs and are at Coors Friday, as noted, for their home opener vs. the Padres.

No player in the modern era has ever hit four HRs in their first three games. Story just did.

Two other Rockies homered in the 4-3 win over Arizona at Chase, JD LeMahieu and Ryan Raburn.

Colorado got a superb pitching performance from Tyler Chatwood, who, in his first game since 2014, went 6 1/3, yielded one earned run, walked none, struck out three.

AT PNC IN PITTSBURGH THE PIRATES WON OVER ST. LOUIS, sweeping all three games played between two teams with MLB's best records in '15.

Someone named Jeremy Hazelbaker hit a HR for the Cards in their 5-1 loss.

Is "Hazelbaker" destined to become a household name?

Maybe.

AT PROGRESSIVE IN CLEVELAND, BEFORE 10,298, the Indians beat Boston, 7-6.

As games go, this was a good one, despite the fact the game winning HR was hit by, oh how I hate to write this, Mike Napoli, ex of the Red Sox; the $60 million 6 year man, who hit all of .207 last season while at Fenway, before the Sox got smart and brought Travis Shaw up from Pawtucket and sent Napoli to Texas.

The Sox hit three HRs of their own in the cold at Cleveland – Brock Holt, Hanley Ramirez, and Big Papi, who sent his 505th HR into the right field seats in the 6th inning.

If 2016 is Clay Buchholz's redemption year, last night's outing was hardly impressive, as Bucchholz gave up five runs on six hits in four dismal innings.

I don't think Dave Dumbrowski reads Notes, but if not, would someone please tell him to trade for James Shields of the Padres. Shields can help the Sox and the Sox have players who can help the Padres.

It would be a win/win for both teams.

THE YANKEES SCORED SIX IN THE FIRST VS. THE ASTROS IN THE BRONX, and went on to win, 16-6, while banging out 17 hits, including four by Starlin Castro, the ex-Cubs shortstop, but now NY's 2nd baseman.

Didi Gregorius, the Yankees shortstop, had three hits. Thus the New Yorkers' double play combo had seven hits between them. Nice.

ONE OTHER GAME NOTE, ROBINSON CANO OF THE MARINERS, hit two HRs in Seattle's 9-5 win over Texas, and now has four to open the new season.

Look for this to become Cano's comeback year, becoming the player he was for NYY.

QUOTE OF THE DAY:

This poem, "Where the Game Waited," is from Tim Peeler, the Poet Laureate of the Carolinas:

I lay my head against the back seat window of that Buick Regal,
Dad's first air-conditioned car
as we rode through heat lightning
summer evenings toward the Denver ball park.

The whole world vibrated for twenty miles
down sixteen south, and I counted
the number of the people I knew,
trying hard as I could to escape myself.

But mornings I woke up as me every time,
a cotton topped preacher's kid
in love with top forty tunes
and batting practice swings.

The little guys always sat in the backseat
where I lay my head, chocked full of belief,
against the easy miles
to where the game waited.

I love Tim Peeler.

BASEBALL NOTES – APRIL 25, 2016

BILL SHAIKIN, WHO WRITES ABOUT BASEBALL FOR THE LA TIMES, led his Sunday column with a terrific idea, have Vince Scully call the All-Star Game in San Diego this July.

I do not know whether that can happen, but Commissioner Rob Manfred and Fox Sports should explore making it happen.

Joe Buck, who is Fox's guy in the booth for the All-Star Game, wants it to happen, calling Scully "the greatest ever."

I have an additional suggestion:

Have Scully do the first three innings, and the second greatest baseball broadcaster ever, Dick Enberg, also retiring, call the next three, and Buck to take it the rest of the way.

George with Dick Enberg, son Tim Mitrovich, and granddaughter Juliette Mitrovich.

Now, that would make this year's Mid-Summer Classic, one for the ages, no matter what happens on the field.

OF THE 15 GAMES PLAYED FRIDAY NIGHT, ONLY FIVE TEAMS, Toronto, NYY, LAA, SF, and Colorado, outdrew the 30,074 fans who watched the Padres beat the Cardinals at Petco, 4-1.

The Nationals, one of the two best teams in the majors, drew only 27,864 to their DC ballpark on a 68 degrees Friday evening.

The Washington, DC, metropolitan area is one of the wealthiest in the world, so why so few fans at Nationals Park?

Especially, when All-World Bryce Harper's in the lineup.

SPEAKING OF HARPER: CHARLES KRAUTHAMMER OF THE WASHINGTON POST, a conservative columnist, very, got off politics last week to write about All-World, saying Harper's the second coming of Mickey Mantle.

Which led me to compare Mantle and Harper's first four years (with an assist from Baseball Almanac).

In his four years with the Yankees, 1951-54, Mantle had 561 base hits in 1,894 ABs, for a .296 average. He hit 84 HRs, drove in 321, and scored 389 runs.

Harper in his four years, 2012-15, has 528 base hits in 1,830 ABs, for a .289 average. He's hit 98 HRs, driven in 248, and scored 328 runs.

Given that Harper lost part of the '14 season to injury, it's clear Mantle and Harper belong in the same conversation.

It's also clear, Krauthammer is better on baseball than politics; the kind of guy you would be happy to hang out with at a game, as long as neither trump/Cruz or Clinton/Sanders came up.

IT TOOK 16-INNINGS AT MINUTE MAID FOR BOSTON TO BEAT HOUSTON, 7-5, IN ESPN's SUNDAY NIGHT GAME.

It was 5-3 Red Sox in the bottom of the 9th and Craig Kimbrel was on the mound with two outs, when Carlos Correa doubled to right field.

He was followed by Colby Rasmussen, who had hit a grand slam against the Sox Saturday, and once again went deep to right center field and a 5-3 win became a 5-5 tie, and the game played on, mercifully ending in the 16th, as the clock ticked past midnight.

The star of the game for Boston was Richard Heath Hembree of Spartanburg, South Carolina, who threw three scoreless innings in relief for the Sox, and received in return his third major league victory against no losses.

With the win the Sox won the three game series from the Astros, which fell to 6-13 for '16 as Boston is even at 9 after 18 games.

The Red Sox are in Atlanta for two, back at Fenway Wednesday night for two more vs. the Braves, before welcoming the Yankees to 4 Yawkey Way Friday night.

SPEAKING OF THE YANKEES, THEY LOST YESTERDAY TO TAMPA BAY AT THE STADIUM, 8-1.

Someone named Steven Souza Jr. hit two HRs on his birthday, as the Rays collectively hit five in the game for the win.

However, NYY won the three game series, with wins Friday night and Saturday afternoon, 6-3 and 3-2.

Jacoby Ellsbury stole home Friday night and Brett Gardner hit a walk off in Saturday's day game to insure a series win.

But even by taking two of three from Tampa Bay, NYY is only 7-10 for the season.

They are in Texas vs. Rangers tonight through Wednesday before Boston and the Sox Friday.

THE CHICAGO WHITE SOX SWEPT THEIR SERIES WITH TEXAS AND NOW HAVE THE BEST RECORD IN THE AL, 13-6.

Yesterday they won 4-1 behind Matt Latos, who is now 4-0 on the season, and his ERA is 0.74.

The two Chicago teams, north and south, are 27-11 for '16.

LAD PAID A LOT OF MONEY TO SIGN KENTA MAEDA, and, it appears early in this '16 season, they invested wisely.

Maeda is 3-0 on the year, picking up his 3rd win Saturday in Denver, as he held the Rockies scoreless through 6.1 innings at Coors Field.

Shall I repeat that?

He held the Rockies scoreless through 6.1 innings at Coors Field.

When you can do that vs. Colorado, a team with Carlos "Gargo" Gonzalez, Nolan Arenado, and

Trevor Story in the lineup, you have done something, my boy.

Oh, Maeda's ERA is 0.36!

MY PAL,TALMAGE BOSTON, THE BIG TIME TEXAS ATTORNEY AND AUTHOR OF TWO BOOKS ON BASEBALL, is a huge fan of Clayton Kershaw, the Dodgers' ace, and took exception to my saying Jake Arrieta of the Cubs is the game's best; a claim I made in Notes following Arrieta's second no-hitter last week.

Talmage believes Kershaw is the game's best, and whoever is next best, ain't close to Clayton.

Tyler Kepner in his Sunday New York Times baseball column, writing about Arrieta since becoming a Northsiders for the Cubs in Chicago:

"In his last 19 regular-season starts, Arrieta is 16-1 with an 0.78 E.R.A. He has not allowed an earned run in 13 of those starts, and the only time he lost was when his opponent — Cole Hamels, then with Philadelphia — threw a no-hitter. Arrieta has also won the Cy Young Award, tossed a shutout in the National League wild-card game and no-hit the Los Angeles Dodgers in that span.

"As a Cub, he is 40-13 with a 2.17 E.R.A..."

But of Kershaw's greatness, there is no dispute.

QUOTE OF THE DAY:

Tim Peeler, the Poet Laureate of the Carolinas, sent me his latest, which he entitled, "Casey's Last At-Bat":

You live beyond the disturbing strikeouts,
beyond the boozy characters you are made of,
beyond the brawn you once became.

One day the sky is sincerely blue
and the field is excitingly green.
It is your temple familiar.

And you make your way
from the circle of preparation
to the rectangle of decision, one last time.

In a world set to sneak into a spotless century,
you dig in and wait
for eternity.

BASEBALL NOTES – MAY 4

JEFF SAMARDZIJA, THE FORMER NOTRE DAME ALL-AMERICAN WIDEOUT, was masterful last night, as he threw eight innings of three hit pitching, striking out nine as SF beat Cincy, 3-1.

His pitching was an act of redemption for all Fighting Irish fans, reeling from the announcement that Lou Holtz, the ex-football coach of this sacred institution of higher learning overseen by the Fathers of the Holy Cross, had endorsed Beelzebub for president.

Now, if I find that Samardzija, like Clay Buchholz and Tom Brady, has also endorsed Beelzebub, then I may have to change the ringtone on my I-Phone from the Notre Dame "Victory March" to "Fight On for 'ol SC."

Pray not.

MEANWHILE, THE RED SOX, FRESH FROM A SWEEP OF NYY, PLAYED THE OTHER SOX and lost, 4-1.

They did this before all of 15,025 fans on Chicago's Southside, as Jose Quintana was wonderful through eight, yielding but four hits, walking none, striking out nine.

Steven Wright was almost as good for the Red Sox, but not quite.

The Pale Hose now stand 19-8 for '16, a remarkable run thus far, and if it keeps up, one hopes Chicago fans will start showing up at U.S. Cellular Field, because at the moment the other team in town, the Cubs, are averaging 18,292 more fans per game than the White Sox.

Not good.

THE CUBS ALSO WON, AGAIN, BEATING THE PIRATES AT PNC, 7-1.

Jake Arrieta was Jake Arrieta brilliant again, as he won his sixth game, shutting down Pittsburgh through seven innings of two hit pitching.

From his six day a week regime of Pilates, it could be said that Jake "Pilated" the Pirates at PNC Park (that should get a "like" on Facebook from Dr. Jennifer Bender, Boston's leading leader on Pilates).

The Northsiders are now 19-6.

So it has come to pass in Kelsey Grammar's fictional "The Boss" Chicago that its two Major League Baseball teams are collectively 38-14 for '14.

Oh, my, but nothing "fictional" about that.

THE PADRES WON AGAIN OVER THE ROCKIES, 5-2, AND HIT TWO HRs, as Matt Kemp hit his eighth of the year and Brett Wallace his first.

The Bearded One, Andrew Cashner, did not pitch great but came away with the win; only fair given the many times he was the loser, while having pitched better.

The Padres bullpen was strong again last night, as Mauer and Rodney faced six batters in the 8th and 9th, striking out four of them.

The Padres go for the sweep vs. Colorado in the sunlight at Petco today, before welcoming the mighty Metropolitans of Queens, NY, Thursday night.

IN JUSTIN TRUDEAU'S CANADA, THE BLUE JAYS BEAT TEXAS, 3-1, AS JUSTIN SMOAK hit a game tying HR in the bottom of the 9th and then hit the game winner with a walk-off HR in the 10th at the Rogers Centre.

A big win for the AL East champions, who have had their struggles thus far, but remain formidable in the pennant chase.

QUOTE OF THE DAY:

THE GREAT CAROLINA POET, TIM PEELER, has gifted us with more of his artistry:

THE IMMORTAL
For the late Dick Stoll
A little guy from Ohio,
Who pitched fine but briefly,
Then married better and stayed,
The way they often did

Just after the war
When the parks refilled
With fans and hope and pride,
Winning on every side,

So that if you played it right
And remembered it well,
Your story and theirs;
When the time arrived to tell.

You became immortal.

BASEBALL NOTES – MAY 5

THE CUBS, NATIONALS, AND METROPOLITANS YESTERDAY SCORED 27 RUNS TO 4 for the Pirates, Royals, and Braves

The NL trio is 56-23 for the season and clearly dominates the Senior Circuit.

But will that hold?

Hey, it's why they play the game.

CLAY BUCHHOLZ, IN A DRAMATIC REVERSAL OF FORM, WON OVER THE PALE HOSE, 5-2, and the Red Sox slipped back into first place in the AL East, as the O's lost 7-0 to NYY at Camden.

It's hard to know what inspired Buchholz more, straight talk from his manager John Farrell or donald trump winning Indiana, but whatever the inspiration, he pitched well, only two runs on three hits in seven innings.

If this is the Buchholz we witnessed going forward, the Sox are a lock to win the AL East.

THE UP THE DOWN-STAIRCASE PADRES WERE DOWN AGAIN WEDNESDAY AT PETCO, losing to the Rockies, 2-0, their seventh shutout; which, over 162 games would result in 40 shutouts.

That would break the all-time record for the number of shutout losses in a season, currently held by the St. Louis Cardinals at 33 (1908).

The number of games played without being shutout, 208 by Cincinnati, the streak ending May 24, 2001 (source: Yahoo Sports).

The Padres lost because Tyler Chatwood pitched brilliantly for the Rockies, throwing eight scoreless innings and giving up only three hits. Great pitching wins most games. That's a truism, and yesterday in San Diego, in 47 degree wind chill weather, was again true, one more time (weather source: MBL AB).

Is Chatwood the real deal?

I think so.

THE MARINERS WON FOR THE 14TH TIME IN 19 GAMES, defeating the A's 9-8 at the Oakland Coliseum, sweeping the three game series and securing, for the moment, first place in the AL West.

Nelson Cruz homered once, his fifth; while Dae-Ho Lee homered twice, giving him four for '16 (how much fun would it be to have Shin-Soo Choo and Dae-Ho Lee in the same lineup).

Seattle won even though their ace, the great Felix Hernandez, gave up all eight runs and nine hits to the A's in four innings.

A shocking outing for King Felix, but the Mariners won.

THE NATIONALS WON IN KC BEFORE 38,610 ROYAL FANS, which I note because it was the biggest crowd in the majors yesterday.

The smallest, sorry to report, 8,766 in Cleveland.

Cy Young Award Winner Corey Kluber deserved better than a minor league crowd for his major league performance – nine innings of shutout pitching.

The Cy Young Award winner of '14 is back.

DAVE O'BRIEN, IN THE NESN BOOTH AT U.S. CELLULAR FIELD LAST NIGHT, was discussing Luke Appling, the legendary "Aches & Pains" White Sox shortstop, who, Dave said, hit a HR off Warren Spahn in an Old Timers' game when Appling was 75.

To which Steve Lyons, sitting in for Jerry Remy, actually said, "Yea, but they were throwing straight pitches"

Dave, sounding somewhat disbelieving at Lyons' response, said, "But he was 75!"

Lyons appeared to get it, because he then said, "That was awesome."

Yes it was.

THIS IS ANOTHER FROM THE POET OF THE CAROLINAS, TIM PEELER:

THE SIGNING OF HOYT WILHELM:

When Hoyt Wilhelm brought
His butterflies to Hickory,
Nobody had ever heard of him;

At the meeting in Hill's Café
Hubbell said "he's got
No curve ball, and he's
Surely got no fastball;
All he's got is that knuckle ball,"

But Sammy Bell, Duke grad
And Hickory manager
Who'd not only played
For the great Jack Coombs

But had also tried to hit
The Iredell farm boy's
Knuckle ball said, "Carl,"

Not Mr. Hubbell as
The Giants' chain of command
And surely his historical
Imminence might demand, but
He said, "Carl," in his cool Carolina drawl;

"It's all he needs."

BASEBALL NOTES – May 6

LAST NIGHT IN CARL SANDBURG'S CHICAGO, IN BALLPARKS AS DIFFERENT AS ADLAI EWING STEVENSON II & EVERETT McKINLEY DIRKSEN, four first place teams played one another – and it had never happened before in major league baseball history.

Let me repeat that: four first place teams played one another – and it had never happened before in major league baseball history.

On Chicago's North Side the Cubs beat the Nationals of Washington, 5-2, while on the South Side the Red Sox of Boston beat the White Sox, 7-3.

At Wrigley 37,564 watched the Cubs move to 21-6 for '16; while at U.S. Cellular 20,126 saw the Red Sox improve to 17-11.

The Nationals continue their series against the Cubs, while the Red Sox are in the Bronx tonight vs. the Yankees, and a repeat of last weekend's sweep of NYY at Fenway, is unlikely, but two out of three would be acceptable.

As for the Pale Hose, they remain in first place in the AL Central, and at home vs. the Twins.

Why MLB schedules both Chicago teams at home at the same time seems utterly ridiculous, and if I am in the ownership group of the White Sox, I think I probably hate that my team is playing woeful Minnesota in a half-empty ballpark while the Cubs are playing a first place team before SRO crowds.

The visuals for the Southsiders are not good. The PR is not good. The scheduling conflict is not good – and, yes, the word stupid comes to mind.

WHAT OCCURRED LAST NIGHT IN CHICAGO, FOUR FIRST PLACE TEAMS OPPOSING ONE ANOTHER FOR THE FIRST TIME IS NO SMALL DEAL.

True, to the great unwashed it may seem just that, a "small deal."

It's not.

Here's why:

In the whole of history no human activity has ever been as well documented as baseball, including the Bible.

If you think I'm wrong, then I invite you to reference the human activity more fully documented than America's Game.

A PITCHER NAMED COLIN REA OUT-PITCHED JACOB deGROM AND THE PADRES WON OVER THE METROPOLITANS AT PETCO PARK, 5-3.

Rea went eight stunning innings, gave up but three hits and one run, a Curtis Granderson HR to dead center field to lead off the 9th, which ended Rea's chance to throw a complete game, but no matter, the young man was terrific, and is now 3-1 on the early season.

The NYM/SD four game series continues tonight. San Diego is experiencing scattered thunder storms this morning, but they should clear by game time.

BY McCOVEY COVE AT AT&T LAST NIGHT NOLAN ARENADO & TREVOR STORY BOTH HOMERED AS THE ROCKIES BEAT THE GIANTS, 17-7.

For Arenado it was his 12th. For the rookie shortstop Story, his 11th. Both figures lead the MLB.

How great is it to have a third baseman and shortstop combine to hit 23 HRs and drive in 52, when your ball club has only played 28-games.

So if we do a Mitrovich Projection on the season for Arenado & Story you end up October 3 with Arenado hitting 70 HRs and Story 64, while driving in 164 and 140 respectfully, or together, 134 HRs and 304 RBIs.

Nice.

AT TORONTO'S ROGERS CENTRE THE BLUE JAYS HAMMERED TEXAS, 12-2, as Edwin Encarnacion hit his 5th HR and drove in six, more than enough for A.J. Happ, who went seven strong innings to win his fourth against no losses.

IN NOTES YESTERDAY I REFERENCED CLEVELAND'S ATTENDANCE Wednesday night at Progressive Field, which was 8,766.

Last Sunday in Dayton, the Dragons of the Single A Midwest League, drew 8,202, or only 564 fans fewer than the major league Indians.

With that game the Dayton team, whose principal owner is Greg Rosenbaum, had their 1,133rd consecutive game sellout, a one of a kind record in professional sport's history – 1,133.

Astounding!

QUOTE OF THE DAY:

MY FAVORITE AMERICAN POET, TIM PEELER, IS BACK WITH ANOTHER GIFT:

HOW TO GET TO HEAVEN:

My dad's magical thinking
Transported him beyond reality.
He believed his sons would
Be major leaguers, and that
Having not worked out,
He believed his grandsons
Would be major leaguers;

Then he eventually believed
That he might just have been
A major leaguer at some point,
About the same time he became
Convinced that someone
Had moved him to the wrong house
During the middle of the night
And had carefully placed
All his furniture where it was
When we sat and talked about it,

And he also believed when
He called me at three in the morning
That if I left my house immediately
And came over to his to transcribe
His life story that his chances
Of being elected to the hall of fame

In honor of his major league
Pitching career might be improved
So I drove forthwith and arrived
With an ink pen and notebook,
After which I sat and he began,

I was born on a dirt farm
Next to a muddy creek
In rural Rowan County,

And I wrote it down
As outside I could hear
The roar of the crickets
And inside I could hear
The buzz of the fluorescent light.

BASEBALL NOTES – MAY 9

SATURDAY NIGHT BEFORE 41,028 AT PETCO PARK, THE METS' BARTOLO COLON CAME TO BAT FOR THE 227TH TIME IN HIS MAJOR LEAGUE CAREER, having never hit a HR.

What happened next was described by the Mets' play-by-play broadcaster; described in a voice that, on an octave scale of one to eight, was an eight:

"He drives one, deep left field, back goes Upton, back near the wall, Bartolo has done it! The impossible has happened! This is one of the greatest moments in the history of baseball."

"Greatest moments?"

No, not close, but a great moment for Bartolo – The Fans' Favorite.

It was 14-years ago when I suggested to Larry Lucchino the Red Sox sign Bartolo, who was done in Montreal. That didn't happen, but the big man has gone on to win 146 games and a Cy Young since at various stops along the way – Chicago (AL), LAA, NYY, Oakland, and yes, Boston, finally in 2008 (he was 4-2).

My man Bartolo, who made, according to Keith Hernandez in the Mets' broadcast booth, an "Hadl to Alworth over the shoulder catch" off a little pop-up behind the pitcher's mound in a game against the Phillies at Citi Field a few weeks back, is now number two all-time in wins among pitchers from the Dominican Republic, trailing only Juan Marichal and two up on Pedro Martinez.

Over 53 major league seasons the win totals for these three stands at 683.

Six hundred and eighty-three victories from an island nation of only 10.4 million people.

Astounding.

Oh, Colon's HR reminds that Hoyt Wilhelm hit a HR in his first major league AB and never hit another in his subsequent 431 ABs.

Let's hope Bartolo does it again, preferably at Citi Field.

THE CUBS PLAYED FOUR VS. THE NATIONALS AT WRIGLEY AND WON ALL FOUR, and now stand 24-6 for '16, clearly the best team in the game.

Which, if Chicago keeps it up, would end up at 132-30 on the year. It has never happened before, that many wins; but Leicester City had never won the Premier League, either.

The four Northside games drew 158,474, or 39,619 a game; meanwhile the White Sox/Twins played three on the Southside, drawing 74,949, or 24,983 a game – all three games won by the Pale Hose.

At 46-16, the two Windy City teams lead both NL and Al Central divisions.

IN THE CUBS 13-INNINGS WALK-OFF 4-3 VICTORY AT WRIGLEY, Joe Maddon, the game's best manager, ordered all-world Bryce Harper of the Nationals walked six times, tying a major league record; and Harper, having been hit in his other AB, was on base seven times – which did nothing for his BA, HR or RBI totals, but his OBP now stands at .432.

THE METS, DOWN TWO GAMES TO NIL AGAINST THE PADRES, came back to win Saturday (thanks to Bartolo) and Sunday, to gain a series split and move a half game up on the Nationals in the NL East. (You can imagine the angst on the Tony Kornheiser Show today.)

George and Tim Mitrovich with Tony K.

The Padres down 4-3 in the bottom of the 8th in yesterday's game, had the bases loaded with no outs, and did not score.

Increasingly, when I think of the Padres, Mr. Churchill's famous Russian metaphor comes to mind, "A riddle wrapped in a mystery inside an enigma."

The Padres, at 13-19 and in last place in the NL West, are in Chicago vs. the mighty Cubs. Perhaps this series will settle the enigma question, but not necessarily in a good way for the team I've rooted for these 73-years.

READING SPORTS IN THE BOSTON GLOBE YESTERDAY ONE MIGHT HAVE ASSUMED THE RED SOX SEASON WAS IN PERIL FOLLOWING CONSECUTIVE LOSSES TO THE YANKEES, but then last night the Sox hit four HRs at the Stadium and Steven Wright pitched a complete game masterpiece and Boston won, 5-1, so maybe it's not over till it's over.

Here's one paragraph from Nick Cafardo's side-bar story on the game, occasioned, in part, by another inept performance Saturday by David Price:

"You could just see the disappointment from Farrell after the game. You could see it in Price. You could just see a team that had been feeling so good after fighting so hard to get to first place suddenly dealing with disappointment again."

I am not a critic of baseball writers. To the contrary I've made much of their abilities to write under the pressure of deadline and write, at times, brilliantly (think Peter Gammons the night Carlton Fisk hit his HR for the ages); this is a very great talent in literature's world, but losing two in a row, especially when one of the losses was the results of perhaps the most inept umpiring performances ever by a man in blue behind home plate, hardly justifies the Sox in peril writing.

The Sox are home at Fenway tonight vs. the A's, a half game back of Baltimore.

THE ROCKIES WON AT AT&T IN SF, 2-0, OVER THE GIANTS, despite a strong outing by my guy, ex-ND All-American, Jeff Samardzija, who went 7.2 innings, gave up the two Colorado runs on eight hits, while striking out eight, but lost to five pitchers employed by the Centennial State team.

Nolan Arenado, the All-World third baseman for the Rockies, was 3-4, including a triple, and drove in one run. His BA is now .322.

THE BLUE JAYS PLAYED THREE VS. LAD AT THE ROGERS CENTRE, but, alas, the Jays lost two and the series.

By losing yesterday Toronto slipped one game under .500; LAD by winning, moved one game over.

The Blue Jays/Dodgers across the 49th parallel outdrew the Red Sox/Yankees at the Stadium in the Bronx, NY, 136,125 to 135,447.

Close, but it appears more people wanted to sing "O Canada" than the "Star Spangled Banner."

But when your Prime Minister is Justin Trudeau, why not.

QUOTE OF THE DAY:

TIM PEELER, WHOSE POETRY HAS GRACED NOTES OFTEN, does so again:

CARRYING ONE WHO'D CARRIED US:

Snow banked the icy graveyard path
Where we carried his red oak casket,
So heavy that we slipped but held on,
As if the box contained as well as him

All the home runs and strikeouts,
Rare triples and overrun bases,
The wave of the crowd roar
That once transported him from
The shore of one season to the next.

BASEBALL NOTES – MAY 10

AFTER THREE INNINGS AT FENWAY LAST NIGHT, IT WAS OAKLAND 4-1 OVER BOSTON, and I can imagine with Clay Buchholz on the mound pitching like Clay Buchholz, a lot of viewers were changing channels; reruns of *Cheers,* with Sam Malone and gang having a certain appeal.

If that was your decision, Ladies & Gentlemen, I hope whatever episode of *Cheers* you watched, was over the top because back at Fenway a whole lot of stuff was going on, as the Sox scored six in the bottom of the 4th, two in the 5th, and four more in the 6th – and the four in the 6th came on Jackie Bradley's second grand slam of the year, a line shot just over the short wall near the Pesky Pole, and gave Jackie six RBIs.

When it was all over Boston claimed a 14-7 win.

Not a good night for Buchholz, but a great night for the Sox, so Boston fans accept it with gratitude.

And, my man Travis Shaw, had another big night, which is what I expect; indeed, his performance is what I saw in Travis last summer when baseball ops thought he belonged in Pawtucket. I knew better.

David Ortiz, Shaw and Bradley were 9-15, including four doubles, one HR, and nine RBIs.

THE WHITE SOX WENT TO TEXAS AND HAMMERED THE RANGERS, 8-4; did it in 87 degree weather, which must felt so wonderful after so many games in cold and miserable conditions in Chicago.

Todd Frazier, the White Sox major pickup from the Reds, had a big night, hitting two HRs and driving across six.

THE CUBS DID NOT WIN AND THE PADRES DID NOT LOSE BECAUSE THEY DID NOT PLAY, as the aforementioned miserable Chicago weather continued.

They will try again today.

THE YANKEES BEAT KC IN THE BRONX, 7-2, AS THE BOMBERS HIT FIVE HRs, but for reasons unexplained by Tyler Kepner in today's New York Times, Ivan Nova, the Yankees' starter was removed after 4.2 innings, having yielded but one run on six hits.

Nova's four successors, including Aroldis Chapman, back from his 30-day domestic violence suspension, pitched effectively for the victory.

The Royals, World Series winners in '15, slipped one game under .500, and have now lost 10 of their last 13 played.

ON THE DAY STEPHEN STRASBURG AGREED TO A $175 MILLION, SEVEN YEAR CONTRACT EXTENSION, the ex-San Diego State ace, celebrated by pitching seven so-so innings at National Park, but it was okay because Washington won 5-4, on a walk-off HR in the bottom of the 9th by someone named Clint Robinson.

THE ROCKIES CAME HOME TO COORS BUT LOST 10-5 TO ARIZONA, as Tyler Chatwood had a bad outing, giving up six runs on seven hits in six innings, but his ERA remains impressive at 3.09.

Trevor Story, who is with Nolan Arenado and Carlos Gonzalez, the 2016 Rockies' story, did not hit a HR, but did drive in two, giving him 27 for the season, tying him with Bryce Harper for fourth best in the NL.

THE GIANTS LOST 3-1 TO THE BLUE JAYS AND ARE NOW 17-17 FOR '16, which in the anyone can win NL West, is nonetheless good enough for first place, as the collective record of SF, LAD, Arizona, Colorado, and SD, is 77-81.

Parity is the name of the game and the NL West has achieved it.

QUOTE OF THE DAY:

ANOTHER FROM TIM PEELER, THE CAROLINA BARD:

THE FOURTH SON

He was eleven years old, seventy pounds,
But he had a rocket arm,
And he could catch every pitch without signals
From a six foot Goliath

Whose minor league pitcher daddy
Had taught him to throw curve balls,
Screw balls, knuckle balls,
Overhand, or side arm.

He was eleven years old,
His parents alcoholics who
Never came to the games,

And my dad fathered him
Like he were his fourth son;

Yet many years later,
When Tim died of cancer,
Dad could not go to the funeral
Even though he had been to hundreds,

Having preached the most of them,
Always finding the strength
To say the last words over the dead,
Though he could not find them
For one of his own.

BASEBALL NOTES – MAY 17

I WATCHED AND LISTENED LAST NIGHT TO THE GAME BETWEEN THE DODGERS & ANGELS IN CHAVEZ RAVINE, because the Red Sox were rained out in KC and the Padres were off, and it gave me a chance to hear Vince Scully – uninterrupted by other things.

To say Mr. Scully is a marvel for the ages is an understatement; in the baseball broadcast booth, he is simply the best ever.

In the top of the 7th LAA scored three times to increase their lead over LAD to 7-3, in what became an interminable inning, solely because the Dodger pitcher, Pedro Baez, was taking a lot of time between pitches, causing Mr. Scully to say that since entering the game Baez had taken up 21-minutes (it would become 30 before the inning ended), and Mr. Scully thought the slowness of Baez's pitching was indicative of a "lack of confidence."

He then asked, "Do you remember Alejandro Pena, wonderful guy, but he took his time doing everything. His nickname was, 'Slow.'"

His nickname was, "Slow." He just dropped that in.

It was perfect, but when you hear this man, perfection is what you get.

He also pointed out that when Albert Pujols came to bat with the bases loaded in the 7th, that Pujols in his career in such situations is hitting .325, with 13 HRs and 193 RBIs (it became 195, as Pujols singled).

And, when you think Vince Scully does this alone, there is no second or third person in the booth, the magnitude of his magic becomes immeasurable.

Thank you, God, for Vince Scully.

THE TIGERS SCORED EIGHT IN THE FIRST AT COMERICA PARK VS. MINNESOTA, but the Twins came back to tie in the top of the 7th, before Nick Castellanos went deep in the Tigers' half and J.D. Martinez followed an inning later and Detroit made it two in a row.

Winning for Detroit was Jordan Zimmerman, who is now 6-2 for '16, despite giving up all eight of the Twins runs (seven earned) in his seven innings.

In Zimmerman's last outing he was on the mound vs. the Nationals when Max Scherzer blew 20 Tigers away in a record tying strikeout feat.

Oh, interesting footnote on that game last Wednesday in Washington, when it was over and Scherzer had his magnificent accomplishment, his ERA was 4.15, while Zimmerman's was 1.50.

TOM CLAVIN, WHO WROTE THAT WONDERFUL BOOK ON THE DiMAGGIO BROTHERS, reminds that Sunday marked the start of Joe DiMaggio's 56-game hitting streak in 1941, one of the most significant accomplishments in sports history; a streak that ended in Cleveland's Municipal Stadium when Indians third baseman, Ken Keltner, made two great back hand stops of Joe D's smashes down the third base line.

In those 56-games, DiMaggio hit .408, with 16 doubles, four triples, 15 HRs, 55 RBIs, and a slugging percentage of .717.

It is often overlooked, after the streak was stopped, DiMaggio would hit safely in his next 16-games; absent Keltner's brilliant plays, the lore would be 72, not 56.

Hitting streaks were not unknown to the Yankee Clipper, as he had a 61-game streak while playing for the San Francisco Seals in the Triple-A Pacific Coast League before his contract was purchased by the Bronx team.

WHICH I NOTE BECAUSE BOB NICOLLS, THE HEAD OF MONARCH INVESTMENTS IN COLORADO, shared with me an article by Sheldon Hirsch, who, while acknowledging the greatness of DiMaggio's streak, writes that in similar 56-game stretches Rogers Hornsby, George Brett, and Ted Williams hit for higher averages.

In 1924 Hornsby hit .476; Brett, .480 in '80, and Williams, in the same year as DiMaggio over the same stretch of games, hit .412.

Hirsch, who co-authored, "The Beauty of Short Hops: How Chance and Circumstance Confound the Moneyball Approach to Baseball," wrote, near the end of his essay:

"In 1941 DiMaggio was already a superstar, the Yankee Clipper, a rags-to-riches son of an immigrant fisherman. At that time baseball was particularly prominent in American culture. We are always partial to finding heroes, and America in 1941 may have been particularly ready. The depression was not far in the rear-view mirror. World War II was raging, Hitler was advancing; six days after DiMaggio's streak started, the first United States ship was sunk by a German U-boat. Perhaps the situation was ripe for defining a super-hero: The right player at the right time with the right feat (pre-OBP and pre-WAR, the base hit was the coin of the realm).

"Then the super-hero married Marilyn Monroe, and was celebrated in song ("Where have you gone Joe DiMaggio?"), literature ("the Great DiMaggio" of Hemingway's "The Old Man and the Sea") and television ("Mister Coffee"). As the DiMaggio aura blossomed, "56" became fixed in the American psyche and grew to transcend sports: The noted commentator Stephen Jay Gould called it "... the finest of legitimate legends because it embodies the essence of the battle that truly defines our lives ... he cheated death."

He ended his provocative essay by writing, "The streak does not warrant the hype."

You can read Hirsch's lengthy article at RealClearSports.com. It's entitled, "Dimaggio's Hitting Streak is Overrated."

QUOTE OF THE DAY:

MORE OF TIM PEELER'S WONDERFUL POETRY:

WILD IN THE STRIKE ZONE 1965:

He was thirty-nine in '65, carting us around
In a Nash four door because it made sense
When you were picking up kids for church
And picking up kids for games and taking
Kids home from school; it made sense

For a preacher and a teacher salary
To drive cheap cars that I never remember
Breaking down on the side of the road,
With a bat bag in the trunk, or a sermon

With the first line in each paragraph
Typed in red CAPITALS on an ancient Royal
Tucked in his jacket pocket like a passport
That he believed could win this game.

George with Michael and Kitty Dukakis.

BASEBALL NOTES – MAY 23

THE CUBS CAME TO AT&T IN SAN FRANCISCO AT 28-11 ON THE SEASON AND LEFT 29-13, as the NL West Leading Giants won the series two games to one, including last night's 1-0 victory behind Madison Bumgarner's masterful pitching.

Are the Cubs mortal, after all?

They were always mortal, but while mortal they are also baseball's best, and will play that into the World Series – most likely against the Red Sox (if Sox GM Dave Dombrowski trades for James Shields).

THE RED SOX WON SUNDAY OVER CLEVELAND, 5-2, and won the series, two games to one.

David Ortiz was 4-4, with two doubles and a HR, and is now hitting .329, with 11 HRs and 37 RBIs.

The Sox have three of the AL's top four hitters – Xander Bogearts (.346), Jackie Bradley Jr. (.342), and Ortiz.

Ortiz's HR yesterday marked the 22nd game in succession in which a Red Sox player has homered – an all-time Boston record.

Which Dick Flavin, the Poet Laureate of Red Sox Nation and a Sox fan since he was a kid, finds surprising, given all of the great home run hitters who have played for Boston – Ortiz, Jimmy Foxx, Jim Rice, Mo Vaughn, Many Ramirez, Carl Yastrzemski, Tony Armas, and Ted Williams (in order of HRs hit in a single season).

George with Dick Flavin and Donna Cohen.

Footnote: The top 10 Red Sox hitters in OBP is Ted Williams – .553, .526, .513, .499, .499, .497, .497, .496, .490, and .479.

Wow!

Oh, Jackie Bradley Jr. has now hit in 27-straight games.

THE PADRES BEAT LA 3-2 SATURDAY NIGHT ON A BASES LOADED WALK-OFF, which followed their 7-6 win Friday night on a walk-off HR by Melvin Upton Jr.

A big crowd of 40,000 plus on Saturday was on their feet yelling as Chin-hui Tsao, in relief for LA, threw four straight balls to Yangervis Solarte, and that was the ball game.

The oddity of this game: 32 batters struck out, as 19 Padres went down and 13 Dodgers. There were 10 bases on balls and only nine base hits, three by Will Meyers.

Yesterday, LAD and SD played 17-innings before 43,100, as the Dodgers scored four to win 9-5 (but the Padres would have swept the series had not the MLB replay crew in NYC not screwed up the replay of Melvin Upton Jr. sliding under Adrian Gonzalez's tag at first in the bottom of the 9th, which was critical, because instead of one out and a runner on 3rd, it would have been no outs and runners at 1st and 3rd).

The Padres continue to confound. They opened the home stand by losing three straight to the Giants, scoring one run in games one, two, and three, but came back, as noted, to win two in a row against LAD, but then Sunday happened – which means that rather than being 5-5 on the season vs. LAD, they are 4-6.

I can't decide whether they are just not very good and a last place team, or actually a good team with a chance to be a serious player for the NL West title, since the NL West appears weakest of baseball's six divisions. Only the Giants, at 27-19, thanks to winning nine of 10, have a plus .500 record.

THE METROPOLITANS OF QUEENS WON OVER MILWAUKEE, 3-1, as one of the game's most exciting young players, Noah Syndergaard improved to 5-2 and his ERA now stands at 1.94.

Love Noah Syndergaard.

The Metropolitans, despite playing a not very good Brewers' team, drew 116,100 to Citi Field for the three game set.

GM Sandy Alderson should be pleased.

THE NATIONALS TOPPED MIAMI 8-2, AS MAX SCHERZER STRUCK OUT ONLY EIGHT, and are now up 1.5 games over NYM in the NL East.

All-World Bryce Harper was 0-2 and his BA has fallen to .260.

Cause for concern? A little, perhaps, but Bryce will be back to being Bryce. Count on it.

THE TWO TEXAS TEAMS PLAYED THREE AT MINUTE MAID AND NORTH TEXAS WON OVER SOUTH TEXAS, THREE GAMES TO NIL.

A very impressive showing by the Rangers, who won 2-1, 2-1, and 9-2.

The Rangers' pitchers held Houston batters to a mere 13-hits during the three game sweep.

Only Atlanta and Cincinnati have won fewer games than the Astros, who were the odds on choice of the game's experts to win the AL West. That may still happen, but we are 45-games into 2016, and so far it ain't happening.

THE GAME WE LOVE IS OFTEN CRUEL, AS WITNESSED SATURDAY NIGHT AT ANGEL STADIUM, when the O's won 3-1 on a 9th inning two out three run HR off the bat of Matt Wieters.

I watched the game's denouement and pulled for LAA to win, but, alas, that didn't happen, despite brilliant pitching by Fernando Salas.

LAA came back big yesterday, however, winning 10-2, as Carlos Perez homered and had a career high, five RBIs.

The three games across I-5 from Disneyland drew 120,404.

So, the Angels and Padres, whose ballparks are separated by 95.6 miles, together played six games over the weekend and drew 235,561 OC/SD County fans.

Nice.

CARLOS BELTRAN OF THE YANKEES BECAME ONLY THE FOURTH SWITCH HITTER IN MLB HISTORY TO HIT 400 OR MORE HRS.

Beltran thus joins Mickey Mantle, Eddie Murray and Chipper Jones, greatly distinguished company, to say the least, and represents for Carlos a huge accomplishment.

QUOTE OF THE DAY:

Another poem from Tim Peeler, who has a new book of baseball poetry coming out – and when published will be celebrated here.

SOMEONE ELSE'S BOY:

Sunlight sewn across the field
Like millions of perfect teeth
You could not settle to watch
The one who never fit in

And you knew that God made him
That God distributed burdens
To those who could handle them
And you heard his mother pray

When it came his time to hit
He stood there confused leaning
Bat on his shoulder watching
A strike then a ball then a
Strike as your stomach tightened

And you hoped with all you had
Uttering your own quick prayer
But he swung late like the gate
That closes after the cows

Are all gone and his mother
Felt angry then bitter and
She turned away as if he
Were someone else's boy.

BASEBALL NOTES – JUNE 7

THE CUBS WON THEIR 40TH GAME LAST NIGHT, beating the Phillies in Philly, 6-4. They stand 24-games above .500.

Jon Lester pitched brilliantly for Chicago through eight, giving up no runs on four hits and striking out nine.

Justin Grimm replaced Lester in the Phillies' 9th and surrendered three runs without recording an out. Hector Rondon followed Grimm and gave up one but was able to close out the game.

THE PADRES FACED ATLANTA AT PETCO AND WON, 7-2, as Christian Friedrich got the win, while pitching 6.2 innings, giving up two runs on six hits, and striking out seven.

It wasn't an overwhelming performance, but Friedrich has been impressive, and the Angels and Rockies surely regret having passed on him earlier this season.

THE ROCKIES MOTORED UP I-5 FROM SAN DIEGO AND BEAT LAD, 6-1, as Trevor Story continued his amazing rookie year by hitting his 16th HR, while driving in three, to reach 42 on the season.

If you multiply the 54-games the Rockies have played times three, you get 162-game, which is the number of games played by MLB teams. If you then project Story's performance based upon his first 54-games, the rookie hits 48 HRs and drives in 126 runs.

I think that wins him Rookie of the Year.

However, the star of the game last night was Colorado pitcher Tyler Chatwood, who went eight innings and yielded but a run on one hit and now stands 7-4 on the season.

ROUGNED ODOR, WHO PUNCHED OUT JOSE BAUTISTA, LAST NIGHT PUNCHED OUT THE ASTROS, as baseball's best AL team won 6-5 in Arlington, 255.7 miles north of Minute Maid.

Odor doubled in the winning run for the Rangers with a wall ball double to left scoring Adrian Beltre from second in the bottom of the 9th.

One Punch Odor also had a solo HR to right.

VERY LITTLE HAS BEEN SAID ABOUT THE AL WEST, so I totaled wins and losses for the three AL divisions, to see how the West looks since media won't tell us, but I will:

The five AL West teams have won 145 games and lost 142; AL East, 150 and 135; AL Central, 145 and 147.

THE O's BESTED KC AT CAMDEN, 4-1, AS MARK TRUMBO HIT HIS MLB LEADING 19th HR, and Matt Wieters and Manny Machado also homered.

Machado, one of the game's very best third basemen, was at shortstop last night for the O's.

Attendance at Larry Lucchino's Camden Yards was 14,878.

Meanwhile, way across the wide Missouri in San Diego, the mostly woeful Padres drew 20,203 vs. Atlanta; that would be the NL's worst team.

Baltimore leads the AL East by one-half game over the Red Sox (who didn't play last night, but face SF at AT&T tonight), while the Padres are mired in last place in the NL West, 11.5 games out of first.

The Padres have averaged 27,997 through 31-games; the O's, 23,776.

THE YANKEES BEAT THE ANGELS IN THE BRONX, 5-2.

But going into the bottom of the eighth, New York trailed 2-0, as Matt Shoemaker had been superb, but then NYY hit back-to-back HRs, and before the inning was over, scored three more, as Carlos Beltran hit his 14th to drive in three and the Halos were done.

MEGHAN MONTEMURRO IN USA TODAY'S SPORTS WEEKLY (June 1-7), wrote about the Phillies, comparing this year's team through its first 50-games to last.

In a "side-by-side assessment" the statistical variations in batting were few, BA, .235 now, to .238 then; runs, 160 to 154; HRs, 38 to 26; RBIs, 148 to 146; OBP, .291 to .280.

But differences in pitching, side-by-side, are more significant:

ERA now, 3.83 to 4.11; opponents average, .242 to .265; walks, 142 to 165; strikeouts, 438 to 339; WHIP, 1.23 to 1.40.

The Phillies through 50-games a year ago were 19-31; this season, 26-24. But the team has struggled the past 10-games, losing eight, and are now two games under .500.

ON THE FIELD AT FENWAY PARK BEFORE LAST FRIDAY'S BLUE JAYS/RED SOX GAME, a famous writer told me, "If donald trump is elected president, he will demand Ted Williams be removed from the Hall of Fame."

What?

The writer's reasoning: Ted Williams was Mexican (his mother was Mexican).

Was my writer friend serious?

I don't think so, but there is no accounting for what the trumpster might do.

*Be afraid, America; be very afraid.

QUOTE OF THE DAY:

WILD IN THE STRIKE ZONE, 2007

I had heard about him for a couple years,
A co-worker told me his daughter who
Tutored him in math went to watch and said,
Daddy, when he throws the ball,
You can hear it singing through the air,

So I left work early, carried my slouch chair
From the high school parking lot
Down a path that led to a red dirt hillside
Overlooking a modest ball field
Where soon every possible open space
Held a lawn chair or blanket of people,

And I perched awkwardly, a face among faces
As he warmed up, taller than expected,
Long-armed, blazing his pitches,
And I sat there amidst talk of radar guns
And cheerleader tryouts and all sorts of
Ho-hum as they were used to the thwack
Of David LePrevost's mitt, Madison's strikeouts,

His ridiculous location; they were
As unaffected as him, having seen
Years of it, and they already knew
Before he became
What he would become.

– Tim Peeler, the Poet of the Carolinas

BASEBALL NOTES – JUNE 28

THE CUBS EMBARRASSED BY LOSING THREE OF FOUR TO MIAMI, came back and whipped the Reds in Cincy, 11-8.

Chris Bryant, the wunderkind out of the University of San Diego (USD), had himself a historic night, with three HRs and two doubles, marking the first time any major league player had ever done that. No, really. And, he also drove in six runs.

Jake Arrieta, the Pilates pitcher, won his 12th game and hit another HR, number two on the season. It was not a normal Arrieta performance, as his ERA "ballooned" to 2.10, but he still got the win.

The win put Chicago into a three way tie with SF and Texas for most victories with 49.

JEFF SAMARDZIJA, THE ALL-AMERICAN WIDEOUT FROM NOTRE DAME, was wiped-out last night at McCovey Cove as the Bay Bridge Athletics beat the Golden Gate Giants, 8-3.

Jeff gave up six runs on eight hits in six innings and lost for the fifth time against eight wins.

THE NATIONALS LOST STEVEN STRASBURG TO THE DL BUT BEAT THE METROPOLITANS, 11-4.

Joe Ross gave up four runs early to NYM but then steadied behind a 17 hit attack by his teammates, including a 4-5 night by center fielder Ben Revere, who raised his average to .220.

All-World Bryce Harper had two hits, drove in a run, and is now hitting .254.

TROY TULOWITZKI RETURNED TO COORS FIELD LAST NIGHT, but the Blue Jays of Toronto were defeated by the Rockies of Colorado, 9-5, despite two HRs by Edwin Encarnacion, giving him 21 on the year.

The Rockies are within two of .500 for '16 and are four games back of LAD for second place in the NL West.

HOW DO YOU STOP AN 11-GAME LOSING STREAK, YOU PLAY THE RED SOX, and last night under the dome at Tropicana the Rays of Tampa Bay beat Boston, 13-7, in what surely is the Sox's most embarrassing loss of '16, now only five games away from halfway to the season's denouement.

Eduardo Rodriquez had a terrible outing, giving up nine runs on 11 hits in all of 2.2 innings.

This is the kid I was so high on last year, lobbying here in Notes for his call up from Pawtucket, but something clearly is amiss.

With the loss the Sox have fallen 4.5 back of idle Baltimore.

Is Dick Flavin's faith fallen in the Sox's journey to the World Series?

I'll ask.

QUOTE OF THE DAY:

Tim Peeler, the Poet of the Carolinas, writes wonderful poetry, but poets labor in the shadows of the larger realm of literature, which is shameful in this 24/7, Twitter, Facebook, email world.

Here is Tim's latest:

THE WILLIS HE WAS:

He was one of the Willises,
Not the musical ones who played
Long front porches on Sunday afternoons,
Not the bar owners who leased
New pickup trucks for their managers
Because it looked good to roll up thusly
And might afford a powerful getaway
Should circumstances call for such,
I'm talking about the baseball ones,
The three barely literate brothers
Who each bothered for a year of college
Because they knew it was a possible way,
Who lived by the crook in the river
Where they'd found slithers of Spanish gold
Buried in the best potters' clay
Known to exist in the county.
He was the one clocked at 90 mph
When he was sixteen threw inside
Rattle snake strikes till he got
A doctor's daughter cheerleader
Pregnant so that her father
Sent her to an aunt's to stay
And threatened him with statutory
If he ever came around again.
That's the Willis he was,
The one who was never the same.

BASEBALL NOTES – JULY 25

HANLEY RAMIREZ HAD SOME WEEK, as the Red Sox won four of six from the Giants and Twins, with Hanley hitting five HRs and driving in 12.

Three of his HRs came Wednesday night against SF, as the Sox won big, 11-7.

Boston has five batters in their lineup who have driven in 60 or more runs – Ortiz, Shaw, Betts, Bradley and Ramirez.

Could all five reach 100 RBIs?

Yes.

The Sox two losses were Friday and Saturday nights. Friday's 2-1 loss came about despite having the bases loaded and no one out and David Ortiz at bat. Saturday's loss 11-9 was just flat out UGLY!

It was ugly and depressing and I needed a break, so I watched Michael Moore's "Where to Invade Next" and my depression deepened.

But back to Friday: What are the odds with the bases loaded and no one out and Ortiz at bat, the Sox don't score?

Anyone?

MEANWHILE, IN BALTIMORE, THE O's SWEPT THE INDIANS AT CAMDEN, winning Sunday 5-3 on a two-run walk-off HR by Nolan Reimold.

Reimold had been 0-16 when he hit the walk-off.

With the sweep the O's keep their 1.5 game lead over the Sox.

JULY 15 THE GIANTS LEAD ALL BASEBALL WITH 57 WINS. It is now 10-days later and SF has 58 wins – and LAD has closed to within three of the lead, as the Giants lost seven of eight to the Padres, Red Sox, and Yankees.

This is not good, because, while a Padres' fan, I am not rooting for the billionaires in Chavez Ravine, who took their four billion in profit and shut down 70 percent of Dodger fans from watching their team on TV.

And the silence of the commissioner and his team at 245 Park Avenue on the island of Manhattan is deafening.

THE BEST STORY OF '16 IS TREVOR STORY OF THE ROCKIES WHO HIT HIS 27TH HR yesterday on Blake Street in Denver, as the Rockies won over Atlanta, 7-2, with Tyler Chatwood pitching five shutout innings to win his 9th game.

The manager of the Rockies removed Chatwood after 93-pitches and replaced him with a guy with an ERA of 5.79.

Way to go Walt, but despite that Colorado got its 47th victory of the year – but the Rockies' redemption is Story, the rookie, and Cargo Gonzalez, the veteran.

They make the team interesting – truly.

TEXAS HANDED KC ITS 13TH LOSS IN THE LAST GAMES 19 PLAYED, winning in Arlington, 2-1.

The game winner was a HR hit by Delino DeShields in the bottom of the 7th, breaking the 1-1 tie. It was only DeShields' 3rd of the season.

AT THE ROGERS CENTRE ON BLUE JAYS WAY IN TORONTO, A.J. HAPP WON HIS 13TH OF '16, thus setting a career high in wins as the Jays won over visiting Seattle, 2-0.

Edwin Encarnacion hit his 27th HR to lead the way, as Toronto won its 55th game.

THE METROPOLITANS OF QUEENS BEAT THE MARLINS OF MIAMI, 3-0, as Steven Matz won for the first time since May.

With the win NYM won the series in Miami and now trail the second place AL East Marlins by one-half game.

THIS IS A 10-PART QUIZ: The Chicago White Sox suspended Chris Sale for five days because of:

1. DUI
2. Spousal abuse
3. Child endangerment
4. Flipping-off fans
5. Assaulting an umpire
6. Assaulting his manager
7. Assaulting a teammate
8. Insulting Jerry Reinsdorf
9. Refusing to remove his cap during the National Anthem
10. Destroying throw-back jerseys

The answer is:

Sale destroyed those God awful, navy blue, throw-back, collared jerseys the White Sox wore in '76 – a look inspired by the Ming Dynasty – which Sale did by using scissors to cut them into little blue shreds.

While the White Sox front office was mightily miffed at their best pitcher – Sale is 15-3 – the Council of Fashion Designers of America (CFDA) voted to make him an honorary member.

Way to go Chris.

I love stand up guys.

Too bad Steve Garvey didn't have the courage to do what Sale did when Steve was wearing Padres' brown and yellow and thinking he was a commercial for Taco Bell.

SPEAKING OF THE PADRES, THEY ARE WEIRD. They sweep SF in San Diego, go on the road to St. Louis, get swept by the Cardinals, fly east to DC and win two of three from the Nationals..

So, playing the East and West division leaders the Padres win five of six.

Nice.

Not so nice, whoever it was sitting in for Dick Enberg and Don Orsillo in the Fox broadcast booth, because whoever he is he sounded like he isn't ready for prime time.

BRANDON CRAWFORD IS THE GOLD GLOVE SHORTSTOP OF THE SAN FRANCISCO GIANTS.

Friday night at Yankee Stadium in the Bronx, NY, that Brandon Crawford, that Gold Glove winner, that oh so impressive fielder, made three errors – not a misprint, three errors – one of which cost his team a victory.

Will we see that again?

No.

CONGRATULATIONS TO DAN SHAUGHNESSY OF THE BOSTON GLOBE, who yesterday was inducted into the J.G. Taylor Spink wing of Baseball's Hall of Fame in Cooperstown, NY.

Since I read everything Dan writes, almost, I can testify the man is good, really; even when some on Yawkey Way are perturbed by what they read (but not so much this year).

But the writer hasn't lived – nor should he or she – who hasn't perturbed someone at some time over some issue.

QUOTE OF THE DAY:

Again, I turn to Tim Peeler, the Bard of the Carolinas for his latest poem, entitled, "Conviction":

He taught me to believe
Beyond my senses, beyond
My limited ability.
He held his mitt knee high

On the outside corner
Willing the ball to arrive
With a gentle pop,
Held the mitt

As if he'd not move it
Though the mad pitch
Might veer toward his face,
And I threw without thinking

About arm angle
Or release point,
Without aiming or
Shifting my shoulder.

I threw that ball
With emotionless belief
And he caught it
The same way.

BASEBALL NOTES – AUGUST 1

"MY HEROES HAVE ALWAYS BEEN COWBOYS," WILLIE NELSON SINGS, but the Texas Rangers aren't cowboys but baseball players. Doesn't matter, because a whole lot of folks are starting to love Texas (the team, that is). They had a good week, as they won five of seven, including a four game sweep of the reigning World Series champs, the Royals of KC.

Mitch Moreland, after hitting an eighth-inning game winner Thursday night vs. KC, came back to hit a walk-off Saturday night, giving him three HRs on the week and 17 for '16.

OTHER IMPRESSIVE WINS SUNDAY – the O's beating the Jays in 12-innings at the Rogers Centre, 6-2; Cleveland and Corey Kluber shutting down the A's at Progressive, 8-0; the streaking Tigers winning 11-0 at home over Houston, and the Cubs topping the Mariners 7-6 in 12-innings at Wrigley and doing it on a two-strike bunt squeeze by Jon Lester (no, really).

WHILE I WAS COMPOSING NOTES AND LISTENING TO MY MAN, WILLIE, the Red Sox were being resurrected across I-5 from Disneyland in Anaheim by a Dustin Pedroia three-run shot to dead center in the top of the 9th, followed by a Xander Bogearts HR to left, and what looked like a 3-1 Sox loss to LAA became a 5-3 Sox win.

Three K's preceded Pedroia's HR, but he quickly got past that with his big bomb. (One of Pedroia'a K's was a chin-high curve ball, called a strike by home plate umpire Gabe Morales, causing John Farrell to get in Morales' face and the ump to tell the skipper to exit the premises; which caused Steve Lyons and Dave O'Brien in the NESN booth to say that might be good because the Sox needed a kick-in-the-pants to get going; and they did, four-innings later.)
But, as big as that was, and it was, maybe Clay Buchholz's three scoreless innings in relief, was ever bigger.

So, staring at a 1-3 start on the road, Boston goes to Seattle at 2-2 to begin a four game series with the Mariners at Safeco.

AT THE END OF THE 8TH INNING THURSDAY NIGHT IN ANAHEIM, I watched David Price on NESN, who had pitched superbly for the Red Sox against the Angels, walk off the mound to the dugout with his team leading, 1-0.

As he did so I thought, if John Farrell pulls Price the Sox lose.

In the bottom of the 9th, with David Price on the bench, the bases were loaded with one out, I had one of those strong *premonitions I sometimes get, that a ground ball would be hit to Hanley Ramirez at 1st, he would field the ball cleanly but throw wildly to home, two runs would score and the Sox would lose, 2-1.

The ball was hit to Hanley, he fielded it cleanly, threw wildly to home, two runs scored, and Boston began its 11-game road trip with their fourth straight loss.

Not good.

Oh, on Farrell pulling Price:

When David left the game, he had thrown eight shutout innings, given up only seven hits, walked one and struck out six on 109-pitches.

I'm just a fan, you know, but I'm not pulling Price unless Price wanted out of the game. If it's me he's pitching the 9th inning – and the Red Sox loss would have been a 1-0 Red Sox win.
But I'm a [Bobby] Kennedy person and we don't do wouldofs, couldofs, shouldofs, but I just did. Sorry.

***MY MOST FAMOUS PREMONITION WAS SEPT. 30, 2013,** when I predicted what would happen in the playoffs, down to winners and games played, and on the day of the 6th game of the World Series I flew to Boston see the Sox beat the Cardinals at Fenway – as predicted.

THE PADRES TRADED ANDREW CASHNER FRIDAY TO MIAMI. I wasn't expecting a birthday gift from my NL team, but there it was – Cashner gone.

I will not miss him, his beard, his maddening inconsistencies – or his 30-49 lifetime record.
I will, however, do my best to forget that he came to us from the Cubs for Anthony Rizzo.

ON SATURDAY THE PADRES TRADED MATT KEMP TO ATLANTA for a player on suspension for domestic violence; traded a player with 24 doubles, 23 HRs, and 62-RBI for a player on suspension.

What?

True.

While having dinner Saturday night with friends of 62-years, I received a very angry phone call from a very angry Padres fan who wanted to know if ownership has lost its collective mind?

This fan then said, "Matt Kemp and Will Meyers are the only reason we go to games, and if the Padres care that little about us, their fans, we're done going to Petco Park."

I do not know A.J. Preller, the Padres' general manager. I do know baseball people who do, smart baseball people. They are not fans of A.J.'s. But, as long as ownership is sold on A.J., and they've made it clear, they are, then Mr. Preller need concern himself only with the job before him, not what people think – because "people" are not paying his salary.

It does seem to me that Preller's model is the ex-GM of the 76ers, who tore down the NBA team in order to score high in the draft. ESPN the Magazine seems to think that "model" may finally work in Philly, but that's a whole lot of years later and a whole lot of losing teams – and that GM is no longer with the 76ers.

In a letter last fall to the Padres' ownership, gentlemen I know, admire and care about, I said I thought their team would lose more games this season than last.

I have not changed my mind.

If you're inclined to feel sorry for anyone in the Padres' organization, feel sorry for those in corporate and season ticket sales. They did a heroic job this season, but next year will test them even more.

FRIDAY WAS MY BIRTHDAY AND ANGELS CHAIRMAN DENNIS KUHL HOSTED SEVEN OF US AT DINNER in the Diamond Club at Angels Stadium.

My brother Dan, his wife, Linda, special friends Lori Mathios, Christy Jaynes, Vincent Bradley, and Dr. John Huffman, were present. Dennis, Sam Kennedy and his son, Jimmy, Angels President John Carpino, and Bud Black, came by to say hello (I loved seeing Buddy, who had lovely things to say about Peter and Tom Seidler).

It was unexpected but wonderful and I am grateful to pal Dennis.

My gratitude extends to all who took time in emails and on Facebook to convey birthday greetings.

My parents taught me well and they taught me the grace of saying, "Thank You."

Thank You!

QUOTE OF THE DAY:

DNA by Tim Peeler:

Papaw balanced peas on a knife.
Daddy threw a string ball he'd made
Against the barn. Grandma lay dying
In a back room of the farmhouse.

The cows drank water in the feed lot.
The other kids all grown and gone

Except little sister Ginny,
A blue shadow in the stale kitchen.

Daddy who had waited and waited,
Holding a warm cloth to Grandma's face,
Went out to "pitch" and chat with God

When he felt his mother
Sweep right through him.

BASEBALL NOTES – AUGUST 9

WHEN ALEX RODRIGUEZ WAS WITH THE SEATTLE MARINERS, I was the guest preacher at the First Presbyterian Church of Spokane, Washington.

In my sermon that Sunday, "The Most Difficult Thing You Will Ever Do," I talked about A-Rod. I did so having read in SI a long profile about the young Rodriguez.

I read about his growing up without a father, of his devoted and loving mother, of his calling her every day when he began playing pro ball, of how he prayed that God's Holy Spirit might lead him to the woman he should marry (it wasn't Madonna).

The story impressed me, as Alex had impressed its writer, and I wanted to share with the wonderful people in worship that Sunday at First Presbyterian, Alex Rodriguez's story.

That was 16-years ago, and there have been a few changes in A-Rod's life.

However, if I am invited back to preach at First Pres., he is not likely to be held up as an example for others to follow.

That said, I remain a fan. I am sorry for what happened to his career. Others may hate him, but I am not a hater. I follow the counsel and enduring example of the great Buck O'Neil, who said he hated cancer, he hated drugs, he hated evil, but he could never hate a fellow human being; a creature of God.

No lovelier human being ever lived than Buck – and if he couldn't hate A-Rod, neither can I.

And you?

BACK HOME AT THE ROGERS CENTRE, the Blue Jays won 7-5 over Tampa Bay, as Edwin Encarnacion had three hits, including his 31st HR and drove in three (he is six shy of 100); all the while underscoring why David Ortiz wants Edwin Encarnacion to succeed David Ortiz at Fenway.

THE GIANTS WON 8-7 IN 14 AT MIAMI AS BRANDON CRAWFORD HAD SEVEN HITS IN EIGHT ABs, as he had five singles, a double and triple, while driving in two. With his seven hits, Crawford tied a major league record for hits in one game.

LAD ALSO WON, 9-4, AS ZACH ELFIN, COREY SEAGER, YASMANI GRANDAL, AND CHASE UTLEY ALL HOMERED, as the Dodgers stayed one behind the Giants in the NL West.

TYLER ANDERSON OF THE ROCKIES PITCHED BRILLIANTLY LAST NIGHT AT COORS, as Colorado led mighty Texas 3-0 through seven, but then, in the monkey see, monkey do, way of managers, Walt Weiss pulled Anderson after only 95-pitches, the bullpen blew up and Texas scored three to win in the top of the 9th 4-3.

All-World Nolan Arenado hit his 30th of the season for the Rockies and Andre Beltre his 17th for the Rangers, but at game's end Texas had its 66th victory of '16, and Colorado fell two under .500 and nine back of SF.

HISASHI IWAKUMA OF SEATTLE FOLLOWED HIS BRILLIANT PITCHING PERFORMANCE VS. BOSTON, with an equally impressive outing against the Tigers last night, throwing seven scoreless innings at Safeco to win his 13th game, as the Mariners won, 3-0.

SOMEONE NAMED CODY REED OF THE REDS, went into last night's game vs. the Cardinals with a record of 0-6 and an ERA of 7.30.

Six-innings later he had given up one hit, zero runs, but the Cards would score five in the bottom of the 9th on a bases loaded walk and a hit batsman to win.

I just love the way pitchers are used today. It really does elevate the game.

Right?

Wrong.

I FORGOT THIS YESTERDAY, BUT SUNDAY NIGHT KENLEY JANSEN OF LAD STRUCK OUT THE THREE RED SOX HE FACED IN THE 9th; which meant he faced six Sox batters Saturday and Sunday and struck out six Sox batters.

IN 49-innings he has struck out 79 batters.

Wow!

QUOTE OF THE DAY:

TIM PEELER'S POEM ENTITLED DNA 6:

We rode that summer river
Of days, outrunning thunder,
Waiting for the bookmobile
To bring those Matt Christopher

Baseball books: Catcher with a
Glass Arm, Return of the Home
Run Kid, The Lucky Baseball
Bat; brother and I would fight

To see who read them first then
I'd read them again at night
Under the covers with the
Secret flashlight I'd pilfered
From the kitchen cabinet.

We rode that summer river
Of days, till the batteries
Died, the games all won or lost,
All of Matt Christopher read,

Our waking, stirred, my dreams fed.

BASEBALL NOTES – AUGUST 19

LET'S START WITH A CORRECTION: Andrew James Happ is A.J. Happ of the Toronto Blue Jays, not J.A. Happ (with thanks to Harry Sherr of the Wellesley/La Jolla Sherrs for pointing out, again, one of my errors).

IF ONLY THE RED SOX COULD DO AWAY WITH THE 8TH INNING, they might have a huge lead in the AL East.

In the Yankees' series last week, two games were lost in the 8th, as the bullpen imploded.

Yesterday in Detroit they went into the bottom of the 8th leading, 3-1, when it was over they were down, 4-3 – and they would lose 4-3 (it was yet another game in which they left the bases loaded and zero runs in).

Apparently Robbie Ross Jr. was exhausted by the 10-pitches he threw in a perfect three up, three down 7th, so John Farrell opted to bring in Junichi Tazawa and save the 8th, but three batters later and three runners on base, the Sox skipper pulled Tazawa, and brought in Brad Zeigler, hoping for more magic from Brad.

But the wick was out on Zeigler's candle and that was that.

It baffles me with all the smarts in baseball ops – any baseball ops – why managers are instructed, when a pitcher comes in from the bullpen and sets down the other team, 1, 2, 3, he is then taken out and another reliever comes in to start the next inning. In my tiny fans' mind, it seems stupid.

Today, when Robbie Ross Jr. exited after inning seven he left with an ERA of 3.68 and was replaced in the 8th by Junichi Tazawa, whose ERA is 4.58.

Am I saying had Farrell left in Ross Jr., that he would have had an 8th inning equal to his 7th, I am. But, while I cannot prove that, neither can you disprove it.

AT WRIGLEY KRIS BRYANT HAD A 5-5, TWO HR, FIVE RBI GAME, and the Cubs beat Milwaukee, 9-6, for their 77th win of the season – and their 15th win in the last 17 played.

Goodness.

BACK IN BALTIMORE THE O's BOUNCED BACK FROM THEIR TWO LOSSES TO THE RED SOX and beat Houston, 13-5, as four Oriole batters hit six HRs, as J.J. Hardy and Chris Davis hit two each, and Mark Trumbo made it 35 for '16.

Kevin Gausman was the winning pitcher for the Birds, his fourth against 10 losses.

THE DODGERS, WHO HAVE BEEN ON A ROLL, were rolled instead by the Phillies at Citizens Bank Park, 5-4.

LAD has moved on to Cincy to face the Reds in a three game weekend series beside the Ohio River, while the Giants are at home vs. NYM. One game separates the two leaders in the NL West.

IN THE WEIRD WAYS OF AMERICA'S GAME, the Padres lost three straight to Tampa Bay, scoring three runs in three games.

Last night, back at Petco in Gaslamp, they scored nine and beat Arizona by two, 9-8.

Alex Dickerson had one hit but drove in four, which led SD to the needed victory.

IN THE PADRES/RAYS THREE GAME SERIES UNDER THE DOME IN ST. PETE, total attendance was 31,461 – an appalling average of 10,487.

I'm told the ownership group who own the Rays are good people, who want a new ballpark. I know the commissioner on Opening Day in Tampa told media he wanted to help the Rays achieve that goal, but I am not convinced a new ballpark would result in a big uptick in attendance.

The Miami Marlins, playing in a stunning new ballpark, have averaged 1,822,571 during the past four seasons, or 367,106 more per season than Tampa Bay; but if you take away 2012, the Marlins' inaugural year in their new ballpark, the difference is only 169,280.

Since the time I was a kid in San Diego, making my weekly trip to our neighborhood Rexall drug store to pick up a copy of The Sporting News, the "Baseball Bible," which carried box scores of every professional baseball team, from the majors to Class D, I have always read attendance figures – I still do.

I knew then Florida teams were not great draws; the consequences, my teen mind told me, of major league teams populating the state during Spring Training; which, I concluded, exhausted the fan base. What I didn't understand was many of those who went to Spring Training games were not Floridians but Snow Birds, escaping the brutal winters of New England and the Midwest.

But a California kid I didn't know this until I went to Florida for Red Fox Fantasy Camp and a Ft. Myers minister invited me to preach at his United Methodist Church and on that Sunday told me that when spring came to the north he would lose half his congregation.

Oh, my.

I had lived more than 70-years and did not know that about churches in Florida or about Spring Training attendance, and I am not dumb – but of that reality I was ignorant.

BASEBALL NOTES – AUGUST 30

BROCK HOLT WAS AT BAT FOR THE RED SOX AND THE BASES WERE LOADED in the first inning of last night's game at Fenway Park, but the Sox were only 4-33 in such circumstances, and the count was 3-2.

A strike out? Pop up? Ground ball? Fly ball? Something bad, no doubt. But no, Brock singled to left field and a run scored.

Up in the NESN broadcast booth, before the base hit by Brock, both Dave O'Brien and Jerry Remy said the bases loaded curse had to end, baseball being baseball.

So, it ended.

And the Sox would go on to win big, 9-4, as Rick Porcello became the majors' winningest pitcher with 18 victories.

Is this how it plays out? Ugly games (Sunday night), followed by great wins (last night).

But, here's the deal:

The Sox should go on to win their next eight – two at home v. Rays, three in Oakland and three in San Diego.

MEANWHILE AT CAMDEN IN BALTIMORE, THE JAYS OF SERGEANT PRESTON'S MOUNTIES, turned back Edgar Allen Poe's Ravens, 3-1.

With the loss Baltimore falls four back of Toronto in the AL East, with Boston two behind.

Josh Donaldson, who hit three HRs at home Sunday, hit one more at Camden, now has 34 on the year.

CHICAGO/PITTSBURGH WENT 13-INNINGS AT WRIGLEY before the Cubbies scored twice to win, 8-7.

There were 30 hits and 14 pitchers used in the game that lasted five hours and five minutes, ending at 12:10 am (CDT).

THE TEAM WITH THE 5TH BEST RECORD IN THE GAME, the Cleveland Indians came home to Progressive Field and won a thriller in 10-innings v. Minnesota, 1-0.

Great game and win for the 11,327 fans who made it to the ballpark.

HAVING BEATEN THE NL EAST LEADING NATIONALS IN DC, the Rockies came home to Denver and beat the NL West leading Dodgers, 8-1.

The first five hitters in Colorado's lineup – Blackmon, LeMahieu, Gonzalez, Arenado, and Dahl – are hitting .325, .344, .305, .293, and .326.

The Rockies lead the NL in base hits (1,240), runs scored (694), doubles (260), total bases (2,073), average (.273), RBI (663), SLG (.457), and OPS (795).

And they have done this without the best rookie in baseball, shortstop Trevor Story, out with a torn UCL.

When he went down, the kid from Irving, Texas, had 27 HRs and 72 RBI. He was well on his way to hitting 40 HR and driving in more than 100. A big loss, but the hope here is he comes back even better next year.

The Rockies are easily the most interesting under .500 team in the game.

TEXAS BEAT SEATTLE 6-3 IN ARLINGTON FOR THEIR 78TH WIN OF '16, giving them a solid 8.5 game lead in the AL West over Houston, the other Texas team.

TOM BOSWELL, IN HIS WASHINGTON POST COLUMN YESTERDAY, WROTE THIS:

"[Trea] Turner is the opposite extreme of the rookie-shock syndrome. Even those who thought he would be very good eventually never imagined what he is doing now. What was San Diego thinking when it traded away Turner and starter Joe Ross in a three-way deal while the Nats only gave up Stephen Souza and a Class A pitcher?

"Since the all-star break, once he was given a chance to play every day, Turner is third in the National League. Third in what? Third in runs scored, total bases and stolen bases. He is also second in hits and first in triples. He has stolen home plate. He scored against the Rockies — with the Colorado infield pulled in — on a one-hopper to the first baseman; he slid face-first across the plate 15 feet sooner than it seemed possible anybody could get there. Against the Orioles earlier in the week, he made a full-speed face-plant catch on the warning track in center field — a position he has played only 20 times. In 41 games in 177 at-bats, Turner is hitting .345 with 20 extra-base hits, 17 steals and 34 runs. Project that to 162 games. No, on second thought, don't do that. It's not fair to anyone. Next year, Turner's not going to get about 240 hits with 24 triples and 20 homers or score 135 runs with 65 steals."

The question Boswell asked, is the same question Steve Peace asked when Padres' GM A.J. Preller made that trade.

Peace, the former State Assemblyman, State Senator, and State Finance Director, thought it was a gigantic mistake to trade away the game's best young prospect, who also happened to be a shortstop, a position once occupied in San Diego by Ozzie Smith and Gary Templeton.

QUOTE OF THE DAY:

This is from Tim Peeler's new book of poetry, *Wild in the Strike Zone: Baseball Poems*, published by Rank Stranger Press, Mount Olive, North Carolina.

NOW YOU GOT 'EM WHERE YOU WANT 'EM:

Nobody told us
The proper way to fall off the mound
In position to field; our junior high coach
Was the seventh grade history teacher
Ironically named John McGraw,
A fact you could not make up,
And our workhorse pitcher was a
Bullet headed lefty from Rhode Island
Whose main claim to fame
Was his John Kennedy It's my ball;
We play by my rules" imitation
Which none of us hicks
Ever really got, and the only time
He wasn't running his mouth
Was when he was pitching
And his batting practice tosses
Came screaming back at him
As he stumbled off to the right of the mound
Leaning over like someone
Looking for a contact lens
and the "Little Napoleon" McGraw
Would shove his stubby hands
Deeper into his windbreaker pockets
And holler "Good job" George
Now you got 'em where you want 'em.

BASEBALL NOTES – AUGUST 31

TWO OUTS, TWO ON, RED SOX DOWN 4-3, BOTTOM OF THE 9th, Sandy Leon pinch hitting for Bryan Holaday.

Three strikes later Leon had struck out; the bat never left his shoulder.

Watching in San Diego, I thought, "You didn't even swing?"

Tim Mitrovich, watching in Arlington, Virginia, sent the following text, "If you're a pinch hitter you're supposed to swing at least once, right? Sheesh!"

So it would seem.

The Red Sox are really good, how could a team be otherwise with players the like of David Ortiz, Jackie Bradley Jr., Dustin Pedroia, Mookie Betts, Xander Bogearts, Rick Porcello, David Price, but games lost to teams like Tampa Bay, frustrate and puzzle the fan base.

This afternoon at Fenway they close out their brief home stand needing a win to finish 3-3, before flying west beyond the Berkshires and landing just beyond the Berkeley Hills in Oakland to face the A's for three games, travel south for three at Petco Park in San Diego, and then to the Rogers Centre in Toronto for three more v. the Jays.

By the time they come Sept. 12 to face the O's at Fenway, we will know how really good the 2016 Red Sox are. What we know at present is this team is better than the 2012, '14 and '15 teams; we don't know if they are as good as the '13 World Series winners.

Oh, my man, Travis Shaw, had a terrible night against Tampa, striking out four times.

Where is Mike Napoli when we need him?

THE O's HELPED THE SOX STAY TWO BACK OF THE JAYS as they won in Baltimore, 5-3, with Matt Weiters hitting a two-run HR in the eighth for the victory.

The game between the first and third place teams in the AL East drew a pathetic crowd of 16,083 to Orioles Park at Camden Yards.

ROUGNED "ONE PUNCH" ODOR HIT A TWO-RUN WALK-OFF HR as Texas beat Seattle halfway between Dallas and Ft. Worth, 8-7.

Odor now has 25 HRs and plays a mean shortstop, but is mostly known for the knockout punch he threw at the Blue Jays' Jose Bautista, which we will see again, many times, guaranteed, if the two teams meet in the playoffs.

The Rangers have more walk-off wins than any other MLB team.

THE CUBS WON THEIR 21ST GAME IN AUGUST BY BEATING THE PIRATES AT WRIGLEY, 3-0.

Kyle Hendricks was strong through seven and Anthony Rizzo hit his 26th HR, a line drive shot to the bleachers in right, while raising his RBI total to 93.

Hendricks' 2.09 ERA leads all MLB pitchers.

The Northsiders need 21 more wins to reach my predicted 105 for the season.

ZACK GREINKE WON HIS 12TH GAME AGAINST FOUR LOSSES, as the D-Backs beat SF at AT&T, 4-3.

With LAD rained out in Denver, SF fell two back in the NL West.

CURTIS GRANDERSON, ONE OF MY FAVORITE PLAYERS, came off the bench and hit two HRs for the Metropolitans of the Borough of Queens, New York, as they defeated the Marlins of Miami, 7-4.

The oddity of Curtis' season is that while he has 23 HRs, he only has 38 RBI.

Trust me when I tell you that Curtis Granderson is a gentleman and he will have a brilliant post-season broadcasting career.

THE PADRES LOST TO THE BRAVES IN ATLANTA, 7-3, and now have lost 76 times, a mark exceeded by only two other teams.

RYAN HOWARD, HIS CAREER MOSTLY DONE, HIT HIS 20TH HR in a losing cause, as his Phillies lost to the Nationals, 3-2.

The great Max Scherzer won his 15th game, throwing eight dominant innings, as he stuck out 11 and gave up but three hits.

Max's 238 K's tops the majors.

COMPLETE GAMES IS A CATEGORY NOT LISTED ON ESPN'S MLB PITCHING STATS, every other stat is there, games played and started, innings pitched, hits, runs, earned runs, strike outs, bases on balls, wins, losses, saves, etc., but not complete games.

ESPN's web site is hugely informative, I check it often, but not to list complete games should be a criminal offense.

There are 30 United States attorneys in 27 major league cites, most of whom are extremely ambitious. I would think several of them might want to examine whether failure to list complete games is an indictable offense.

QUOTE OF THE DAY:

Another poem from Tim Peeler, entitled "Rebels 2":

The contracts always looked the same:
400-500 month, so the hat passed
By the fans of College Field after a winning start
Or a home run made the difference
In a hard winter as the post-war country
Regained its land legs and the general manager
Who was also an elementary principal
Would meet you in the gray twilight
Behind the school's coal bin
To deliver an extra hundred
From your games' gates,
Yet the real prizes were the girls
That cruised Main Street
Till the line of ballplayers
In front of the town hotel
Diminished to the ones
That were really just there
To pitch pennies or whose fears
Of their wives or girl friends
Back home were greater
Than their current desires.

BASEBALL NOTES – SEPTEMBER 1

THE ROCKIES ALMOST SWEPT A DOUBLEHEADER & SERIES FROM THE DODGERS, but didn't.

In game one at Coors yesterday they won, 7-0. No, really, they shutout the billionaires. Did that because their starting pitcher, T. Anderson, went 6.1 innings with zero runs scored, and was followed by Rusin, Logan, and Estevez, and zero runs scored.

In game two, Colorado led 8-0 going into the top of the 8th. That would seem safe enough, right? The doubleheader and series sweep was a mere six outs away. Only three games away from .500 and only eight games back, six outs away.

Doable, right?

Not exactly.

Because you have to figure that Rockies' manager Walt Weiss would find a way to screw it up for his ball club, and he did.

After getting two shutout innings from relievers Lyles and McGee in the top of the 6th and 7th, Weiss went to his bullpen to bring in Casariti, clearly thinking he could do this, that a pitcher with an ERA of 13.03, would get the job done.

Wrong.

In 1/3rd of an inning the immortal Casariti threw 18 pitches, yielding two runs, three hits, and one base on balls.

Weiss then turned, again, to Estevez, who got his team out of the 8th without further damage, and Colorado still leading, 8-5.

But, Weiss, figuring, no doubt, that Estevez must be gassed, having thrown all of 29 pitches in games one and two, would not go out for the 9th. So the manager turned to Ottavino, who in that fatal 9th threw 27 pitches, yielding five runs, three hits, two bases on balls.

End results: the Dodgers of Los Angeles, 10, the Rockies of Colorado, 8.

So, why should I care what happens to the Rockies, when I have the Red Sox and Padres in my life?

Because, as president of The Denver Forum, that great city has been in my life for 31 years, and because the people I care about, John Hickenlooper, Bob Nicholls, Jim Kennel, Jeff Hart, Andy Newell, Martha Bennett, Norm Brownstein, Steve Farber, Doug Price, Mitch and Maggie Morrissey, Erin Holleman, Nancy Hestera, Ron Tilton, and a whole bunch more, are all Colorado fans, and since the Padres are done for '16 (and a few years beyond), I root for the Rockies.

And, I am not a fan of Walt Weiss.

THE CUBS WON 6-5 OVER THE PIRATES AS KRIS BRYANT HIT HR 36, and Aroldis Chapman came on in the top of the 9th at Wrigley for the save.

For Chapman, no sweat, in 43 career innings v. Pittsburgh he has struck out 76 batters and his ERA against the Three Rivers team is 0.87.

It was Chicago's 85th win of the season. They need 20 more to reach my predicted goal of 105. They have 30 games left in which to do that.

THE RED SOX WON 8-6 AT FENWAY DESPITE ANOTHER 8TH INNING BULLPEN IMPLOSION, and headed west to Gold Rush country having won two of three from the last place Rays.

Abad and Tazawa pitched to form, as they gave up two runs, two hits, and walked two in the hated 8th, but lucky for them the Red Sox hitters are world class and came back from the tie to produce two winnings runs.

Down 4-1 earlier, Hanley Ramirez delivered a grand slam HR, and helped turn the game around.

The Sox are off today before playing three against the A's this weekend.

SECOND BASEMAN ROUGNED ODOR HITS HRs 26 AND 27 AND TEXAS BEAT SEATTLE, 14-1.

Odor, he of one-punch fame, is having a heck of a year, with his 27 dingers, 76 RBI, and a .276 BA.

This is only his third big league season and the kid is only 22.

I would seriously suggest to the owners of the Rangers, they find a way to keep this young man in the USA this off season. You cannot risk his going home to the turmoil in Venezuela, where he would clearly be a kidnap target, so have him file for political asylum.

And tell donald trump Odor is a Venezuelan not Mexican.

THE NATIONALS WON 2-1 OVER THE PHILLIES & SWEPT THE THREE GAME SERIES, and stay 9 up on the Metropolitans, who also won, beating Miami, who have now lost seven of 10 and fallen 11 games back in the NL East.

IN OTHER GAMES: the Jays beat the O's at Camden, 5-3 (in this critical series, no crowd exceeded 17,000 at glorious Oriole Park at Camden Yards; the three game total, 47,776, or approximately a one game total in Toronto); Cleveland won 8-4 over Minnesota, which has now lost 13 straight; the Giants beat the D-Backs at AT&T, 4-2, to remain two back of LAD, and the Padres lost to the Braves, 8-1, and after playing Atlanta again today, fly to LA for three v. the Dodgers, and then home for three v. Boston.

QUOTE OF THE DAY:

"Sherry" from "Wild in the Strike Zone" by Tim Peeler:

Two boys, one to hit, and one to field,
Then to switch. She'd mapped the yard
and knew where the bushes were,
where the clothesline ran.
Her back to the plate, she marked off
this year's spot with confident steps,
turned till the sun glinted off
The thick shades she'd worn
since she left the hospital,
since her husband slammed
her face into the stone fireplace,
destroying her eyes.
She felt the seams of the ball, aligning them with her first two fingers.
She knew the boys' height
from hugging them every day.
She knew you had to come forward
and when to let go.
She knew to duck
But would sometimes
get hit by grounders.
Sherry threw strikes
that only her sons could see.
No wonder they became
all-star players.
No wonder they became good men.

PREFACE: I'm in Boston for a Great Fenway Park Writers Series luncheon with Brian Kenny of MLB Network today at the Residence Inn, down Brookline Avenue from America's most beloved ballpark.

Brian will speak on his new book, "Ahead of the Curve: Inside the Baseball Revolution."

Thus, in brevity:

BASEBALL NOTES – SEPTEMBER 13

DAVID ORTIZ HIT HIS 33RD HR OF THE SEASON AND 536TH OF HIS CAREER and the Red Sox won over the O's at Fenway, 12-2.

With his HR, Ortiz tied Mickey Mantle for 17th all-time, as the Sox pounded out 16 hits, including HRs by Hanley Ramirez (24) and Chris Young (9).

David Price, whose pitching has been superb post all-star game, won his 16th game of '16, as he and Rick Porcello have accounted for 36 of the Sox's 81 victories.

THE NORTHSIDE CUBS OF CHICAGO MADE IT WIN NUMBER 92, as they defeated the Cardinals, 4-1, at Busch in St. Louis.

Kyle Hendricks won his 15th, as he pitched a one hitter through eight and lowered his major league leading ERA to 2.03.

With the win the Cubbies are 13 away from 105, which has no significance other than it is what I predicted.

IF THE CUBS & RED SOX MAKE IT TO THE WORLD SERIES, that will be a great thing for America's Game.

A pairing that will accomplish two things:

It will 1) result in the highest television ratings ever, and 2) distract us from Clinton/trump.

Theologically, I don't think God concerns himself/herself with who gets to the World Series, but this year, maybe.

THE TIGERS WON OVER THE TWINS IN MOTOWN, 4-1, and are now only one game back in the Wild Card contest.

THE DODGERS, BACK AT THE STADIUM IN THE BRONX, won over the host Yankees, 8-2, as the Giants fell four back of LAD in the NL West, losing to the Padres at AT&T, 4-0.

San Diego's shutout was achieved through the efforts of six pitchers.

Dick Enberg, in the Fox San Diego broadcast booth last night, pointed out that Yangervis Solarte, the Padres' 3rd baseman, has more HRs and RBI than the Giants' vaunted Buster Posey, 15 and 66 to 12 and 64, while being one point off in BA, .286 to .285.

Who knew?

Dick Enberg, knew.

FINAL WORD ON DAVE ROBERTS:

There was significant and substantive dissent to my tear down of Roberts' decision to remove Rich Hill from Saturday night's game v. Miami, when Hill was pitching a perfect game.

Notable among the dissenters – Red Sox Chairman Tom Werner and MLB Network's Brian Kenny.

Both of whom pointed out Hill's problems with developing blisters on his throwing hand, and therefore Roberts' decision, placing the team's interest above Hill's chance to achieve immortality, came first.

I am, of course, respectful of both Mr. Werner and Mr. Kenny's views, but if only Yasiel Puig had not made that falling down catch on the warning track in left field for the third out in the bottom of the 7th, all of this would have been mute.

QUOTE OF THE DAY:

Tim Peeler, the Carolina bard, is back with "McGwire":

I understand spectacle:

Falstaff, the fat country lawyer,

Long home runs, the poor man's

Big car, the night sky's black art,

Games that are both foolish

And random, how mysteries

Wait for time to sift,

How hearts lift

Joyously in song

How hugs are

The parentheses

That can save us

From this sentence.

PREFACE: It's probably best not to compose Notes at midnight (EDT) as I did on Alaska Airlines flight's 769 from Boston's Logan to San Diego, because a slight tweaking is then required (I concede, not a concern of yours, but of mine).

BASEBALL NOTES – SEPTEMBER 15

ANTHONY RIZZO HIT HRs 31 & 32 OF '16, while driving in three to up his RBI total to 101, as the Cubs won 7-0 over the Cardinals at Busch in St. Louis.

Jon Lester was brilliant through eight, giving up three hits, one walk, and eight strike outs, while winning his 17th game against four losses.

It was Chicago's 93rd win and puts them 17 up over the Cardinals with 17 to play.

RICH PORCELLO PITCHED EIGHT GREAT INNINGS FOR THE RED SOX, but Kevin Gausman was a run better and O's won at Fenway, 1-0.

Porcello lost his 4th game against 20 wins, while Gausman won only his eighth against 10 losses.

Gausman's ERA is now down to an even 4.00, but his post All-Star Game pitching has been fascinating, as he has turned in several superlative performances – not least last night.

The Sox lead the AL East by one game over Baltimore, and with the Jays' losing to Tampa, they slip two back, while the Yankees, who come to Fenway tonight for four, lost to the Dodgers, 2-0, falling four behind.

By losing, the Red Sox continue their puzzling pattern of play.

Monday night they scored 12-runs; Tuesday, 3; and last night, none.

In Oakland on Friday, July 3, they scored 16 runs; 11 the next night; none on Sunday, followed by one in San Diego on Labor Day, before winning the next two. Then in Toronto last Friday, they put 13 up on the board, followed by only two on Saturday, and then, of course, 11 on Sunday

As noted, puzzling.

THE UP THE DOWN STAIRCASE PADRES WERE UP IN SF AND BEAT THE GIANTS, 3-1, to sweep their three games series from Bruce Bochy's team; a team that had completely dominated the Padres before the All-Star break.

Having heard MLB Network's brilliant Brian Kinney at Tuesday's Fenway Park Writers Series luncheon, I think it's safe to report that Brian would approve of the Padres having used 14 pitchers to accomplish their sweep.

To understand Brian's thinking, you need to order from Barnes & Noble, "Ahead of the Curve: Inside the Baseball Revolution," an in-depth look at the rise of the geniuses in baseball ops.

Why Barnes & Noble?

Because Barnes & Noble is a bookstore not a warehouse!

Remember:

If you are a lover of bookstores and desire a bookstore in your city, then know if Barnes & Noble goes away most American cities will not have a bookstore, including San Diego.

QUOTE OF THE DAY:

Another from the great Tim Peeler, entitled, "Fences":

We played little league ball on
Fields without fences before
Rotary Club money strung
Chain links across the landfill
Known as Kiwanis Park and
Out by left field a sink hole
Collapsed halfway through summer.
One six foot twelve-year-old sent
Towering fly balls to the
Gravel parking lot while
His little brother toppled
Into the abyss; firemen
Roped him and plucked him back
To his Momma who busted
His ass and gave him money
To go buy a Pepsi dope.
Now that park is named for an
Australian girl who
Got dismembered by the step-
Mom her father met online.
Forty-eight years ago we
Didn't really need fences.

2017

BASEBALL NOTES – APRIL 7

THE COLORADO ROCKIES, TIED FOR THE NL WEST LEAD, OPEN VS. LAD AT COORS THIS AFTERNOON.

The idiosyncratic ways of Denver weather – snow Wednesday, 70 yesterday, 46 and rain this morning – will turn away no fans, because they are Coloradans and they're weather proof.

Good luck to Bud Black, who makes his home managerial debut on Blake Street (and speaks to The Denver Forum at noon on Tuesday at the Denver Athletic Club).

The Rockies won yesterday, 2-1, over Milwaukee, as Nolan Arenado and Mark Reynolds homered, and five Colorado pitchers yielded only five hits for the win.

THE PADRES ALSO OPEN AT HOME VS. THE GIANTS, a mid-afternoon start at Petco Park. Weather will not be an issue.

Both teams won one in four to start '17, as the Padres lost their series to LAD and SF to Arizona.

Starting for SD is Luis Perdomo; for SF, Matt Cain.

THE RED SOX WHO WERE RAINED OUT YESTERDAY AT FENWAY VS. PITTSBURGH (they will make it up next week), are the guests of the Tigers in Detroit's home opener at Comerica this afternoon.

The Sox won two against the Pirates, including a dramatic Sandy Leon walk-off three run HR in the 12th inning for the win Wednesday.

Some Boston scribes want Christian Vazquez not Leon behind the plate. We'll see how that plays out.

Chris Sale, the Sox's major acquisition during the off-season, pitched brilliantly in his Sox debut, as he threw seven shutout innings, giving up but three hits, one walk, and seven K's.

THE MARINERS STAVED OFF A HOUSTON SWEEP AT MINUTE MAID, as they rallied for two in the top of the 9th and pulled out a 4-2 victory.

Seattle, 1-3 after their South Texas visit, remain on the road, playing the Angels across Disneyland from I-5 for LAA's home opener.

The Angels opened against the A's across the Bay Bridge from AT&T and gained a split in their four game set.

THE MINNESOTA TWINS, WHO HAVE ENDURED BAD BEGINNINGS TO NEW SEASONS, actually began this season by winning all three of their games against KC at Target.

Way to go, Twins.

OTHER THAN CAROLINA'S TIM PEELER'S POEM THAT FOLLOWS, that's it for Notes today, as my wife, La Verle, who suffered a catastrophic break to her right leg, remains in recovery, and when that happens to the woman who has shared 60 years of your life, there is distraction, even amid ongoing duties in San Diego, Denver and Boston.

Each day she gets better, but she's still two weeks from coming home.

Oh, you should know, at Pasadena Nazarene College, she played a terrific third base – and her baseball knowledge is second to none.

QUOTE OF THE DAY:

JACKIE ROBINSON WAS A BUNT

Every bunt is a fresh attempt,
a brain's radar tuned to the pitcher's release,
the batter's body in blunt stance.

Bunting is like drawing a charge,
laying a good block,
baiting someone else's hook.

The man who bunts well
is the man you would hunt with
or even take to war.

The man who bunts well gives up
the pawn of the moment
for a bishop later,

a black bishop
angling toward a white plate.

BASEBALL NOTES – TUESDAY, APRIL 18

THE BRONX BOMBERS HAVE WON EIGHT IN A ROW, as they beat the Pale Hose, 7-3, last night across the Harlem River at the Stadium.

They are now 9-4 for '17, and while most experts do not expect them to keep that up, it's a nice beginning.

Which leads. Me to ask, is it necessary to write this again? – a game won in April counts as a game won in September.

A couple of years back, here in Notes, I did the *tedious research to prove my point of how many times a pennant winner was determined by one game over a long season – the Red Sox lost by one game in both '48 and '49, for example – but that research is lost amid more than 450,000 words of Notes, but trust me – every game counts!

*"Tedious" is defined as examining 114 years of AL and NL standings.

THE RED SOX BEAT THE RAYS AT FENWAY ON PATRIOTS' DAY, 4-3, another comeback win for the Sox, who did that three times in three days of the four game series.

Dave O'Brien, in the NESN booth, told The Nation of the 20 games played between of the two teams of recent vintage, 12 have been decided by one run.

Overall the Sox have a clear advantage since the Rays debuted in '98, having won 200 of 349 played, but from 2010 on the record is closer, 84-90 (according to mcubed.net).

The Sox are in Toronto at the Rogers Center to play the team Alex Speier of the Boston Globe says will win the AL East.

Perhaps, but at the moment Justin Trudeau's Jays, Canada's National Team, are 2-10.

THE D-BACKS BEAT LAD IN THE RAVINE LAST NIGHT, 4-2, to gain a split in their four game set, as Robbie Ray pitched brilliantly through six to win his first game of '17.

There were 20,552 empty seats at Dodger Stadium, perhaps due to the fact the investment bankers who owned the team have the most expensive "cheap" ticket in the majors at $20 (the Rockies, is $4).

When you add the high cost of going to Dodger games, the team's absence on television to some 70 percent of their fan base, a downturn in LAD attendance may continue.

THE SAN DIEGO PADRES, A TEAM THAT HOPES TO EMULATE WHAT THE CHICAGO CUBS, just did, as both have lost four in a row.

The Padres went to Cumberland, GA, to play the Braves, and proceeded to lose all four games of the series, a 5-4 loss yesterday capping that feat.

Meanwhile, the Cubbies were losing four to the Pirates (3) and Milwaukee, all at Wrigley Field 6-3.

Why it's enough to cause George Will to drop his membership in the Republican Party (actually, he already did, but I believe it was Trump related, not Cubs related).

George with Tim Kurkjian, Christine Brennan, Justice Alito, David Brooks. Talmadge Boston, and George Will.

Attendance at Sun Trust for the Braves' inaugural home opener was 41,149, followed by the same count Saturday of 41,149, plus 37,147 Sunday, and a more Turner Field like crowd of 24,516 last night.

QUOTE OF THE DAY:

Tim Peeler is back with another of his poems. Love his work. He is Special:

The Yearning

To write baseball poems
Is really the yearning to see
Dad's ugly brown four door
Studebaker backing into a spot
At Robinson Field an hour early
As he was for every event in his life;
To watch him shoulder the bat bag
And carry it across the packed red dirt
To the first base dugout where he sat
With the scorebook, formulating
The lineup for fifteen minutes as if
The Yankees were coming
To play the Red Sox at Fenway;
To hear him greet players and parents
As he did at the sanctuary door after
Three thousand church services,
Then to see him watch little Coffey
Squatting on shin guards,
A chest protector bigger than him,
The way one dead man
Watches another
In a dream
Or a memory
Or a poem.

BASEBALL NOTES – THURSDAY, MAY 4

THE RED SOX BEAT THE O's AT FENWAY LAST NIGHT, 4-2, with the series now standing at 2-1 Sox, with game four tonight.

Which I note because Baltimore/Boston has become a big deal, some fans believing the rivalry tops that of Sox/Yankees, Dave O'Brien said during last night's NESN broadcast.

In Tuesday's Boston Globe, The Peerless Pundit, Dan Shaughnessy, wrote:

"The Red Sox were the Orioles' daddies in the 5½ seasons preceding [Buck] Showalter's arrival in the Baltimore dugout. From 2005 to mid-2010, the Sox went 81-31 vs. Baltimore, including seasons of 16-2 and 15-3.

Since Buck landed, the Orioles are 71-55 vs. Boston after Monday's wedgy win over the stumbling Sox."

But the rise of the O's v Sox rivalry is less game related than incident related.

Manny Machado's spiking of the sainted Dustin Pedroia last week at Camden and team pitchers throwing at one another's batters and attendant media obsession is more likely the cause of fan interest.

SAM KENNEDY'S NESN INTERVIEW ON ADAM JONES and the racist behavior of some Fenway fans toward the great O's center fielder, was a signature moment.

It was in that moment, I believe, when in the public mind, Sam Kennedy became President of the Boston Red Sox.

He was so good in that interview, his remarks so completely appropriate, that if fans had not paid attention to him before, they now will.

It's not easy following Larry Lucchino, but Sam Kennedy has made his mark.

WELL, WHAT WILL KORNHEISER SAY NOW ABOUT WASHINGTON'S RELIEF PITCHERS?

"Mr. Tony" as he is called by his Podcast crew, has been raving about how good the Nationals are, while ripping their relief pitching, even suggesting that one of them, following a recent poor performance, should catch a boat to somewhere and not come back.

Then yesterday happened, and a relief pitcher for Washington named Jacob Turner, came into the game, replacing Gio Gonzalez, and delivered four – count them – four scoreless innings of brilliant relief pitching, in which he gave up but two hits, walked none, struck out four, and, deservedly, got the 2-1 victory for the Nationals, and is now 1-0 for '17.

Ryan Zimmerman, the much maligned Ryan Zimmerman of '16, had two more hits for DC and is now batting, .427.

Which astounds many fans, not least Tony Kornheiser.

Who, by the by, now has his own restaurant just inside the DC line on Wisconsin Avenue, NW. He and his partners named it, "Chatter."

It is open for breakfast at eight, and you can watch the Podcast live.

If it wasn't for the distance, 2,686 miles, I would certainly drop in, because I love Tony's show. I can't explain why, because it makes zero sense to listen to a Washington centric mostly sports show while living in San Diego, other than to blame Tim Mitrovich, who works for the US Senate, who put me onto it, and now I'm hooked.

But I may consider therapy.

IN ONE-HOUR AND TWENTY-NINE MINUTES, MAY 4, 1977, RANDY JONES OF THE PADRES beat the Phillies, 4-1. It was the fastest nine-inning game in Padres history, and the second fastest ever in major league history.

The story of Jones' win and the time of the game, written by Kirk Kenney, led sports today in the *San Diego Union-Tribune*.

Kirk's story goes on to chart game times from 1920-2016.

In the 20s, an average major league game lasted 1:48; in the 30s, 1:57; 40s, 2:04; 50s, 2:20; 60s, 2:33; 70s, 2:30; 80s, 2:34; 90s, 2:48; 2000, 2:58; 2005, 2:46; 2010, 2:55, and last season, 3:00.

On the night Jones won his game, attendance was 10,021 fans. But in '77, when games lasted on average, 2:30, an average crowd in the majors was 18,598.

Last year, when games averaged three hours, average attendance was 30,131.

So, does anyone really care about time of games? I think it matters, but it's not keeping them at home.

***BASEBALL NOTES – TUESDAY, MAY 16**

I WROTE IN NOTES YESTERDAY:

"THE WEATHER MOTHER'S DAY IN BOSTON WAS MISERABLE and the Red Sox made the weather seem 75 and sunny."

The following word was dropped:

"Not!"

Dick Flavin, the Fenway Park public address announcer, told me it was indeed as miserable a day weather wise as he could ever recall on Yawkey Way.

IF I SAY ST. LOUIS CARDINAL FANS ARE BASEBALL'S BEST, you might disagree. If I say they are the nicest, probably not.

Walking away from Busch Stadium in '04, with the Red Sox having just won their first World Series in '86 years and wearing Sox gear, Cardinal fans were unfailingly congratulatory.

Perhaps it was a display of common humanity from fans whose teams have won 11 World Series toward the less fortunate, but whatever it was, it was notable and appreciated.

That said, the Sox are back in the Mound City tonight to meet the NL Central leading Cards, who've won eight of 10.

The Cardinals broke the two million attendance mark for the first time in '63 – they've since repeated that 53 times.

HUNTER RENFROE, AS PROMISING AS ANY PADRES' PLAYER, came to bat in the bottom of the 9th at Petco Park last night, and with a slight flip of his wrists, sent a two-run walk HR into the third row of the left field bleachers for a 6-5 win.

Renfroe, whose record in '16 with Triple A El Paso and the Padres, included 40 doubles, five triples, 37 HRs, and 122 RBIs, is franchise making stuff.

BUD BLACK, THE ROCKIES MANAGER, texted me a get well note and wrote how pleased he was with the team's home stand and says he looks forward to keeping it up on the road for 10 games in Minnesota, Cincinnati, and Philly.

Seven and three always from Coors would be nice.

MATT CAIN PITCHED SUPERBLY FOR SF AND THE GIANTS WON OVER LAD AT AT&T, 8-4.

Buster Posey had two hits and homered for Bruce Bochy's lads, and Posey is now hitting .370.

Nice.

QUOTE OF THE DAY:

The Granite Falls Rocks by Tim Peeler:

The Granite Falls Rocks
Who played on 115-year-old
MS Deal Field, then 49
Have been often mentioned
For their 14-90 record
The worst in minor league history
Their losing streaks of 33
And 26, because after
The story is done cooking,
All that's left is the numbers,
Just the facts as they say,
But their 1951 tale is better
As I heard it from this humble
Local historian who
Pointed out that the town
Had a winning semi-pro team,
And when the local Class D
Needed an eighth club
They thought what the hay,
And the rest is almost history,
Except in August, the whole
Season wilted on the vine
They signed the first three
Black players to contracts
In North Carolina history,
The Paul Harvey part
Of their mystery.

George the lay-minister.

BASEBALL NOTES – TUESDAY, MAY 29

THE GREAT JON MILLER WAS RINGSIDE AT AT&T MEMORIAL DAY, when All-World, Bryce Harper of the Nationals, enraged by being hit in his right hip by a 90 mph plus fastball from Giants' reliever, Hunter Strickland, fired his batting helmet onto the infield grass and charged the mound.

Up in the Giants' broadcast booth, Miller said, "There's a right to the jaw, a left to the chin!"

In other words, Boys & Girls, fisticuffs were underway.

This was no scrum. This was real. And, of course, everyone charged the mound, including some players who stand 6'4 and weigh 240 lbs.

Some fans love the excitement, but not me. Real injuries can result from these altercations (ask Bill Lee of the Red Sox what Craig Nettles of the Yankees did to his left arm in a brawl at Fenway Park).

But, yes, I know, boys will be boys, and stuff happens.

I assume some heavy fines and suspensions will result, which would be appropriate.

The scene that unfolded on the field in SF, underscores why I think Giants' catcher Buster Posey is a very smart dude. He did not enter the fray, nor remove his catcher's mask. I do not know what his teammates think about that, but Buster did the right thing.

He's already lost one season from a violent collision at home plate; why risk a second?

THE SOX (RED) LOST TO THE SOX (WHITE) AT WHATCHAMACALLIT PARK ON CHICAGO'S SOUTHSIDE YESTERDAY, 5-4.

With Boston up, 4-3, in the 7th, John Farrell, Boston's manager, called in Joe Kelly, he of the 1.54 ERA, to hold the lead, which he did.

Farrell then did what he does, he called on Matt Barnes to pitch the 8th, apparently because Kelly was exhausted from having thrown 29 pitches in the 7th.

And, of course, when I saw Barnes coming in I knew the Red Sox would lose – and lose they did.

I have zero confidence that when Matt Barnes enters a game good will result for Boston.

Whether my impression is fair, I do not know, but I don't think it's going away.

PLAYING BEFORE AN SRO CROWD AT PETCO PARK, the Padres beat the Cubs, 5-3.

Trailing 2-0 in the bottom of the 4th, the hometown nine had loaded the bases, when up stepped The Rookie, Hunter Renfroe, who proceeded to deliver a grand slam, and with it the game to SD.

As I have noted here on several occasions, I believe Renfroe is the real deal – and the Padres have a big time star in the making.

CANADA'S NATIONAL TEAM, THE BLUE JAYS, SCORED 17 RUNS, while Cincy scored two at the Rogers Centre in Toronto.

The Jays, picked by Alex Speier of the *Boston Globe*, to win the AL East, appear to be turning it around from their woeful start.

THE O's, HAVING LOST SEVEN STRAIGHT, CAME HOME TO CAMDEN MEMORIAL DAY and beat the Yankees, 3-2.

Aaron Judge, who may be the second coming of Mickey Mantle, hit his 17th HR in NYY's loss.

***THEY WERE 15 GAMES IN THE MAJOR LEAGUES MEMORIAL DAY WITNESSED BY 483,448.**

The top crowd, 46,241, was in St Louis, where the Cardinals lost to the Dodgers, 5-1.

The smallest, oddly, 16,938, was in Pittsburgh, where the Pirates beat the D-Backs, 4-3.

Five teams drew more than 40,000 – St. Louis, San Diego, Colorado, Baltimore, and San Francisco.

The 15 game average – 32,229.

*You do realize, do you not? that you are not reading this anywhere else. It's not that the "research" is tedious, because it doesn't rise to that level, but attendance figures have fascinated me since I was in junior high school in San Diego and reading *The Sporting News*, the "Baseball Bible," which listed the attendance for every major and minor league team.

QUOTE OF THE DAY:

Tim Peeler has made "Quote of the Day" more than any other writer, because the Poet of the Carolinas, is that good.

In this poem baseball is not mentioned, but I believe baseball players believe in heaven, too:

The Convinced

He went to his grave believing
That he would be reunited
With his parents and his siblings
With friends who'd gone before
That there was more to this world
Than the smells and sounds
The pain and fear and heartbreak
The joys and laughter and light
The darkness of endless night.
He went to his grave believing
That we are all in this together
That love and truth would triumph
That every moment held weight,
Gospel sure of his heavenly fate.

BASEBALL NOTES – THURSDAY, MAY 8

THE DODGERS OF LOS ANGELES BEAT THE NATIONALS OF WASHINGTON in the sunlight of Chavez Ravine yesterday afternoon, 2-1.

Clayton Kershaw was the winning pitcher for the Dodgers and is now 8-2 for '17.

Stephen Strasburg was the losing pitcher for the Nationals and is now 7-2 for '17.

The scores of the three games played in Los Angeles were: 4-2, 2-1, and 2-1, with Washington winning two of the three.

It was a pitcher's series as the two teams only scored 12-runs. Batters were held to 29 hits over the three games, they walked 13 times, while striking out 58 times.

Of the games Tuesday night and yesterday afternoon, no doubt many will say, "Now, that is what I call baseball; the game as it was intended to be played."

Those three low scoring games were no more baseball as "intended" than the Phillies beating the Cubs at Wrigley Field, 23-22 (17 May 1979).

There is no as "intended." There is, rather, Baseball – America's Game.

ON THE OPPOSITE SIDE OF THE CONTINENT, the Yankees beat the Red Sox in the Bronx last night, 8-0, as C.C. Sabathia won for the seventh time this season against only two losses.

He pitched brilliantly through eight innings, yielding but five hits and striking out five, with zero bases on balls.

Rick Porcello, who won the Cy Young last season for the Red Sox, performed more like the Rick Porcello of '15, which is not what Boston expected. Hardly. In 6.3 innings he gave up eight hits and six runs.

The series stands 1-1 and tonight the Sox pitch David Price, looking to him to be David Price.

The loss put the Sox two games back of the Yankees, so a victory tonight would be welcomed north of New Haven.

Which means what?

If you live south of Yale U. you are generally considered a Yankees fan, but north is Red Sox Nation.

BUD BLACK'S BLAKE STREET BOMBERS BEAT CLEVELAND 8-0 yesterday, which followed Colorado's 11-3 win Tuesday night. Nineteen runs in two games against last year's AL champions is impressive. Very.

The Rockies lead the NL West by two games over LAD and the D-Backs.

And thus far it's been a dream season for my friend, Buddy Black, and the agnostics among us believe the dream will shatter and the Rockies will become the Rockies again.

But to women and men of faith, agnosticism is an intellectual dead end, and I believe this is the Rockies' year.

And what should that mean to you?

What it should mean is this:

September 30, 2013, in Baseball Notes, I predicted the following:

In the AL playoffs, Boston over Tampa; Detroit over Oakland; Boston over Detroit.

In the NL playoffs, St. Louis over Pittsburgh; Los Angeles over Atlanta; St. Louis over Los Angeles.

I then predicted the Red Sox would beat the Cardinals in six games, and on the morning of the sixth game I flew to Boston to be present at Fenway Park to see the fulfillment of my predictions.

So, as the Rockies are in Chicago today for the first of four vs. the World Series winners, you might consider what I wrote, "This is the Rockies' year."

However, in the interest of full disclosure, you should know I predicted Hillary over Trump, and I said it wouldn't be close.

So, there's that.

THE AWESOME ASTROS OF HOUSTON FELL TO THE ROYALS OF KC, 7-5, and with that win KC won the three game set at Kaufmann.

While Houston is running away with the AL West, KC is only 4.5 back of Minnesota in the AL Central, which has the tightest race of baseball's six divisions.

THE TORONTO BLUE JAYS, THE NATIONAL TEAM OF CANADA, thanks to a tie-breaking two run HR in the top of the 10th, beat the A's, 7-5, and did it in the city where "there is no there there," as Ms. Stein opined about Oakland.

Justin Smoak also homered in the 10th, his second long ball of the game.

The Jays started poorly, and immediately doubts were cast on Alex Speier of the *Boston Globe's* bold pre-season prediction that the Jays, not the Red Sox, would win the AL East.

With Toronto only six back, despite their inauspicious start to '17, it is possible that we may yet witness the redemption of both the Blue Jays and Alex Speier.

You should know that I tease about Alex, who has been a guest of The Writers Series, and is, as Peter Gammons says, "The best of the young writers covering America's Game.

QUOTE OF THE DAY:

Tim Peeler, the Poet of the Carolinas, is back:

GAME DAY

Over the washboard dirt road
Leaning into the handle bars
Carrying two bats each, one glove
The smell of oil if it was hard summer,
Dust if the trucks hadn't been there.
The neighbor boys were waiting
As we had to lunch first,
Fried bacon and Velveeta
On toasted hotdog buns.
Earlier we'd picked up the party line
Rang it two times and stopped
Which meant a ball game.
The sun blasted through the pines
Onto a field we'd nearly worn
The grass off, and it was just us
Except for the sand trucks pounding
The washboard like hungry dinosaurs
Charging toward the river.

BASEBALL NOTES – WEDNESDAY, JUNE 14, 2017

MONDAY NIGHT AT TARGET FIELD IN MINNEAPOLIS, the Mariners of Seattle beat the Twins of Minnesota, 14-3.

Tuesday night at Target Field, the Twins beat the Mariners, 20-7, with the 20-runs setting a franchise record.

Why do we love America's Game? Those two back-to-back games will tell you why.

Inexplicable and unexplainable.

Last night, the Twins had 28 base hits, including five HRs, three of which were hit by the immortal, Eddie Rosario.

Five Twin hitters had three of more base hits, including third baseman, Eduardo Escobar, who was 5-6. Three had four, Jason Castro, Kennys Vargas, and Rosario.

Of the 28-base hits, only seven were for extra bases.

Oh, not one of the starters in the Twins' lineup is hitting .300.

IN 1950 THE " Whiz Kids" of PHILADELPHIA won the NL pennant over the Brooklyn Dodgers by two games (but were shutout by the Yankees in the World Series, 4-0)

For reasons I cannot explain I remember the Phillies' lineup – Andy Seminick, behind the plate; Eddie Waitkus at first; Mike Goliat at second, "Puddin Head" Jones at third; Granville Hamner at shortstop, with Del Ennis, Richie Ashburn, and Dick Sisler in the outfield, and Robin Roberts and Curt Simmons the team's two aces on the mound, with Jim Konstanty in the bullpen.

I was a kid of 15. I lived in San Diego. I was not a Phillies' fan.

But if asked today why I remember a team's lineup from 67-years ago, when I cannot tell you the players and positions of any other team – neither the San Diego Padres of '98 nor the Red Sox of '04, I am clueless

Why should that be? I do not know? Perhaps I will leave my brain to SABR and let them do the requisite research.

Oh, in a taxi ride across Manhattan in 1970 with Gloria Steinem and Richard Reeves of The Times, however it happened, the subject of the "Whiz Kids" came up between Reeves and me, and I proceeded to recite, as I have above, the Phillies' lineup.

At the end of which, the estimable Ms. Steinem said, "This is the most useless conversation I have ever been subjected to." (However, a whole lot of years later, I was able to persuade my friend, Gloria, to come to Fenway and speak at a luncheon of The Writers Series; and to do it wearing Red Sox warmup jacket.)

WHICH LEADS ME TO SAY that last night at Fenway, the Phillies, more woebegone than whiz kids (they have the majors' worst record), lost to the Red Sox, 4-3, but once again took the Sox into extra innings, this time 12; Monday night it was 11.

The four game set continues, but tonight in the City of Brotherly Love rather than Puritan Boston. (There is a book by that name. A very good read, but it is not about the Sox or Phillies, more Benjamin Franklin, et al.)

THE ROCKIES LOST THEIR THIRD STRAIGHT, as the Pirates beat them at PNC, 5-2, and with it their sole possession of first place to LA's Investment Bankers, otherwise known as the Dodgers.

Buddy Black's team will try and get back to their winning ways tonight, as they close out their three games in the Steel City, before returning to Denver and four vs. SF at Coors Field.

THE PADRES WERE ON THE RECEIVING END OF EIGHT AND TWO-THIRD INNINGS OF SUPERB PITCHING FROM CLAYTON RICHARD and won over Cincy at Petco Park last night, 6-2, as the Reds lost their fifth in a row.

Rookie Franchy Cordero had three hits, including two 400-ft. plus HRs (his third in the two wins over Cincy).

The two close out their three games today at 12:40 pm (PDT).

THE ALL-WORLD ASTROS OF HOUSTON, lost once more to their inner-state rivals, the Texas Rangers at Minute Maid, 4-2.

But no worries, the Astros still lead the AL West by 11.

THE ANGELS OF ANAHEIM WON OVER NYY IN ELEVEN INNINGS, 3-2, opposite Disneyland in So. Cal.

Eric Young, who had tied the game at 2-2 with a HR in the 8th, singled in the bottom of the 11th for the walk-off win.

FOR ALL THE SCORES AND STATS GO TO MLB.COM.

QUOTE OF THE DAY:

A repeat from Tim Peeler, the Bard of the Carolinas:

FAILURE SEMANTICS:

My youngest son never played the game,
Never ran out an infield hit, stole second,
Made a running catch or dropped one,
Never did infield chatter or missed a signal,
Never walked or threw a man out at the plate,
Never stopped halfway between bases
Unable to decide which way to go.
His brother scared him with hit by pitch stories
So he stuck to the soccer field while I felt
Because I'd played and coached
Watched and written about
And even quit the game,
That I'd failed him in some basic
And even tribal way,
That he had been caught by
The comet tail of my bad karma,
But now he is a coach,
The first official one in the family,
And he tells me he could coach
The game if he had to, that it's
All websites and youtube vids now,
Nothing as difficult as experience,
And I nod because he has a winning record
And all I have is these poems.

BASEBALL NOTES – TUESDAY, JUNE 20

I HATED THE TRADE THAT SENT ANTHONY RIZZO TO THE CUBS FROM THE PADRES, as I knew, and said then, the trade was a mistake, that Rizzo was destined to be a star – and a star he has become.

And until yesterday he was one of my favorite players, but then he crashed into Austin Hedges, the Padres' catcher, crashed into him with the full force of his 240 pounds, resulting in Hedges tumbling backwards, and out of the game.

Ever since Buster Posey, the Giants' catcher was sidelined for a season due to also being run over at home plate, the major leagues adopted a rule (7.13) to protect defenseless catchers; a rule that says, in effect, a catcher cannot block the plate and a runner cannot deviate from a straight line to home.

In the Padres/Cubs game at Wrigley last night, with Rizzo on third, Chris Bryant lined to center field, Rizzo tagged and made for home, as center fielder Matt Szczur made the catch and threw a strike to home plate; Hedges, clearly set up to the right of the plate, as the rule calls for, caught the throw, applied the tag, and despite being crushed by Rizzo, who clearly deviated from the line, held onto the ball, and Rizzo was out.

Rizzo was out, yes; so too Austin Hedges.

At that point, Rizzo should have been thrown out of the game, but wasn't.

Dennis Lin, who covers the Padres for the *San Diego Union-Tribune*, wrote in today's paper that the play "ignited a fire storm on social media," with Rizzo the target of fans' ire.

After the game, the Cubs, of course, defended their first baseman, with Joe Maddon, the Cubs' manager, who I have called "baseball's best," idiotically saying he "absolutely loved it," Rizzo taking out Hedges.

Shame on Joe Maddon.

What will be the results? Well, if Major League Baseball is serious about Rule 7.13, Rizzo will be fined and suspended – for at least as long as Hedges is gone from the game.

Will that happen?

No, the Cubs *are* Chicago *and* the World Champions, and the Padres are the Padres, so who cares?

I do.

Oh, the Padres who swept the Cubs in San Diego, lost to the Northsiders, 3-2.

Too bad, the Cubs didn't deserve the win.

IN THE NL WEST, COLORADO WAS IDLE, AS WAS ARIZONA, but the Dodgers played and won, 10-6, over the Mets in the Ravine, as Clayton Kershaw won his 10th game of the season, despite giving up six runs on six hits in 6.1 innings; a very Kershaw unlike performance, but he'll take the win, as will LAD, who moved a half-game back of the Rockies, who are home tonight against the D-Backs, who are only one game back in baseball's winningest division.

THE RED SOX, FOLLOWING THEIR GREAT GAME SUNDAY NIGHT VS. HOUSTON, played last night in KC at Kaufmann Stadium, but it wasn't a great game for the Sox, but maybe KC, who won 4-2.

THE GIANTS TUMBLED TO THEIR SEVENTH STRAIGHT LOSS, as they were shutout by the Braves and R.A. Dickey, 9-0.

Tough year for Bruce Bochy, one of the game's finest managers and gentlemen, as his team is mired in last place, 20-games back of Colorado.

No one saw this coming, but then no one saw the Giants' pitching ace stupidly deciding to go dirt bike riding, either.

THE NATIONALS CONTINUE TO LEAD THE NL EAST, but they have also lost six of their last 10 games, with the most recent last night, 8-7 to the Marlins in Miami.

The Nationals had been up by six, but then things fell apart, and Miami came back, scoring six times off Washington starter, Tanner Roark, who couldn't hold his big lead, as he imploded in the third inning, and was out of the game.

The much maligned Nationals' bullpen – much maligned on the Tony Kornheiser podcast – did itself proud, yielding but two runs over the next 6.1 innings, but, alas, one of those was the Marlins' winning score.

LAST GAME TO NOTE, the AL champs, Cleveland Indians, are playing like the champions they are, beating the O's at Camden behind the complete game shutout of Corey Kluber, who three hit Baltimore, walked zero and struck out 11.

A performance certain to get you a win, and it did, as the great Kluber is now 6-2 for '17.

NOLAN ARENADO, WHO HIT THE WALK-OFF TWO-RUN HR FOR COLORADO Sunday vs. SF, also hit for the cycle, which I stupidly missed, even though I saw it happen (in part, not the whole).

BASEBALL NOTES – THURSDAY, JUNE 22

THE PADRES WON AT WRIGLEY OVER THE CUBS, 3-2, thus saving the season series, winning four of six, including their sweep at Petco Park.

But the Rizzo/Hedges controversy did not go away, as the Padres manager, Andy Green, came under social media attack because Rizzo escaped being hit by a Padres' pitcher in retaliation for Rizzo's Dick Butkus like hammering of the Padres' defenseless catcher Monday night.

Saint Rizzo didn't get plunked, didn't get fined, didn't get suspended, because Saint Torre, a baseball lifer – and gutless in this instance – said that while Rizzo clearly violated Rule (7.13) there was no cause to punish the poor lad.

Meanwhile, Austin Hedges, missed his second game, while Saint Rizzo plays on.

DR. EINSTEIN FAMOUSLY DEFINED INSANITY AS DOING THE SAME THING AND EXPECTING A DIFFERENT RESULT.

Which brings me to John Farrell, the Red Sox manager, who yesterday afternoon in KC, with the Sox leading, 4-2, in the eighth, once again went to the bullpen and brought in Matt Barnes, who did what he too often does – as he did Sunday night in Houston – walked the first two batters he faced, so Farrell replaces him with Robby Scott, who walked the bases loaded, as he and Barnes threw 15 pitches, only two for strikes.

Fifteen pitches. Two strikes. Not good.

With the bases jammed, Scott then faced Salvador Perez, who had a brilliant AB, fouling off numerous pitches as Scott kept the ball low and away, but then came inside and the KC catcher swung mightily, and the ball disappeared into the left field bleachers at Kaufmann for a grand slam; Perez's first ever, and with four runs in, the Royals would achieve a 6-4 win.

I have looked at Barnes' record at Baseball-Reference, and in 31.2 innings this season, he has given up 26 base hits and 16 bases on balls, which means that every inning he pitches, 1.2 runners get on base.

Last year, Barnes gave up 62 base hits and 31 bases on balls in 66.2 innings, or 1.4 base runners for every inning pitched.

I will say this for Barnes, he has the distinction of providing me with one of my most memorable baseball moments, as in last season, when Farrell brought him in from the bullpen at Fenway, and, Barnes being Barnes, proceeded to walk the first three batters he faced.

At which point, one thought, Farrell pulls him from the game. But Farrell being Farrell, leaves his erratic reliever in. To do what, walk a fourth batter?

But then, Matthew D. Barnes of Danbury, Connecticut, strikes out the next three batters, and sprints triumphantly to the Sox dugout, a cascade of cheers ringing in his ears.

That moment, memorable and all, has not altered my view of Mr. Barnes, so that while Farrell has confidence in him, I have none, and will continue to cringe every time the bullpen gate opens and he walks out – as in yesterday in KC and Sunday night in Houston.

HAVING ORDAINED THE ROCKIES AS NL WEST TITLE WINNERS, should I reconsider my prediction, given that Colorado lost yesterday to Arizona, 16-5?

And with their loss, lost their first place standing to the Dodgers, who have pulled a half-game up on Buddy Black's boys.

No.

IN THE MERCURIAL WORKINGS OF MY MIND, however, I thought of the up the down staircase nature of America's Game, such as when the Phillies of Philadelphia beat the Cubs of Chicago at Wrigley Field, 23-22 – 17 May 1979.

The Phillies had won the day before over the Cubs, 13-0, but the day after their 23-22 win, they lost in Montreal to the Expos, 3-5.

In the 23-22 game, the greatest ever played (if you like offense, I do), the two teams combined for 45 runs, 50 base hits, nine doubles, two triples, 11 HRs (three hit by the immortal Dave Kingman), 15 bases on balls, and 11 strike outs.

The loss left the Cubs at 16-16 for '79; the Phillies, 24-10-1.

Philadelphia would end the season at 84-78-1; the Cubs, 80-82.

Game time was four hours and three minutes and was played before 14,952 fans.

Oh, the wind was 18 mph, and, although not indicated, was blowing out, as it is impossible to believe it was blowing in.

OTHER STUFF:

Max Scherzer's bid for his third no-hitter, ended with one out in the 8th, as Miami scored two unearned runs, and the Nationals lost, 2-1. They remain, however, 9.5 games up on the second place Cobb County Braves.

The Yankees ended their seven straight losses by beating LAA at the Stadium, 8-4, as Matt Holiday and Didi Gregorio's hit go ahead HRs for NYY, who reclaimed first place from Boston in the AL East.

A bunt single in the 6th ended a perfect game effort by the Tigers' Justin Verlander, and Seattle stormed back to win at Safeco, 7-5.

QUOTE OF THE DAY:

Another poem from Tim Peeler, with the added note that today I begin my campaign to have the great Peeler designated North Carolina's Poet Laureate, and I believe I am safe in saying that Dick Enberg will serve as co-chair of the Peeler for Poet Laureate.

Tim's offering today is entitled:

Availability Heuristic

Two doors down, the neighbor's dad
Had played minor league baseball,
Done a stretch in the Coast Guard,
Been an amateur boxer.
The next door neighbor had been
The best semipro player
Folks had ever seen round here.

On past the church down the road
Toward Hollywood Heights a
New house with a boy born
Ready to play, rocket armed
Shortstop, cotton topped cocky.

The other kids already
Knew bunt and run, field and throw,
As if some native union
Of knowledge, heredity,
And spirit conjoined their brains,

And though I was small for small,
I could short arm a fastball
Or steer my Sears bike past them
Because I was connected,
No, welded, to the things I knew.

BASEBALL NOTES – THURSDAY, JUNE 29

THE INEXPLICABILITY OF AMERICA'S GAME, came to mind once again last night, while watching the Twins and Red Sox at Fenway.

First, Boston lost to Minnesota, 4-1, as Rick Porcello, the Cy Young award winner in '16, was dreadful once again, losing his 10th game against four wins, with his ERA climbing to 5.06.

Second, Dave O'Brien, in the NESN booth at Fenway, pointed out that the Twins' 3, 4, and 5 hitters, Joe Mauer, Miguel Sano, and Max Kepler, had gone 0-34 before last night's game, but ended their collective failure when they went 5-11 against the Red Sox, including a double and HR, drove in 4 and scored 4.

Third, Julian Benbow, writing yesterday in the *Boston Globe* about Hanley Ramirez, wrote:

"Ramirez is hitting .241 with 10 homers and 29 RBIs. He's struggled mightily against lefthanders, hitting just .143 with eight strikeouts in 35 at-bats. A year ago, Ramirez dominated lefties with a .346 average and 11 homers."

Isn't that quite extraordinary, Ramirez in '16 and Ramirez today? Porcello last season and this?

The Mauer, Sano, Kepler 0-34 streak, followed by 5-11, doesn't rise to the Porcello/Ramirez level, but all three underscore the game's inexplicability.

Today the Sox pitch David Price, another huge disappointment, against Minnesota; while someone named Gibson pitches for the Twins. It's a battle of ERAs, Price's 4.76 vs. Gibson's 6.23.

AND, HERE'S ANOTHER INEXPLICABLE: LAST SEASON THE GREAT BARTOLO COLON was 15-8 for the New York Metropolitans, with an ERA of 3.43.

But last night, pitching for the Atlanta Braves, Bartolo lost to the Padres at Petco, 7-4.

For the 44-year old Colon, it was the eighth time this year he has lost against only two wins, and his ERA, at 8.14, is over the moon.

Colon is one of my favorite players – cannot say why, he just is – and who can forget the HR he hit at Petco two years ago; becoming the oldest major league player to hit his first HR at age 42.

Invoking Colon's name always reminds me of an email I sent Larry Lucchino in Colon's out year with Montreal (2002), urging him to sign Bartolo. Larry wrote back and said Colon was "too fat." I wrote back and said, "No, he's not, that's just his body type."

The Red Sox passed on Bartolo, and two years later he won the Cy Young for LAA.

Lucchino's a genius, as I am not, but he erred on Bartolo.

HAVING WITNESSED THE PADRES WIN, I TURNED TO DODGERS/ANGELS IN ANAHEIM, where LAA was leading in the top of the 9th, 2-1.

Two were out and Yasmani Grandal was at bat for the Dodgers. On the mound for the Angels was Cam Bedrosian, with two strikes on Grandal, when Bedrosian threw a letter high slider over the middle of the plate, which Yasmani hit high and deep to slightly left of dead center field. As 44,669 held their collective breaths, Cameron Maybin raced to the wall, positioned himself for a game saving catch.

As the ball descended, Cameron ascended, rising 30-inches above the playing field, his glove held high, but, alas, the ball fell just beyond his reach for a * game-tying HR.

However, LAA would come back in the bottom of the 9th to win, 3-2, because on a swinging third strike by Maybin, who belatedly ran to first base, as the pitch had slipped past the Dodgers' catcher, who, retrieving it, then threw wildly past first, allowing Ben Revere, who was on second from a fielding error, to score the winning run.

It wasn't the most artful on walk-offs, but the Angels will take it, and tomorrow they will try and win the four game I-5 Freeway Series. But with Clayton Kershaw on the mound for LAD, look for a series split.

*it was 9:52 pm (PDT) When Grandal hit his HR. Sitting on our couch in the family room, expecting something untoward to happen, as it did (I do not like LAD), I yelled, "No!"

Not knowing what was going on, my wife, La Verle, still recovering from her catastrophic leg break, managed to get out of bed, and using her walker, came down the hallway from her bed-room, anxiously inquiring, "George, are you all right, what happened?"

I answered, "Grandal just hit a game tying HR." She responded, "OMG, will you ever grow up?"

Doubtful.

OUR SON, TIM MITROVICH, WHO WORKS FOR THE U.S. SENATE, was at Nationals Park last night when he texted me at 8:45 pm (EDT) that Stephen Strasburg, a San Diego State grad (as is Tim and his wife, Lisa), had just struck out his tenth Cubs' batter, and it was only the 5th inning.

Strasburg would pitch two more innings, strike out three more Cubbies, while winning his ninth game against just two losses, as the Nationals won, 8-4.

DC now leads the NL Central by nine and a half games, while the Cubs have slipped one back of Milwaukee in the NL Central; which means, with only six and a half games separating first and last place teams, the division is wide open.

OTHER STUFF:

APPARENTLY PLAYERS ON THE COLORADO ROCKIES do not read Notes, and are, therefore, unaware I've predicted they would win the NL West. Clearly that is the case, because yesterday at AT&T they lost their eighth straight game, falling again to the Giants, 5-3.

They lost because Jae-Gyun Hwang, playing in his first major league game, homered to drive in two, the game difference.

THE YANKEES BEAT THE WHITE SOX IN CHICAGO, 12-3, as Aaron Judge hit his 27th HR of the season in game 76, if he hits three more by game 82, he will be halfway home to 60 for the season. No rookie has ever hit that many HRs, and it would better by 11 Mark McGwire's 49 for the A's in '87.

Oh, debuting for NYY last night was another rookie, Miguel Andujar, who had three hits and four RBIs.

QUOTE OF THE DAY:

This is Tim Peeler, the Carolina Bard, with a poem about Mickey Mantle, entitled, "Solar System"

Mickey made his sons
His drinking buddies
If they wanted
To hang with the Mick
In a Manhattan bar,
A powdered girl
On either arm.
It was a twisted circumstance:
A great star
And his eager satellites,
Their only way
To orbit.

BASEBALL NOTES – TUESDAY, AUGUST 22

I WAS JUST WALKING INTO MY HOME IN SAN DIEGO, returning from a five-day trip to Boston and Denver, when my cell phone rang.

The caller was a Wellesley, Mass., friend, "Are you watching the Sox game in Cleveland?" "No, I just got home. Why?" "Because", my friend said, "The Sox are up by one in the 8th inning, but [John] Farrell just brought in [Matt] Barnes."

"OMG," I said. "Not again."

Boston was up 4-3 over Cleveland at Progressive Field, but Barnes was entering the game, and Barnes being Barnes, immediately put two runners on.

But Sox manager Farrell, rather than wait until Barnes had loaded the bases or someone had homered, removed Barnes from the game. But even at that it was too late, as Edwin Encarnacion singled to left off Barnes' successor and the game was tied, with the Tribe winning on a Sox miscue in the bottom of the 9th.

There is a "sense" that some of my pals who root for the Sox have that when Barnes comes into a game, the Sox will lose; that he will walk his first batter or hit him, give up a single or HR, and just like that, the Sox's lead will vanish – and with it the game.

Why we know this and Farrell doesn't is a question worth pondering.

THE WASHINGTON NATIONALS LEAD THE NL EAST BY 14 GAMES, but while they play in the majors' weakest division – 288 wins, 326 losses—their record against their division rivals, 32-21, is not substantially different when playing the other 25 MLB teams, 42-27.

Against the majors' best teams – Arizona, Colorado, Chicago (Cubs), Los Angeles (Dodgers), Milwaukee, St. Louis – Washington's record is 19-13, and against the AL's best – Baltimore, Los Angeles (Angels), Seattle – 5-4.

Thus we learn the Nationals are the Nationals and their record against the other 29 teams is remarkably consistent. They're good, not overwhelmingly good, like LAD or Houston, but good.

The Nationals will be in the playoffs. That's certain. What is uncertain is what follows.

YASIEL PUIG HOMERED IN THE 12th at AT PNC and LAD had its 88TH WIN, beating the Pirates, 6-5.

It was Puig's 22nd HR of'17, and the young Cuban is enjoying his Redemption Year, even if only hitting .251, as he plays a mean right field and possesses the game's strongest throwing arm.

The Dodgers' new acquisition, Curtis Granderson, obtained from the Mets, hit his second LAD HR and drove in four.

OTHER STUFF:

THE O's BEAT THE A's AT CAMDEN, 7-3, as San Diego's Morse High grad Adam Jones hit his 23rd and 24th HRs of the year, putting him within one of 25, which would be his seventh consecutive year to hit 25 or more.

THE PADRES INEXPLICABLY SENT HUNTER RENFROE DOWN TO EL PASO. The why of it escapes me, as I consider him one of the team's more exciting players, even if he's hitting only .230 and has struck out 125 times, because he also has hit 24 HRs, played exceptionally well in right field, and among the team's outfielders, has the strongest throwing arm.

So, with some irritation, I would ask, why Renfroe and not Wil Meyers, who has struck out 145 times (seventh highest in the majors), is hitting only seven points higher than Renfroe, with the same number of HRs, 24?

Clearly, the baseball ops people think they have made the right decision, and since they are all knowing and I am just a fan, what would I know? But superior intel or not, they've made the wrong decision.

"TOUCH 'EM ALL", THE VOICE SAID, "TOUCH 'EM ALL."

Sounded like Dick Enberg to me, but since it was a Dodgers/Tigers game in Detroit and Enberg had retired as the voice of the San Diego Padres, how could that be? And, if it was Dick Enberg calling the game, how could he do that and not shout it out? Because he's Dick Enberg and shoutouts are not his style.

I asked Enberg, was that really you broadcasting from Coamerica?

Here is what he said:

"Jeff Byle, who was my boss in SD, has moved to Fox Sports Detroit and invited me last Spring to do the three game weekend series with the Dodgers.

"It was a chance for me to go back to my Michigan homeland. Good fun. They gave me an Ernie Harwell Award on the field, Sunday. Royal company!

'It felt good to be back in the saddle and the response was terrific. Maybe another series next year."

Why only one? He is Dick Enberg. He is a Hall of Fame broadcaster. And he still has it!

QUOTE OF THE DAY:

Tim Peeler, the Bard of the Carolinas, is back with, "Standing on the Monster with the Lions,"

Here's his poem:

On the precipice
At the holiest of baseball places –
I had been to the shrine
By Coopers' lake
Had seen where the light
Broke through the ceiling
On the gallery of heroes,
But never here,
A hundred years, time struck
In the August afternoon glow,
While a melodious voice that lived
In this emerald city
Recited a poem
For a lucky group of tourists,
And my septuagenarian host
Gently swayed to the rhythm
Of Red Sox history.

Dick Flavin, Boston Red Sox day game public address announcer does impromptu poem. Dick Flavin recites hundred year Fenway Park celebration poem from atop the green monster. Aug 13, 2013.

I watched through my camera lens
As Flavin finished and Mitrovich
Stood by him for a moment
Speaking quietly,
And it was like that great scene
In Picket Fences
Where the old judge and counselor
After a fierce day in court stand in the moonlight,
Wading the river, and one of them says,
"I feel just like I did when I was twenty."

BASEBALL NOTES – THURSDAY, AUGUST 24, 2017

RICH HILL OF LAD HAD THROWN SEVEN PERFECT INNINGS VS. MIAMI IN '16, but his manager, Dave Roberts, pulled him from the game.

Last night at PNC in Pittsburgh, where the Allegheny and Monongahela flow together to form the Ohio River, Mr. Hill threw nine no-hit scoreless innings, but stayed to pitch the 10th, when someone named Josh Harrison hit a walk-off HR and the Pirates won, 1-0.

After the game, Roberts said, "I think (I am) sad for Rich, It's a game that we got beat, but I think that you look at opportunities that a player has to have a chance at a no-hitter, and he gave himself every opportunity. It's more a feeling of I'm very excited for Rich because he threw the ball so well tonight but disappointed that he didn't get that no-hitter."

You think?

I do not root for the Investment Fund team that plays in Chavez Ravine, but if you are throwing a no-hitter, Dodger or not, I am rooting the pitcher gets his no-hitter.

A pitcher should never be removed from a game when pitching a no-hitter – ever. That opinion lacks unanimity among the game's experts, but this is my blog not theirs, and I've had 75-years to think about it – and I am not changing my mind!

THE YANKEES SCORED 23 RUNS ON 30 BASE HITS, INCLUDING SIX HRs, in the first two games of their series vs. the Tigers at Coamerica, winning 10-2 last night and 13-4 Tuesday.

Gary Sanchez homered for the third time in two games, and now has 26 for '17 – 47 HRs in 147-games.

By winning big NYY stays 4.5 back of Boston.

THE CLEVELAND INDIANS NO LONGER PLAY IN THE "MISTAKE BY THE LAKE," but in beautiful Progressive Field, but baseball is baseball, whether played in League Park (see painting below), Municipal Stadium or in a state of the art ballpark, where last night the Tribe fell to the Sox of Boston, 6-1.

Drew Pomeranz threw 5.2 innings, but won his 13th win against but four losses, while walking four, striking out nine, and lowering his ERA to 3.09.

He was succeeded out of the bullpen by Kelly, Reed, and Kimbrel, only one of whom gave up a run (Reed).

OTHER STUFF:

THE CUBS AGAIN BEAT UP ON THE REDS, winning last night, 9-3, to move 3.5 games up on the Brewers, who lost to SF, 4-2. In the Cubs/Cincy game at Great American Ballpark, five HRs were hit – Schwarber (21) and La Sella (4) for Chicago; Votto (33), Schebler (24), and Suarez (24) for the Redlegs.

SIXTY STRAIGHT TIMES, ZACH BRITTON successfully closed a game for the O's, but that is done as Britton blew a two-run lead in the 9th at Camden, but despite the record breaking streak ending, Baltimore won in 12 over the Athletic, 8-7. Note to Britton: You're forgiven.

THE ROCKIES WERE ROCKED when Eric Hosmer hit another walk-off HR for KC, scoring three when two were out and the Royals beat Colorado, 6-4. Bud Black's team has hit a rough patch, losing seven of 10, but remain 10-games over .500 and a half game back of the D-Backs for the WC in the NL West.

THE PADRES WHO TRUMPED THE CARDINALS BIG TUESDAY NIGHT, lost last night in St. Louis, 6-2. When your starting pitcher walks four and hits three in 4.1 innings, you probably lose, and SD did.

TYLER KEPNER OF THE NY TIMES, wrote in his Sunday baseball column that Chris Sale of the Red. Sox, went into Saturday's game with 241 strikeouts (now 250), and arrived at 200 K's in his 20th start last month; a record held by only three other pitchers, all Hall of Famers – Randy Johnson, Pedro Martinez, and Nolan Ryan.

WORLD SERIES BASEBALL NOTES — OCTOBER 27, 2017

THE GAMES OF OCTOBER RESUME TONIGHT AT MINUTE MAID IN HOUSTON, perhaps a welcome distraction for the thousands still dealing with the disaster of Harvey; while off the front page and no longer leading the nightly news, remains an everyday crushing reality to those flooded out of their homes — their lives upside down, their futures at risk.

President Franklin D. Roosevelt believed the playing of baseball would help ease the nation's angst during WWII; so too may we hope the citizens of Houston and Beaumont, of Galveston and Port Arthur, and all those places in-between, will find a measure of reassurance in their Astros.

Pitching for Los Angeles tonight is Yu Darvish and for Houston, Lance McCullers. Darvish was 10-12 on the season; McCullers, 7-4.

Darvish struck out 209 batters in 186.2 innings for the Rangers and Dodgers; McCullers, 132 in 118.2 innings.

LOS ANGELES MEDIA, ESPECIALLY THE *TIMES*, is in a tizzy due to the Dodgers loss Wednesday night to the Astros, 7-6 in 11-innings.

This was the estimable Bill Plaschke's lead in his column yesterday:

"The first blast shocked. The second blast stunned. The third blast silenced. The fourth blast finished.

"Bam, bam, bam, bam, the Dodgers have lost a World Series game, a World Series advantage, and every bit of World Series momentum."

Plaschke is strong on alliteration (Pat Buchanan writing speeches for Spiro Agnew, is called to mind), but slightly overboard on the Dodgers' demise two nights ago.

If the Astros win again, I will see if Plaschke's alliterative powers may rise once more to the occasion.

CLAYTON KERSHAW WAS TYLER KEPNER'S LEAD IN SPORTS SUNDAY FOR *THE NEW YORK TIMES*, but I wasn't interested in reading again about the great Kershaw (I know the man's story), but a graph that accompanied Kepner's story, did catch my attention.

It featured Cy Young Winners in the World Series — Roger Clemens, Randy Johnson, Steve Carlton, Greg Maddux, Sandy Koufax, Pedro Martinez, Jim Palmer, Tom Seaver, and Kershaw.

Clemens won seven Cy Youngs, pitched in eight games in six World Series, was 3-0, with two World Series championships.

Randy Johnson won five Cy Youngs, pitched in three games in one World Series, was 3-0, with one World Series Championship.

The other six pitched in 21 World Series games, were 14-14, with 11 World Series championships, with Kershaw winning his first World Series game in Tuesday night's game one.

THE NEW YORK YANKEES BROKE WORLD SERIES PROTOCOL BY FIRING JOE GIRARDI, which seems absurd, seriously.

A Boston friend tells me that Girardi was fired because the Red Sox fired John Farrell and the Nationals fired Dusty Baker, so the Yankees had to fire Girardi or lose face.

In the case of both Farrell and Baker, their two ball clubs were heavy favorites to win their respective divisions, and did, but couldn't get to the World Series.

However, no one picked the Yankees to win the AL East, which they didn't, but they did win the Wild Card over the Twins, and then had a remarkable comeback vs. Cleveland, as down 0-2, they won three in-a-row — and took Houston to seven games in the ALCS.

I think Girardi did a great job with his young team and played a significant role in the ascendancy of the Linden Legend, Aaron Judge.

Girardi deserved to come back. So, shame on Brian Cashman and the Steinbrenners.

Oh, there is this: The Yankees also won the season series from the Red Sox. I mean, really how can you fire a guy who does that?

Final note on Joe: My unnamed Boston pal also told me that the Padres should bump Andy Green to the front office as A.J. Preller's assistant, and hire Girardi.

That ain't happening, but he would be the team's most credible hire ever.

QUOTE OF THE DAY:

"The result cannot be considered unthinkable, because October baseball expands the realm of possibility and exposes the soul to untold anguish. The Dodgers had avoided this fate for so much of these playoffs. They were the team who broke hearts, who snuffed out dreams. Except until this week, they had not stared down an opponent like the Houston Astros.

"On Wednesday evening, in the final innings of Game 2 of the World Series, the veneer of invincibility surrounding the Dodgers' bullpen shattered beneath the might of Houston's offense in a 7-6 defeat that tied this series at one victory each.

"Kenley Jansen blew a save by yielding a solo homer in the ninth. Josh Fields surrendered two more in the 10th. After scoring two runs in the bottom of the 10th, the Dodgers turned to Brandon McCarthy for the 11th.

"There was no one left in the bullpen. McCarthy had appeared in only five games since the All-Star break. The Astros pilloried him. George Springer boomed a two-run shot. McCarthy seethed with anger afterward. Jansen contemplated the fallibility of man." — Andy McCullough, *Los Angeles Times*, Thursday, October 26

WORLD SERIES NOTES — SUNDAY, OCTOBER 29, 2017

THE DODGERS HAD ONE RUN THROUGH EIGHT, SCORED FIVE IN THE 9TH AND WON GAME FOUR, 6-2, to tie the World Series at two games apiece.

But give LAD the advantage tonight, as Kershaw the Great is on the mound facing the lesser Dallas Keuchel for Houston at Minute Maid.

Through 5.2 innings last night, Alex Wood for the Dodgers had a no hitter, when George Springer of the Astros homered to put the AL team up one nil over the NL ball club, but just like that Dave Roberts was out of the visiting team's dugout, not quite trudging to the mound (he's not a trudger), but neither was he skipping (he's not a skipper), his sole intent was to remove the ball from Wood's right hand and remove Wood from the game.

At which point, in the Colorado Governor's Mansion (I assume), one John Hickenlooper, the Rocky Mountain state's remarkably effective chief executive, emailed to say that Roberts' decision to pull Wood was ridiculous.

Of course, the governor, the former star pitcher for Wesleyan University, was spot on. It was ridiculous, but Roberts is Roberts and he routinely pulls pitchers from games who are throwing no-hitters, so why leave in a game a failed pitcher, who had just given the team opposite a 1-0 lead?

But while John Hickenlooper is governor of Colorado, and possibly the next president of the United States, the question may be asked, what does he know about managing? Did the governor win 104 games this season? Well, did he?

It was either Bill Plaschke or Andy McCullough in the LA Times who said that people may question Roberts' managerial method, but it is hard to argue with the man's success.

Yes, it is.

However, unless Donald Trump has suspended the First Amendment to the Constitution of the United States (he didn't, did he?), the governor is well within his right to question the Dodgers' manager.

And, there is this: when I received the governor's email I had just remarked that it was really a dumb decision for Roberts to take Wood out of the game.

Yes, the Investment Bankers' backed team won, and may well go back to the Ravine east of LA's City Hall, up three games to two, but the governor's judgment on pulling Wood, stands.

When the late Eugene McCarthy said to me that Baseball is a "game for intellectuals," a judgment I wholly agree with, I do not think the senator was thinking of baseball managers or players. I think he was thinking about you and me, patriots all — who truly believe that Baseball is America's Game.

And to know America, as Jacques Barzun, one of the great intellectuals of our history, famously said, "You must know baseball."

IN THE MATTER OF YULI GURRIEL AND HIS RACIST GESTURE DIRECTED AT YU DARVISH, the actions taken by the commissioner of baseball, one Rob Manfred, in suspending Gurriel for the first five games at the start of the 2018 season, I deem wholly inadequate.

He should have been suspended from the World Series and fined $250,000 (he wouldn't miss it; he makes $14,400,000).

If Darvish were black and Gurreil had called him the "N" word, would the commissioner have leveled a mere five game suspension? Were Darvish Jewish and Gurriel called him "Jew Boy?" Would the commissioner have ruled the five game suspension next year sufficient to the obscenity committed by Gurriel?

The answer is, of course not. But because Darvish is Japanese, the commissioner thought, five games should do it.

The commissioner, faced with a moral test, failed it.

Shame on him.

WORLD SERIES NOTES — WEDNESDAY, NOVEMBER 1, 2017

HAIL TO THE VICTORS VALIANT, HAIL TO THE CONQUERING HEROES, HAIL, HAIL TO…"

Houston?

No.

Not last night, as the Dodgers won, 3-1, over Justin Verlander and the Astros in Chavez Ravine, where the ghosts of displaced Hispanic families past still haunt the land where their homes once stood — their haunting appropriate on Halloween.

Game six was neither game two nor five, which were other worldly, but a mostly pedestrian affair — save to the 30 percent of Dodger fans still able to watch their team play on television during the regular season — but nonetheless one that set the stage for the certain drama and anticipated theatrics of game seven.

The one non-pedestrian moment occurred when Dave "The Hook' Roberts pulled Rich Hill from the game after 4.2 innings, when Hill had surrendered but one run on four hits, but Roberts, mesmerized by his own genius, decided it was time and Hill was gone from the mound and to the Dodgers' dugout, where he promptly destroyed a water cooler, so great was his justifiable anger at his manager.

Actually, Roberts allowed Hill to pitch two-thirds of an inning longer than he did in game two, but no doubt it was still fresh in Hill's mind that his manager had also pulled him from a game last season; pulled him when Hill had pitched seven perfect innings against the Marlins in Miami (September 9, 2016), which caused Andy McCullough of the LA Times to write in sports the next day:

"The suffering stretched across the face of Dave Roberts. His eyes brimmed red. His stomach roiled with discontent. He had never before experienced a win that felt like a loss, not until Saturday's 5-0 Dodgers victory over the Miami Marlins, when he made a decision that protected Rich Hill's health, incited Hill's rage and invited heartache into the manager's office.

"'I'm going to lose sleep tonight,' "Roberts said." "'And I probably should.'"

You think?

In his two Series appearances, Hill pitched a total of 7.2 innings, gave up only two runs, allowed just seven base hits, walked four and struck out 12.

He deserved to stay in the game. He deserved a chance to win a World Series game, as he deserved the chance to pitch a no-hitter, but the redundancy of his manager's mind precluded that from happening.

Because of Eve Rosenbaum's front office position with the Astros — she, the former Harvard softball player and Red Sox intern — now directing Houston's international scouting operation, I'm rooting for the Astros.

It's been 29-years since LAD last won a World Series, but I'm good with it being another 29.

Oh, I'm sure the Investment Bankers will bill Hill for the cost of replacing the water cooler.

WATCHING LAST NIGHT'S GAME ON FS1, I was surprised when MLB.com informed me the Dodgers had won, 3-1, while Houston was just coming to bat in the top of the 9th.

What?

Was the Fox telecast that far behind the actual game?

If I'm Fox paying that kind of money to exclusively broadcast the World Series, I might want to ask the commissioner why are you co-opting our broadcast?

I have no brief to make in behalf of the Murdoch/Trump network, but fair is fair and this wasn't fair — so, an explanation is in order.

MEMO TO TONY KORNHEISER:

Yes, Mr. Tony, that is Mary Hart sitting in the front row boxes behind home plate at Dodger Stadium. The gentleman to her right is her husband, or significant other, and to his right, Larry King (Mr. King's seventh or eighth wife, not in evidence).

I note this because on your recent podcast you and your crew seemed uncertain if that was Mary. Yes, it is.

Having watched the Dodgers play at home this season, most notably vs. the San Diego Padres, Ms. Hart is always in her box seat — which suggests she's a true fan of America's Game.

Another reason to love Mary Hart.

QUOTE OF THE DAY:

Dick Flavin is the Poet Laureate of Red Sox Nation and at every Red Sox's Writers Series event, Flavin has his five minutes to amuse and entertain — which he does to the unfailing gratitude of the faithful who, while having gathered to hear some famous writer, Dan Barry say, or Peter Gammons, perhaps Jackie MacMullan or Richard Haass, but are no less thrilled to hear Flavin, this quite extraordinary fellow, who crafts for each new event a fitting poetic tribute.

In his Musings this week, he wrote about Boston's hiring of Alex Cora as the new Red Sox manager, and the inevitability of his ultimately being fired, because all managers are, as John Farrell, Joe Girardi, and Dusty Baker know, but Flavin found one who wasn't — the immortal Chick Stahl:

CHICK STEEL

Are you one of those wise guys,
Those blowhards, those jocks
Who thinks you can manage
The Boston Red Sox?

Well, it's not all that easy,
Oh no, not at all.
Just take, for example,
The case of Chick Stahl.

He managed the Sox
In 1906,
But the fact the team stunk
Put Chick in a fix.

Next year in Spring Training
They still couldn't win.
So Chick took bold action,
He did himself in.

The boo birds that season
Would not get to Chick.
Carbolic acid
Is what did the trick.

He gulped the stuff down
And quickly expired,
The only Sox skipper
Who never got fired.

So if the job should
Become yours to fill
Before you accept it

Please make out your will.

WORLD SERIES NOTES — THURSDAY, NOVEMBER 2, 2017

HOUSTON'S JOURNEY TO THE WORLD SERIES BEGAN APRIL 10, 1962, WHEN THE THEN COLT 45s OPENED AT HOME BY BEATING THE CHICAGO CUBS, 11-2.

The winning pitcher that day was Bobby Shantz, the 37-year old left hander from Pottsville, Pennsylvania. Bobby, who pitched a complete game for the new team, was in his 13th major league season, topped by the 24 games he won for the Philadelphia Athletics in '52.

The Colt 45s would play 483 games thereafter, but underwent a name change in '65, becoming the Houston Astros (the gun culture of the Republic of Texas actually lost one), and over the next 52-years would play an additional 8,458 games before winning their first World Series, as they did last night in Chavez Ravine, 5-1.

THERE HAVE BEEN MORE THAN A FEW LESS THAN MEMORABLE WORLD SERIES — 2017 IS NOT AMONG THEM.

Was it the greatest? Since I eschew the term "greatest", other than when applied to Babe Ruth, who was the greatest ball player who ever lived, I am unwilling to characterize the '17 World Series as that; but if the question is, does it belong among the greatest? Yes — games two and five justify that distinction.

In winning, the Astros used four pitchers before settling on Charlie Morton, who threw innings six, seven, eight, and nine, for the win. In those four innings he threw 89 pitches, 52 for strikes, gave up two hits, one run, walked one, and struck out four.

But by the time Morton entered the game, it was already over, as Yu Darvish imploded in the biggest game of his life, surrendering five runs (four earned), before departing after one out in the second.

The Dodger pitchers who followed Darvish, Morrow, Kershaw, Jansen, and Wood, pitched superbly, most notably Kershaw, who went four scoreless innings, but it was, as it is clichéd, too little, too late.

The Astros had won, the Dodgers, despite winning 104 games during the regular season — winning 104 in the major league's most competitive division, the NL West — are done for 2017; as its players depart for the four corners of the U.S., and other lands in other places the wide world over; burdened by the memory of their failure, as LA's fans now count 29-years since their last World Series win in '88 over the A's — the one memorialized by Kurt Gibson's one-handed walk-off home run and gimpy circling of the bases to win game one.

Yes, 29-years is a long time, but compared to the Cubs waiting 108 and the Red Sox 86, 29 is nothing to fret about, but trust me on this, many will, not least the LA Times' Bill Plaschke, who led his column this morning by writing, "The drought continues. The emptiness remains. The ache returns…"

IT IS CERTAINLY TRUE THAT LOSING A WORLD SERIES should not over-shadow a stunningly successful season as the Dodgers enjoyed, but that is already happening — as it is, unfortunately, within the perversity of our humanity to hail winners and forget losers.

But I will remember three things about the 2017 Dodgers — their 43-7 run in mid-season and then losing 16 of 17 played (the one win was Kershaw beating the San Diego Padres, 1-0), and Bill Plaschke's campaign to have the team call up Cody Bellinger from Oklahoma City, which they did, then thought about sending him back down, only to have Plaschke start a new campaign, writing that Bellinger needed to stay and the kid proceeded to hit 39 home runs — and is the clear choice as National League Rookie of the Year.

Score one for the columnist.

AS FOR THE NEW CHAMPIONS OF AMERICA'S GAME, here are three take always from today's *Houston Chronicle*:

1. The Astros' Game 7 victory Wednesday night lit up Twitter, generating 62,000 tweets per minute as the final out was recorded, company officials said.

2. The marriage proposal everyone saw on TV after the World Series was something Astros star Carlos Correa had been planning for a while. In fact, Correa said he wanted propose to his girlfriend Miss Texas USA Daniella Rodriguez sooner, but he was patiently waiting, hoping he could do it on a national stage. The Astros' 5-1 win in Game 7 over the Dodgers provided just that stage.

"I was like OK, so we have a championship caliber team, so let me wait it out to see if we can be champions and do it at the big stage," Correa said. "So, we were able to win the game, which was the first part of my day to accomplish, and then I was able to do it."

3. When the grueling, thrilling, stress-filled seven games ended, George Springer ran toward his teammates from right field. The Astros had just done it. They'd won the World Series.

Three years ago, Springer's photo on the cover of *Sports Illustrated* predicted the moment. And he never doubted it would happen. Through ups and downs, wins and losses, hurricanes and floods, injuries and comebacks, the outfielder and leadoff hitter has been a constant and steady force for the Astros. He put together a World Series for the ages in 2017 and celebrated the sweetness of victory after the Astros subdued a beast of a Dodgers team with Wednesday night's 5-1 victory in Game 7.

After the clincher was over, he stood on a podium in the middle of Dodger Stadium to collect the Willie Mays trophy, given to the Most Valuable Player of the Fall Classic.

NOW THAT IT'S OVER, WE CAN GO HOME, stare out the window and wait for spring, as Rogers Hornsby famously said.

Peace and Blessings to you.

2018

BASEBALL NOTES — TUESDAY, APRIL 17

THE BIGGEST PITCHING MATCHUP OF THE EARLY SEASON TAKES PLACE TONIGHT IN ANAHEIM, where David Price faces Shoehei Ohtani, as the AL East and West leaders, Red Sox and Angels, with combined records of 26-5, play their first engagement of '18 — perhaps a window into the AL championship come October.

Oh, game day temperature at Angels Stadium will be 73, or 47 degrees warmer than the 26 wind chill equivalent degrees the Red Sox averaged during their nine game home stand.

Since the Sox were 8-1 in Arctic conditions at Fenway, what effect will the salubrious surroundings of Southern California have on Boston's team?

To be determined.

We do know one player thrilled to be gone from the ice age conditions in the northeast, that would be Chris Sale, who said pitching Sunday was the "most miserable I've ever been on a baseball field, by far, not even close."

ACROSS THE EAST RIVER FROM U.S. DISTRICT COURT JUDGE KIMBA WOODS' CHAMBERS, where a different kind of proceeding was taking place, Tony Kornheiser's Nationals won only their fourth game in the last 13 played, as Sports Illustrated's Cover Boy of years past, Bryce Harper did the unthinkable — hit a HR with a shattered bat (see MLB's highlights).

There have been broken bat singles, but it's doubtful anyone has ever hit a HR with, not just a broken bat, but a shattered bat.

When the ball left the bat and the bat above Harper's hands went flying into the screen down the first base line, nearly decapitating the bat boy, Harper began his HR trot, still holding in his hands what was left of his barely discernible bat, because it was at that point it shattered.

Up in the Nationals broadcast booth, color analyst F.P. Santangelo, called it a Roy Hobbs' moment, while play-by-play broadcaster, Charlie Slowes, almost missed the ball disappearing over the right field fence, because he had followed the shattered bat's terrifying trajectory to the protective screen above the bat boy's head.

Goodness, is Mr. Harper some kind of strong, as the baseball's speed coming off his bat was clocked at 99.2 mph, with a launch degree of 30 — and it carried 406 ft!

Oh, the Metropolitans finally lost, as DC prevailed, 8-6.

THE DODGERS SCORED 10 RUNS AGAINST THE PADRES AT PETCO LAST NIGHT, eight of which were driven in by two former Padres — Matt Kemp with three and Yasmani Grandal with five.

Kemp hit two HRs and Grandal one, but Yasmani's was a grand slam.

The attendance on a cold night by the bay was 23,082, who watched the home town nine lose, 10-3.

One positive note is that SD's Christian Villanueva hit his sixth HR of'18 (Christian who?). Villanueva's six puts him in a three way tie for most in the majors.

Was that expected? I don't think so, making it all the more fun to watch.

CAPSULE COMMENTS ON MONDAY'S PLAY:

COLORADO BEAT THE PIRATES AT PNC, 6-2, as the Rockies won their eighth game of 10 played away from Coors. Playing that well away from the Mile High City bodes well for Bud Black's team going forward, with only 144 left to play...THE REDS OF CINCY stopped their eight game losing streak by winning over Milwaukee, 10-4...PLAYING AT SAFECO IN SEATTLE the Mariners defeated the Astros, 2-1. The winning margin was provided by Nelson Cruz, who hit his third HR of many more to come. Inexplicably, only 12,923 watched, and when you play at Safeco you can't blame the weather...SPEAKING OF WHICH, the Jays/O's game at the Rogers Centre in Toronto was postponed because, pay attention here, icicles fell from the closed roof of the stadium. What? They play two today.

SIX GAMES WERE POSTPONED SUNDAY, THREE MORE YESTERDAY. Twenty-four games have now been postponed, and with 13-days left in April, the MLB record of 26 postponements for the month will be broken.

QUOTE OF THE DAY:

"PARAMNESIA 2

The deluge of nighttime dog barks
Pauses for the after storm gutter drip.
There was a game, he says, can't
Remember if it was 47 or 8, but we had
A two run lead in the bottom of the ninth.

Crickets like a crowd roar and the faint
Leaving of a train across the river gorge.
You got a light. Thanks. Well they got
The bases loaded, drunk as they say.

The old man's profile, a Hemingway
Hillbilly with bifocals in porch light.
And coach, he hollers for me to get in there
To pitch to this Babe Ruth no neck left hander.

A bawling cow somewhere, the Judge's braying
Donkeys, hungry in their dark pasture.
So I say a little prayer 'cause I believed back then,
Hid the ball in my glove behind my back.

A neighbor's old pickup truck inching
Through the front yard of his trailer.
I throw it hard and outside at the knees.
He swings and misses. Lights was so bad.

An owl in the maple top, sounding out a
Whole summer of loneliness.
When he struck at the third bad pitch, that was
The game, but then he come after me with his bat.
A Hmong woman across the field, singing by the
Lanterns in her vegetable garden.
Our first baseman, Rosenbluth, stopped
Him out between the bases.

The hiss of traffic on the wet road,
River like a belly against the old dam.
We piled on him, beat the s..t out of him
Before his teammates got out there, must have
Been 48, same year I met your mother.

— Tim Peeler, Poet Laureate of the Carolinas

BASEBALL NOTES — WEDNESDAY, APRIL 25

THE YANKEES, BEHIND CC SABATHIA AND FOUR HRs, won again in the Bronx last night over the Twins, 8-3.

CC was superb through six innings, giving up but one run on two hits, while on offense, Aaron Judge, Didi Gregorius, and Gary Sanchez, homered, with Sanchez doing it twice.

New York had 10 hits in the game, with Judge and Gregorius accounting for six of them, but 13 times Yankee batters struck out.

Overall, NYY leads the majors in runs scored with 127 in 21 games played, and is tied for the lead in HRs with 32.

Johnny Costa, who I partnered with on Bryon Williams' podcast the day before the season began, is a major Yankee fan, and wanted us to know that New York's rookie, Miguel Andujar, through Monday night's game, had an extra base hit through seven consecutive games, which only Joe D. and the Mick matched before their 23rd birthdays.

SHOHEI OHTANI, PITCHING IN HIS FOURTH GAME FOR THE ANGELS, was mostly mediocre through 5.1 innings, but one fastball was clocked at 101 mph, and many more topped 95, as LAA made it two straight over Houston at Minute Maid, 8-7.

While striking out seven, Ohtani had control issues, as he walked five, but his presence on the mound for visiting LAA drew 36,457 to the game. Absent an unlikely meltdown, he will continue to draw big crowds wherever he plays for the Halos.

Hitting stars for the Angels were Mike Trout, who hit his MLB leading 10th HR and their Gold Glove shortstop, Andrelton Simmons, who homered twice and drove in five, while raising his average to .317.

With their win, LAA moves back into first place in the AL West.

Can they continue to play at this level? I believe so, as the Angels did more in the off-season to improve their ball club than any other team. But the question's determinative will be known 138 games from now.

CURTIS GRANDERSON, ONE OF MY FAVORITE PLAYERS, did in the Red Sox last night at Toronto's Rogers Centre, when he hit a walk-off HR against the game's best relief pitcher, Craig Kimbrel, as the Blue Jays won in 10, 4-3.

The Sox, down 3-0 going into the top of the 9th, rallied to tie, thanks to Brock Holt, who had a three hit game and drove in the tying run with the bases loaded.

On Holt's single to left field, the Sox third base coach, Carlos Febles, made the mistake of sending Eduardo Nunez home, and Granderson's throw easily beat Nunez, who didn't even bother sliding, because he was way out.

Curtis, who has faced Kimbrel only five times since '15, Peter Abraham's wrote in today's Boston Globe, was hitless until he wasn't.

His walk-off-off was only the third time that has happened to Kimbrel since '13, Abraham's also informed.

Boston has dropped three in a row and their AL East record has slipped to 17-5.

Suicide watches are up on bridges over the Charles.

THE CUBS AND INDIANS MET FOR THE FIRST TIME SINCE THE WORLD SERIES OF '16 and Chicago won, 10-3, as Kyle Schwarber hit two HRs, as Tyler Chatwood pitched six strong innings, allowing but one run, to gain his first win of'18 against three losses.

The temperature climbed all the way to 56 in Cleveland, but it felt like 43 with wind chill, and only 16,407 made it to Progressive for the game.

The Indians are 12-9 on the season, which leads the AL Central, while the Cubs are in third place in the NL Central with a 11-9 record.

They play again tonight, with Jon Lester pitching for Chicago and Trevor Bauer for Cleveland.

A REVIEW OF LAST NIGHT'S PLAY:

THE PADRES WHO SCORED 13 against Colorado Monday night, scored zero last night and lost to the Rockies, 7-0. Eric Lauer, in his first major league start, gave up seven runs in his first two innings. He's a high draft pick, so he'll get a second chance...The Marlins beat LAD in the Ravine, as Cameron Maybin doubled in the winning run in the top of the 9th, as [Kenley] "Jansen watches as [Pedro] Baez botches" the save (the LA Times headline writer wrote)...THE ATHLETICS, who are 8-2 in their last 10 games, won again last night, beating the Rangers in Texas, 3-2, as Jed Lowrie hit a tie-breaking double in the 7th. Lowrie, hitting .363, leads the majors... THE CARDINALS lost at home to NYM, as Jay Bruce hit a tiebreaking HR in the 10th to give his team its 15th win against only six losses.

QUOTE OF THE DAY:

1947

Jackie black as an old coal hod,
drew 1.8 mil from Flatbush
out to Harlem--crossed the
marble, strolled under the
chandelier into emerald Ebbets
where Stanky and Reese and
Walker drawled their chatter
and rolled their blue sleeves
out by the left field line looked
like a church full of negroes
emboldened by a hard war,
come for a look see,
a roaring sea of suits, hats,
yellow dresses, holding
their breath for Jackie,
raising thankful prayers
even as the borough fled
to Long Island then Tampa
of the mind.

—Tim Peeler, Poet Laureate of the Carolinas

BASEBALL NOTES — TUESDAY, MAY 15

I'M SEATTLE BOUND FOR AN ADVISORY BOARD MEETING OF THE SCHOOL OF THEOLOGY AT SEATTLE PACIFIC UNIVERSITY (SPU), and today I've given Notes over to Tim Peeler, the Poet Laureate of the Carolinas.

Tim's magical work is featured often here in Notes, and it was on one of those occasions that after reading Tim's poem, "Aunt Lucille," that Dick Enberg called to say how much the poem had moved him, that he had placed it in a folder with instructions to his family that when he died "Aunt Lucille" was to be read at his memorial service.

Dick's passing was shocking to who all who knew, respected and loved him. And when the Padres honored his life and memory at Petco Park, his son, Ted, read "Aunt Lucille."

I invited Tim Peeler to the Fenway Park Writers Series to share his brilliant work, and we became friends.

Notes returns Thursday, as the work of the Advisory Board of Seattle Pacific is a priority.

But for now, pay attention to Tim's poem.

PLANNED LIVES AND HUSHED MEMORIES:

There is no finish line,
Only the sun on our faces,
The smells of laurel
And horse droppings,
Under the road and then
Across the unmown meadow
Past the Cone grave,
Textile magnate, apple grower,
Bones above Blowing Rock,
We slowly wind the crushed
Gravel path to the fire tower
I'm afraid to climb,
But not you Sergeant
Army Marathoner,
Black Indian man with a scar
I see in your gray crown
As I stride one curve above.

There is no finish line,
A father pitches everything
He's got in a side yard hoping
Boy swings can scatter
Dogwood blossoms
In the tree beyond the mound.
The past exaggerates
The pointed limbs of
Snow ball bushes
And who remembers
The clothesline placed
So that the snow melted
First there, and how a boy
Learned to ride a Christmas bike
Till the training wheels lay
Beside half a snowman
With Dad's old preacher hat
Slumped across the torso,
Church bells ringing, dog barks
Answering religiously,
A tractor spinning as it turns
The box blade, scraping the
Church parking lot.

There is no finish line
And we are babies crawling
And dust, all at once.

We ride buses to tether ball mornings
And kick ball afternoons because
One cannot be stolen and the other
Cannot be torn up.

The other game is touch football
And in the fourth grade
The quarterback is already
The quarterback and the linemen
Are already crazy wanting something else.
Three times a day
The mill whistle drowns
The school bells.

Each class works on the trail
Behind the school which is
The only place that is not
Mill property.

We race from playground
To the town ball field to watch
Fearless mill hands:
Brothers and uncles
And daddies.

The red dust from the
Drag panned infield settles
In our hair. Even then,
We cannot let go of
What we love, but must
Watch the sundown march
Of everything toward
The great convergence,
The only sound that saves us
Each evening, our mothers'
Tired voices calling
Supper Time!

There is no finish line,
Walt Disney Wide World
Of Sports Bonanza
Have Gun Will ask
For a second serving
Of banana pudding. . .
Parsonage doorbell ringing
Another mother and two sons,
Hungry and beaten, crying,
Seated in the "breakfast" room,
While Mother warms up more
Liver mush and white beans
And Father calls "somebody."
Middle of summer we cannot see
The town or Grandfather's
Rocky chin without climbing
The rickety tower — I don't
And run harder to punish

Sargent for his old man
Confidence, kicked gravel
Flying flinty in gray shadows.
Abominably human,
I run faster than
The smell of flowers,
The laughter of
A church group of hikers,
Back to the Manor,
Back to our car,
Back to our planned lives
And our hushed memories.

BASEBALL NOTES — FRIDAY, MAY 18

HAVING WON TWO OF THREE FROM THE RED SOX, the A's crossed the International border bound for Toronto, where last night at the Rogers Centre they beat Team Canada, 10-5.

I can hear Dick Enberg saying, "Oh, my!"

I mean, what is going on with the Athletics?

The Baseball Writers Association of America (BBWAA), that professional organization of sanctified scribblers, were telling us pre-season Oakland would not be very good, that they would be last in the AL West, but thus far that is not how it's played out.

With their win over the Blue Jays, they have evened their record at 22-22 and have won four of seven on this road trip from the Yankees, Sox, and now Jays.

Looking at their lineup, you find one three hundred hitter, Jed Lowrie at .324, with shortstop Marcus Semien next best at .274; but the team's BA, at .250, is higher than that of 17 other clubs.

The A's pitching staff, however, has an ERA of 4.37, placing them 20th in the majors.

They won't beat the Astros or Angels, nor likely the Mariners, but they may be better than Texas, so there's that.

THE ANGELS, SHUTOUT BY JUSTIN VERLANDER WEDNESDAY NIGHT, managed but one run last night vs. Tampa Bay, losing 7-1.

Tyler Skaggs held the Rays to a single run through six (remember, the new nine), but that was it, Mike Scioscia wanted his bullpen in the game. That was a big mistake, as LAA's three relievers imploded, giving up six runs on eight hits in only three innings.

Game, set, match.

Mr. Scioscia, who has held a manager's card for 19-years, made a similar cranium error last week vs. the Twins, pulling his starter, only to have his bullpen implode then, as well. Thus the Halos, who are 25-19 and down 2.5 games to the Astros, might be 27-17 and a half-game out.

Oh, my guy, Shohei Ohtani, drove in the Angels' only run with a HR. Great bounce back for the kid who was out thrice by K's against Verlander.

ROBINSON CANO OF THE MARINERS WENT ON THE DL WITH A HAND INJURY, which was bad enough, because he's one of Seattle's key players, but then came the shocking announcement of an 80-game suspension due to an MLB drug policy violation.

In Seattle for a Seattle Pacific University Seminary Advisory Board meeting, I read Larry Stone's column in the *Seattle Times* on Cano's fall from grace.

Stone made a big deal of the suspension, saying he doesn't believe Cano's claim of innocence, citing other major leaguers who entered not guilty pleas when suspended, specifically that of Rafael Palmeiro and Ryan Braun, only later proven to have lied.

But I'm a Seminary board member, not a cynical sports writer like Stone, so I'm giving my man Cano a break, because I actually believe in innocence before guilt, a standard of American jurisprudence.

Don't know Mr. Stone, but his column was over the line, but it's endemic to his profession; a profession I otherwise honor because I greatly admire the sports writer's art, the ability to write under deadline and often to write glorious prose.

Maybe Robinson Cano can hire Michael Avenatti.

THE PLAY OF YESTERDAY:

THE RED SOX BEAT THE O's AT FENWAY, 6-2, as David Price took a shutout into the 9th inning, but despite two runs scoring, pitched a complete game. Imagine…THE PHILLIES WON OVER THE CARDS, 6-2, as Odubel Herrera was on base three times, which he has now accomplished in 43 straight games. Wow…BUD BLACK'S ROCKIES, who have struggled of late, beat the Giants in 12 at AT&T, 5-3 to close within two of idle Arizona…THE PADRES WERE AT PNC PARK in the city of three rivers, but perhaps awed by the beauty of the Pirates' ballpark and rushing waters, they lost, 5-4.

QUOTE OF THE DAY:

OLD MAN ODE:

When she used to come to my games,
My girlfriend wore such short shorts
And had such long legs, lounging low
In the cement bleachers by herself
Right behind the catcher
That errors were committed
And even the plate umpire

The Fellowship of the Ring

Charley Loulakis at National Cathedral Service.

Victoria Picott, assistant women's basketball coach Houston University.

Couple seated next to George at Fish Market in Solona Beach, California.

E J Dionne, Washington Post Columnist.

Dailin from Cartagena, Columbia.

Flight crew of American Airlines Number 587 Washington to Kansas City.

Jimmy Lee Rose, first member of the 2018 FWSR, HOF college football player in California and Kansas State.

Lauren Passero-Brooks, owner of Kensington Cafe.

Keith, who works at Trader Joe's in La Mesa, California.

Marc Sterne, producer of Tony (Tony K) Kornheiser Show.

Natalie Floyd, First Bank, Denver, Colorado.

Rory Devine, NBC 7, San Diego, California.

Sneaked a look between batters.

Those were the malicious days
When every local expert thought
I'd be the next Tony Cloninger,
And I assumed that Kathy was but the first
Of a string of beauties that would
Pursue me as I climbed toward
My imminent destiny, and
I treated her as such.

When she facebooked me
Out of the blue deep Internet last week,
I studied her supposedly recent picture,
Still the big Fawcett blond smiling
On the deck of a yacht
In a picture tagged by a ballplayer's name
I barely remembered, then checked
On the Baseball reference to see
He'd played five years,
Gotten the one big contract
That changed his water to wine.

Doing fine, I replied to her
Mention of her new blues CD
That she wanted me to buy,
And I settled in for another night
Of everything that never happened.

— Tim Peeler

BASEBALL NOTES — THURSDAY, MAY 24

THE PADRES BEAT WASHINGTON IN THE DAYLIGHT AT NATIONALS PARK, 3-1, to save game three of the series.

Tyson Ross was splendid, yielding but one run in 6.2 innings, giving up but five hits, one walk, while striking out nine.

Ross is now 4-3 for the season, and the Padres need him to stay strong, if they are to climb past the Dodgers in the NL West — that would be the fourth place Dodgers.

Bryce Harper, who graced the cover of SI when he was 16, was 0-4 in the game, with three strike-outs vs. Padres' pitching, but in the series he was 4-12, with two HRs, numbers 14 and 15 for '18.

Harper is hitting only .231 this season, and while there is time to turn that around, two years back he didn't, as he hit .243.

Some *Washington Post* sports writers think that Harper, whose Nationals' contract expires at season's end, can command $300,000,000 on the open market from some team next year.

$300,000,000?

Okay, maybe Tom Boswell and Chelsea James of the Post are right, but only if Harper raises his average to, oh, .243.

$300,000,000 million for playing baseball.

Is this a great country or what!

THE YANKEES WERE UP 10-5 OVER TEXAS AFTER FIVE IN HOT & HUMID ARLINGTON; they had hit another four HRs.

Being, generally, a logical person, I thought that's it, New York wins and stays a half game back of Boston, who beat Tampa, 4-1, but that's not the rest of the story.

The Rangers came back to score seven more runs and won, 12-10.

Oh, my.

Neither CC Sabathia nor Doug Fister, who started for NY and Texas, were effective, to say the least.

Their totals through 4.1 innings each — 17 runs, 15 hits, and four bases on balls.

A REVIEW OF WEDNESDAY'S PLAY:

THE COLLAPSE OF ARIZONA is quite stunning, as they lost again in Milwaukee to the Brewers, 9-2, as my man, Travis Shaw, hit his 12th HR of the season…THE ROCKIES went down to LAD, 3-0, in the Ravine, but remain in first place in the NL West thanks to the inexplicable drama of the D-Backs descent…CLEVELAND BEAT THE CUBS AT WRIGLEY, 1-0, to go up one game over .500 and restore some dignity to the AL Central...SHOHEI OTHANI DROVE IN TWO RUNS in the top of the 9th at Toronto's Rogers Centre, as the Angels scored four to beat the Blue Jays, 5-4, for a big comeback victory…JAKE ARRIETA PITCHED BRILLIANTLY for the Phillies, as they shut out the Braves in Philly, 4-0, to pull within a half game of first in the NL East.

THIS IS PETER ABRAHAM IN THE BOSTON GLOBE WEDNESDAY ON MOOKIE BETTS:

"'He's the best player in the league. I don't think there's any arguing that,' [Chris] Sale said. 'It seems like he's hitting a homer every other day . . . you're in awe of it.'

"Betts [Tuesday night's game] was 2 for 4, raising his batting average to .368 and OPS to 1.211. He already has 63 hits, 49 runs, 36 extra-base hits (16 of them home runs), and 35 RBIs.

"There are 114 games remaining and it's almost a certainty Betts will fall into a slump at some point and the cold grip of statistical regression will be felt.

"Advance scouts, statistical analysts, and pitching coaches are good at what they do and they'll provide useful advice on how to pitch Betts. That or they'll give up and decide to pitch around him.

"But just for fun, consider that Betts is on pace to finish the season with 165 runs, 212 hits, 54 homers, 64 doubles, and 118 RBIs.

"No one has scored 165 runs since Lou Gehrig had 167 in 1936. Ted Williams set the Red Sox record of 150 in 1949.

"It's possible to have 64 doubles but it hasn't happened since Joe Medwick in 1936.

"Suffice it to say no player has ever had 165 runs, 212 hits, and 54 home runs in one season.

"Babe Ruth came close when he had 177 runs, 204 hits, and 59 homers in 1921. Old George Herman didn't get too many infield hits."

When Abraham wrote about how challenging it is to pitch to Mookie, he wrote, “or they’ll give up and decide to pitch around him.”

That amused me, because, how do you “pitch around” a lead-off hitter?

QUOTE OF THE DAY:

RACING THROUGH GHOSTS:

I went out there every day,
The Westside Jaycee Park
Before I knew that
The Newton Conover Twins
Once played to packed grandstands there
When men wore Clark Kent hats after
The war, all those optimistic survivors—
I went out there, sometimes twice,
Running eight laps on the
Crushed gravel and sand track,
Where Don Stafford bashed line drives
That sent Dick Stoll scrambling to back up third,
And Eddie Yount, local hero who’d
Made it to the show in the 30s
Launched home runs that would
Have landed in the Elk’s Club pool.
I went out there every day
Between teaching adjunct classes
And tried to run the fastest
I had ever run it,
Blazing sun prickling my head,
Heart in mouth as I shaved time,
Fought through the back stretch beyond
The softball field’s outfield fence
By the two paved basketball courts,
A half dozen horseshoe pits,
I went out there even when
I was dragging or exhausted,
Monster face to the finish,
Driving myself to defeat yesterday
And last week and a year ago,
Becoming a noon time apparition long
Before I knew I was racing through ghosts.

—Tim Peeler

BASEBALL NOTES — TUESDAY, MAY 28

FIRST, THE PADRES PLAY THE REDS AT PETCO FRIDAY NIGHT, Cincy being in Denver Sunday not San Diego, which hosted Miami yesterday, who enjoyed being hosted, beating SD, 7-2.

I think I got carried away when either Kevin Acee or Jeff Sanders, who cover the Padres for the *Union-Tribune*, wrote the home town nine had a chance to improve their standing in the NL West by playing seven games against the Reds and Marlins, both anchoring the bottom of the NL Central and East divisions.

Putting the wrong team in Petco is embarrassing, but nothing quite like NBC's Ann Curry delivering the commencement address at Wheaton College in Boston and confusing it with Wheaton in Illinois and referencing it as Billy Graham's alma mater.

Oh, my!

Indeed.

So, the Padres are home tonight, tomorrow, and Thursday against Miami, and then face Cincy for three Friday, Saturday, and Sunday.

Oh, the 27,932 who watched Miami/SD yesterday, was 17,365 more fans than see the Marlins on average play at home.

SOMETHING STRANGE IS HAPPENING AT SAFECO IN SEATTLE, where the Mariners continue to win one run games, as they did yesterday, beating Texas, 2-1.

They are 9-1 in their last 10 played, seven of which were won by a single run — 5-4, 3-2, 3-2, 1-0, 2-1, 4-3, and 2-1, with their one loss also by one run).

The Mariners have played 53 games this season, 23 of which were decided by one run and 17 of which Seattle won.

They have pulled to within one game of Houston in the AL West, and they have accomplished their rise without Robinson Cano, who broke his wrist May 13, and was then suspended by MLB for a drug violation.

MEMORIAL DAY REVIEW:

ANTHONY RIZZO OF THE CUBS, whose BA had fallen way below .200, was 3-4 vs. the Pirates yesterday, as Chicago won, 7-2, and Rizzo raised his average to .228…JUSTIN VERLANDER Beat the Yankees again, as the Astros won in the Bronx, 5-1…LAA LOST TO DETROIT, 9-3, but the great Mike Trout assumed the HR lead in the majors with 18, with the Red Sox's Mookie Betts and J.D. Martinez one behind with 17. J.D. hit his 17th yesterday at Fenway as the Sox won over the Jays, 8-3…TAMPA BAY AND THE A's went 13 innings before the Rays prevailed in Oakland, 1-0…SPIRITS SHOULD BE HIGH FOR THE KORNHEISER PODCAST TODAY, as the Nationals have won four straight and have closed to within one of the Braves in the NL East…THE D-BACKS WON OVER CINCY, 12-5. It was only their third win in the last 18 played, but despite being in free fall, they are but 1.5 games back of Colorado in the NL West…MILWAUKEE WON AGAIN, beating St. Louis, 8-3, for their eighth victory in their last 10 games.

.

I'M A CHARTER MEMBER OF THE KENSINGTON GROUP, which has been meeting for breakfast every Saturday morning for 22-years.

We call ourselves the "Kensington Group" because that's the San Diego community where many of us lived, and thought it had a rather highbrow sound to it, especially when we bought a full page ad in *The Paris Review* to celebrate my friend George Plimpton's 50th year as its publisher.

Our group meets for friendship and conversation. The subjects covered vary with the week's news, often dominated by our accidental president and America's Game.

During the week, there is also an exchange of emails, which most recently focused on the Angels' Mike Trout and a member's claim he's the game's greatest.

Entering the dialogue, I wrote:

"I do not doubt Trout's greatness, but there are many great players, no one great player, save Babe Ruth."

In a stream of consciousness, I then wrote:

"In the years 2012-17, Mike Trout struck out 1,424 times in 3,276 ABs.

"In the years 1937-42, Joe DiMaggio struck out 157 times in 3,750 ABs. In '41 alone Joe D. struck out only 13 times in 622 ABs.

"But those astonishing numbers pale in comparison to the great Tris Speaker, the Red Sox/Indians Hall of Famer, who in a 22-year career came to bat 10,195 times and struck out only 220 times.

"In the years 1913-18, Speaker batted 3,178 times, and struck out 85 times."

"There are some major league players today who strike out that often in two months of play."

As to the question why today's players strike out so often, compared to DiMaggio and Speaker, or Ted Williams or Tony Gwynn, I have no answer, beyond invoking a dreaded cliché, "It is what it is."

Or perhaps I should just say, a transcendent mystery.

QUOTE OF THE DAY:

WHO TORE DOWN HOTEL HICKORY?

This main street building yawns through its cracked glass,
Yields no history in a town where
Time is a cover up, an imported,
Trowel-ed over façade. Even in
Trade Alley, forgetfulness shadows

Useless as outdated parlay cards.
Hickory, its greatest building
Imploded for the townspeople
Who swarmed to see, somber, like at a hanging.

Only the pool hall hotdogs and shoeshine chairs,
Only the black and white tile beneath
The disordered clack of a broken billiards game,
Only the grilled sizzle of city ham and American cheese,
Only the ghosts of penny pitching Ohio boys,
Minor league ball players waiting for their fans,
The local girls to get off from dime store jobs,

All of the us that is them,
Herded toward an indifferent pash,
Because the First National Bank knows better,
War-driven, cross-carrying, touched with fire,
White socked, cologne splashed,
Future dreaming, men of a former condition,
Gullible in a sweet sort of way, proven in another.
Museum pictured now, sans veneer.
Who lost the bet? Who left a copper leaning
By the gutter? Who tore down history
To make room for money?

— Tim Peeler

BASEBALL NOTES — TUESDAY, JUNE 12

IT TOOK 12-INNINGS AT ORIOLES PARK AT CAMDEN YARDS IN H.L. MENCKEN'S BALTIMORE last night for the Red Sox to beat the O's, 2-0.

It was, on both sides, a pitcher's night, as 10 pitchers threw 335 pitches against 22 players in 80 ABs, resulting in 11 base hits, 26 strikeouts and 11 bases on balls.

The win was the Sox's seventh in eight games vs. the O's this year, and the victory moved Boston into a tie with New York for the lead in the AL East.

The reported attendance at Camden was 15,934, but as the game went into OT it appeared the only fans left in Larry Lucchino, Janet Marie Smith, and Donal Shaefer's ball park were Sox fans, with one exception, a rather handsome, gray haired gentleman, sitting a couple of rows above the Baltimore dugout wearing a smart black leather jacket with an O's logo.

I like Buck Showalter and Adam Jones (a San Diego kid), Jonathan Shoop and Manny Machado, but the O's are woeful, as their record stands at 19-46.

So many great players. So many great teams. Sad.

Oh, I did not know that since Camden opened in '92, every HR that lands on Utah Street, between the bleachers in right field and the warehouse, is immortalized with a baseball plaque embedded in the side walk with the player's name, distance of the HR, and date.

The Sox's Jackie Bradley has one from April of '17, as his HR carried 416 ft.

My compliments to NESN's Guerin Austin for the story, told during the game.

THE CUBS MOVED INTO FIRST PLACE IN THE NL CENTRAL, as they beat the Brewers in Milwaukee, 7-2, scoring five runs in the top of the 11th for the win.

The Brewers' relief corps of Wilson, Strop, Rosario, and Bass, were quite spectacular, yielding but four hits in five innings, walking none and striking out six.

The winning hit for Chicago was a HR off the bat of Anthony "Pardon My Slide" Rizzo.

A big Monday night Miller Park crowd of 37,578 saw the game.

A BRIEF REVIEW OF MONDAY NIGHT'S PLAY:

THE MARINERS CONTINUE TO AMAZE, as they won again, beating LAA at Safeco, 5-3, as Nelson Cruz homered twice. Seattle is now 42-24 on the season…THE PADRES PLAYED THE CARDS at Busch and St. Louis won, 5-2, as Marcel Ozuna, Jose Martinez, and Jeff Gyorko homered…CARLOS CARRASCO THREW TWO HIT BALL OVER SEVEN, as the Indians beat the White Sox on Chicago's South Side, 4-0.

DAN SHAUGHNESSY ON THE RED SOX IN MONDAY'S BOSTON GLOBE:

"It is interesting to note that despite the phony notion that they are annual World Series contenders, the Red Sox have won three playoff series since 2008, all coming in 2013. Take away 2013, and the Red Sox since 2008 are 1-9 in the postseason with three last-place finishes…

"Call me a dope but I still don't understand the abrupt release of Hanley Ramirez two weeks ago. We still don't know exactly what happened, but it's pretty clear the Sox could have used Hanley in Friday's 1-0 loss to the White Sox. Cora these days regularly sends out a lineup with two or three guys hitting below the magical Mendoza Line (.200)…With Mookie Betts still on the shelf, Boston's vaunted offense drops off a cliff after J.D. Martinez in the cleanup spot."

QUOTE OF THE DAY:

INTERVIEW WITH MR. LITTLE:

Said when I was younger
Saw ball games in four New York parks,
John Billy's Uncle Herschel used to take me,
Saw Robin Roberts once.
Smokey Burgess from Caroleen
And Rube Walker from Lenoir
Both hit home runs
Then Shotgun Shuba
Won the game with a double.

Said when we were kids
We played bicycle games
We'd all ride our bikes
To another part of town
And play the kids there
And yes, there was usually
A fight at the end
Or more likely a fight that ended it.

Then he told me about
His perfect season at Davidson
Where he had a football scholarship
Said he played first base all year
No errors never missed a throw
A grounder a liner
Then he told me how he'd stood
Waiting under a pop up
Out behind first
How it hit the heel of his mitt
And bounced out
Costing them the championship.

His voice softened
And then broke
Fifty-five years later
A successful banker with
A wonderful wife
And a beautiful family
All over the country.
I shoulda let the right fielder have it.
He knew it
Everybody at the game knew it
He was my roommate
And he never said anything to me.
Nobody did but I knew it.

— Tim Peeler, Poet Laureate of the Carolinas

BASEBALL NOTES, SECOND EDITION — MONDAY, JUNE 25

I HAVEN'T DONE THIS BEFORE, written a second posting of Baseball Notes on the same day, but my objective is to keep Notes under 1,000 words, which is necessary if Facebook allows the art I select to be included with my postings, and today I was closing in on my word limit and I want the art included, so this Notes II:

KEVEN ACEE, IS A SPORTS WRITER FOR SAN DIEGO UNION-TRIBUNE, who worshipped the Chargers, but when the Bolts broke for LA, Kevin gave up his column in sports to become the newspaper's Padres beat reporter, where I believe he's aced the assignment.

This is Kevin in today's newspaper:

"Even before Andrew McCutchen tagged a belt-high fastball from [Brad] Hand to the gap in right-center field with one out, what [Andy] Green knew more than anything is his team could not afford to play a 12th inning.

"Green knew if he looked at his bullpen all he would see is hanging arms and a submarining right-hander who he'd been compelled to promote just that morning and was around essentially only to eat innings.

"Green was going to win or lose with the pitcher who had saved so many Padres victories over the past 13 months…"

From this except of Kevin's reporting, I wish to lift one phrase, "hanging arms."

What?

"Hanging arms?"

Seriously?

Of course, Kevin, is serious, because this has become the mindset of sports scribblers all over the USA, why it's even leaked into the NESN and Fox San Diego broadcast booths, where brilliant broadcasters and smart analysts, have been duped, along with their ink stained wretched colleagues, to writing about "hanging arms" and "exhausted bullpens," etc.

I can't take it!

For God's sake, get a clue.

You cannot possibly convince me, not in this life time, that a relief pitcher who has, thrown, what?

64 pitches over eight days as has Mr. Hand, is part of a crew with "hanging arms."

Because if you are trying to tell me that they are fatigued, tired, exhausted, worn down, I am telling you, and anyone paying attention, I will accept "fatigued, tired, exhausted, worn down" as a description for mine workers, housing construction crews, farmers, or any other true laborer, but not for millionaires who play baseball for a living.

Or, let me take it to the next level:

I will accept "fatigued, tired, exhausted, worn down" as a description of our heroes on duty in Afghanistan or the Middle East, but I am not accepting, again, for millionaires who play baseball for a living.

My new friend, Lt. Colonel William Walker, United States Marine Corps, did six tours of duty in Iraq and Afghanistan, was in the middle of the killing fields, now stationed in San Diego, would never, ever tell you or me that he is "fatigued, tired, exhausted, worn down."

So, Peter, Nick, Kevin, Jeff, Alex, Julian, Ian, Dave, Jerry, Dennis, Don, Mark, Love ya all, but please stop insulting our Intelligence by telling us, through either the written or spoken word, that grown men are "fatigued, tired, exhausted, worn down" because they were called in from the bullpen in one week to throw a couple of dozen pitches.

Because, gentlemen, it's ridiculous!

And, you're better that that.

JEFF MILLER, WHO COVERS THE ANGELS FOR THE LA TIMES, wrote this in Sunday's newspaper:

"They've had shoulders, elbows and ankles, an adductor and an oblique, a forearm, a knee, a wrist, a hamstring and a lumbar.

"They've had strains, sprains and tears, a subluxation and an impingement and an absurdly swelled amount of inflammation.

"The one thing the 2018 Angels haven't had, medically speaking at least, is a hurt Mike Trout.

"Only now, they have a hurting Mike Trout, the best player in baseball limited to designated hitting for the second consecutive game [last] Thursday...

"'It's weird," Trout said, looking down at his right index finger. Got a little sprain in there.'

"Still, for a team that has a dozen names on the disabled list, has had eight of its top nine starting pitchers miss time and has employed a baseball-high 46 players, any irregularities concerning Trout are, in fact, quite concerning.

"He's the only player on this club to have appeared in all 75 games, the only Angel who, until this week, hadn't experienced some form of debilitating ailment..

"He's also Mike Trout and all that means every year. Entering Thursday, that meant leading the majors in home runs (23), walks (64), runs (60), on-base-plus-slugging percentage (1.158) and WAR (6.6).

"Appearing in career game No. 1,000, Trout is the only player to surpass 200 homers and 175 stolen bases before his age — 27. He hit more home runs (224) in his first 1,000 games than Barry Bonds (172)."

QUOTE OF THE DAY:

12 FATHER'S DAYS DEAD:

His remains are scattered
In sermon stacks and financial records,
In Little League scorebooks
Which report the chronicle of his coaching,

In his last glove left to a grandson
Who now coaches,
In a voice that loops on cassette reels,
Marking the fragments of his outrageous faith.

And his remains are scattered
In the memories of his congregants,
In the family that has gone on
Without him a dozen difficult years,

Crossing the bridges between the innings
Of the game he loved every summer. — Tim Peeler, Poet Laureate of the Carolinas

BASEBALL NOTES — WEDNESDAY, JUNE 27

THE RED SOX & ANGELS HAVE MET FOUR TIMES THIS SEASON. The Red Sox have won all four games, outscoring LAA 36-4, as last night at Fenway they again beat Mike Scioscia's team, this time, 9-1.

The other three games in April were played across I-5 from Disneyland in Anaheim, were won by scores of, 10-1, 9-0, and 8-2.

Christian Vasquez, Mookie Betts, Jackie Bradley Jr., and J.D. Martinez, all homered for Boston. J.D.'s was his 24th of the year, which leads the majors, one more than Cleveland's own Jose Martinez and LAA's Mike Trout.

Perhaps, at season's end, the signing of Julio Daniel Martinez, may be viewed as one of the most significant in Red Sox annals; but for now up in the WEEI radio booth at Fenway, Joe Castiglione is talking J.D. and MVP.

And why not? The man is hitting .326, has 19 doubles, one triple, the 24 HRs, an OBP of .393, and a SLG average of .646, plus his 61 RBIs also tops MLB.

Will it last?

To answer the question, go to J.D.'s performance last season with Arizona and read what he did for the D-Back's from August on, when he became the toughest out in the game — he was quite unbelievable.

Oh, in last night's game, Jackie Bradley Jr., the game's best outfielder, had three hits and is now 6-7 in his last two games; a most welcomed sign from JB, who has struggled at bat, but never in the field.

THE CUBS STOPPED THEIR FIVE GAME SKID BY BEATING LAD, 9-4, as Jon Lester won his 10th game before 53,904 at Dodger Stadium.

Javier Baez, Chicago's second baseman, had a big night in the Ravine, as he hit two HRs, including a grand slam, collected two other hits, drove in five and now has 56 on the year. In addition, Mr. Baez is an outstanding fielder, routinely making highlight plays.

With Milwaukee winning over KC, 5-1, Chicago still trails the NL Central's leader by three games.

OVERNIGHTS:

HOUSTON BEAT TORONTO AT MINUTE MAID, 7-0, as Charlie Morton won his 10th against one loss. It was the Astros' 53rd win of '18, tying them with the Red Sox for most in the majors, one up on NYY.

SPEAKING OF WHICH, the Yankees also got a shutout, beating the Phillies in Philly, 6-0, as Luis Severino won his 12th. The young man has been quite sensational for the Bronx team, with his wins piling up, his ERA down to 2.10, and his strikeouts rising to 132, placing him number seven among hurlers.

THE PADRES WON IN TEXAS, defeating the Rangers, 3-2. Tyson Ross gave up two runs and five hits through six, another credible performance for SD, but the bullpen three of Strahm, Yates and Hand, were lights out through their three innings of relief, as Hand saved his 22nd, to lead the NL.

THE WONDERS OF '18, the Athletics of Oakland, were down six to the Tigers in Detroit City, but came back to win, 9-7. Jed Lowrie, who's having a career year, was 4-4. The A's have won eight of 10, to go four up over losses n the win column.

THE NATIONALS SUFFERED THEIR SECOND STRAIGHT SHUTOUT, a truly tough loss to Tampa, 1-0. The losing pitcher for DC was the truly great Max Scherzer, who I want to win every time out, save if he's facing the Red Sox, Padres or Rockies. But, hey, that gives him 26 other teams to beat.

CHELSEA JAMES COVERS THE NATIONALS FOR THE WASHINGTON POST. In her game day story yesterday, writing about the team's 11-0 loss to Tampa Bay the night before, the Nationals' eleventh in sixteen games, writing about its apparently abused bullpen, Ms. James wrote the following:

"In the unique society of the baseball clubhouse, [Justin] Miller and his fellow innings-eaters qualify as martyrs regardless of their performance, revered because their statistics suffered for the good of their fellow relievers. The Nationals have required too many martyrs lately."

Did you read that?

Ms. James' description of the members of the Nationals' bullpen as "martyrs?"

Excuse me.

No, Ms. James.

Jesus was a martyr. Joan of Arc was a martyr; so too Socrates, Thomas Beckett, Thomas Cranmer, William Tyndale, Jan Huss, Nathan Hale, Joseph Smith, Dietrich Bonhoeffer, and the *4,384 African-Americans murdered by white lynch mobs in the South, who became, by that savagery and evil, martyrs to their color and to the mistaken belief, as pledged in the Declaration of Independence, that all men are created equal.

Words matter, equating relief pitching with martyrdom, is an affront to human dignity; an affront to those saints and heroes of history who died in behalf of their faith and their cause — and were never paid millions for throwing a baseball.

*Source: The Legacy Museum, Montgomery, Alabama

CORRECTION: When I wrote on Monday that the Red Sox/Yankees have had the same number of playoffs appearances since the intro of the WC in '93, a friend and Yankees fan, Mike Vignogna, emailed to say that was wrong. The scorecard has NYY in the post-season, 19 times; Boston, 12.

QUOTE OF THE DAY:

AUTOMATIC SAVE:

The brain remembers every
Click of its camera so
Somewhere in there are all of
Dad's batting practice pitches,

All of my pitching practice
Tosses, endless infield he
Fungoed, two a day practices
At Longview Elementary,

Older boys from the hood
Who came to challenge our squad,
Raring to fight when they lost,
Blue collar textile kids,

Sons of alcoholics,
Generational abusers,
Cross-handed hitters,

Scab-legged Scots-Irish,

Sun-beaten in a film of red dust—
They are all there, captured in
A crafty substance called time.

— Tim Peeler, Poet Laureate of the Carolinas

George and Matthew Mitrovich.

BASEBALL NOTES — FRIDAY, JUNE 29

OREGON STATE WON ITS THIRD COLLEGE WORLD SERIES, as the Beavers beat Arkansas in Omaha, 5-0.

They won behind the shutout pitching of a freshman, Kevin Abel, a kid from San Diego's Madison High. Abel, by allowing just two-hits, won his fourth game, thereby setting a record, as no one had ever done that before in the CWS.

The victory by OSU was the 34th championship for the PAC-12, far and away the most by any conference. USC alone has 11 of those championships.

The SEC may reign in football and basketball, but the college crown in baseball, belongs to the PAC-12.

Yes!

THE RED SOX WON OVER LAA AGAIN LAST NIGHT AT FENWAY, this time, 4-2.

With the win, number 55 on the season, they move a full game up on the Yankees, who they face tonight at the Stadium in the first of a three game set.

Big series?

Yes.

Season maker or breaker?

No.

Whether playing the Yankees or Yakima, every win has equal value in the standings.

Boston and LAA played six times this season. The Red Sox won all six. They also hit 20 HRs in those six games, the most ever by any team in major league history in a series of six or fewer games.

OVERNIGHTS:

CLAYTON KERSHAW WAS BACK ON THE MOUND AT DODGER STADIUM, but exited after five innings and a 3-1 lead, having allowed but one run on five hits. His departure was all the Cubs needed, as they scored seven in the 7th to gain a series split and a 11-5 win. Anthony Rizzo, who began '18 battling to get his BA above .200, had a 4-5 night.

J.D. LeMAHIEU had a big game for the Rockies. vs. the Giants at AT&T with a two-run HR in the 9th, setting a career high with five RBIs, as Colorado won for Bud Black, 9-8.

ZACH GREINKE PITCHED SEVEN STRONG INNINGS IN MIAMI, had two base hits, drove in a run and stole a base, as Arizona defeated the Marlins, 4-2. The D-Backs, who went into an unfathomable losing streak, appear to be back to their NL West norm, as they've won eight of 10, and lead their division by three and a half over LAD.

WHATEVER THE AILMENT BESETTING THE NATIONALS, remains beyond medical relief, as they lost in Philly to Philly, 4-3. It was their seventh loss in 10 games, not good for the team the experts said would win the NL East. Still could happen, as we've just started the season's second half, but meanwhile at Chatter Restaurant in Washington, DC, Tony Kornheiser and his podcast crew, are anxious.

Oh, Tuesday night, Tony will be wearing, on his and Michael Wilbon's Pardon the Interruption (PTI) show over ESPN, the 4th of July Nationals' baseball hat I sent.

THANKS TO TWO ERRORS BY THE O's in the 10th inning, the Mariners won at Camden, 4-2. Three of Seattle's runs came from Nelson Cruz's 21st HR. They have now won four in a row.

MATT KEMP RETURNED HOME TO THE DODGERS after an absence of three years. His homecoming has been rather splendid.

Through 76 games this season, he has hit .311, while accounting for 16 doubles, 13 HRs, and 47 RBIs, which leads the Dodgers.

In his sojourn with the Padres and Braves, he played 425 games, hitting 78 doubles, four triples, 65 HRs, while driving in 233 runs. He batted in years 2015, '16, and '17, .265, .268, and .276.

The *trade that brought him to the Padres was a big deal. He was an authentic major league star with LAD. In 2011 he led the NL in runs scored, HRs, and RBIs. There was palpable fan excitement in California's border town, 122.8 miles south of Dodger Stadium. It was a big deal.

But for reasons unexplained, Kemp annoyed people in San Diego; people in the clubhouse, in the broadcast booth, and he annoyed team chairman, Ron Fowler.

I do not know the details. I haven't asked. But knowing Mr. Fowler, knowing his standing in San Diego, especially his remarkable philanthropy, I have to believe Mr. Kemp's conduct was offensive.

That said, he's gone from the Padres and Braves, but as Helen Elliott wrote in the *LA Times* yesterday, he's happy to be back at Chavez Ravine — and LAD is happy he's back.

*The trade, Yasmani Grandal for Kemp, was, as it turned out, a bummer for SD. The Dodgers got a player, Grandal, who's become key for them — and now they have Kemp back.

QUOTE OF THE DAY:

SWINGERS:

Bull-necked Norman Small
Came to Hickory from Mooresville
For one year, lefty who'd played
In Durham, married his sweetheart
On the field, ducking under
The crossed bats of teammates
Though rumor had it that she
Was often busy when he was gone.

New Jersey farm boy, played
Into his mid-thirties,
For the Moors at the end
Of a downtown street,
Leading the league in homers
Nearly every season,
Over three hundred
Even with the war years
Like four missing teeth.

Bull-necked Norman Small,
The Mooresville Moor
Likely never read Othello
Nor flashed his jealousy
While playing the local hero
At his flirty young wife,
And they had a great life.

— Tim Peeler, *Poet Laureate of the Carolinas

*How did Mr. Peeler become "Poet Laureate" of the Carolinas? Because that's the title I chose to give him.

And who gave me that authority?

Was it the legislative bodies of the Carolinas, North and South?

No.

It is The First Amendment to the Constitution of the United States.

Have A Great Weekend!

BASEBALL NOTES — WEDNESDAY, JULY 4

IT WAS 96 AT GAME TIME AT NATIONALS PARK LAST NIGHT and the Red Sox hitting matched the weather index, as they beat Washington, 11-4.

The Nationals would be first in the NL East, the experts said, but at the moment, the capital's team stands at .500 on the year.

The legendary Tom Boswell's column in the Post today, is headlined, "Nat's crisis point has arrived in a hurry." So it seems.

The team that had a 20-9 record in May, self-destructed starting on June 1, winning only nine times and losing 19.

The fate of DC's team doesn't concern me, beyond its effect on Tony Kornheiser and crew, but what perplexes is the seeming high regard media continues to hold for Mike Rizzo, the Nationals' GM. When he fired Dusty Baker, that was a mistake, compounded by his hiring of a rookie manager, David Martinez, who, I'm told, half-way through the season, has lost his clubhouse.

A team lucky enough to have Max Scherzer on it should be better than .500, but we'll see.

In my brief visit to Washington, the smart baseball people I spoke to, were in one agreement: the game's best are the Red Sox, Yankees and Houston — and then everybody else.

But we won't know that denouement until the shadows of fall have made their way across ballparks east and west.

In last night's game, Xander Bogearts had a grand slam and J.D. Martinez hit his MLB leading 26th HR, while driving in four. His 71 RBI also top the majors.

Both teams had 12 hits, but Boston left only three runners on base; Washington, nine.

Standing outside Nationals Park last night with Tim Mitrovich, waiting for Uber, I saw for the first time the ballpark's west front, and decided that it's really unattractive. The ballpark's interior, is fine, the west exterior, not.

OTHER GAMES PLAYED ON THE THIRD:

THE YANKEES BEAT THE BRAVES IN THE BRONX, 8-5, as Aaron Hicks hit his fifth HR in seven games, and Kyle Higashiocka and Giancarlo Stanton, also homered.

JOSH REDDICK AND TONY KEMP HOMERED IN THE THIRD as the Astros won over Texas in Arlington, 5-3.

BUD BLACK'S ROCKIES ARE BACK TO .500, as they beat the Giants at Coors, 8-1. Charlie Blackmon homered in the first and Nolan Arenado added his NL leading 22nd before 47,072 on an 87-degree night in Denver.

YOAN MOCANDA'S TRIPLE IN THE 12TH gave the White Sox a 12-8 victory over Cincy. Daniel Palka and Avisall Garcia hit two HRs for Chicago, as they rallied for four in the top of the 9th to send the game into OT.

WITH TODAY'S 4th OF JULY GAME, the San Diego Padres will have played 19 games on the road, only five at home. That disparity in home and away games doesn't explain why the border town team has been so woeful of late, but one cannot dismiss out of hand, either, its effect.

I would think, given the close relationship that team chairman, Ron Fowler, and principal owners, Tom and Peter Seidler, have with the commissioner's office, they will insist such indefensible scheduling never happens again.

Oh, the Padres lost again yesterday, this time to the A's, 6-2, in that city where there is no there there, claimed, famously, Gertrude Stein.

A NOTE ON NOTES:

This is being composed on United Airlines flight 229 from Dulles to San Diego, as my one day in DC is over, but the trip was worth it, as we had a most successful Fenway Park/Washington Writers Series luncheon yesterday with Joe Castiglione and Dave O'Brien, as the radio and television voices of the Red Sox were terrific, and more than compensated for the absence of players, who facing a six o'clock start time, couldn't attend.

It was, literally, a standing room only crowd in attendance, comprised, in part, of Congressional staffers for Massachusetts and New England delegation members.

You cannot be a part of something like our event without realizing anew, the utter and complete love affair Red Sox fans have for their team. Wherever I've gone with the Sox, I have experienced this, up close and personal. Time after time, Red Sox fans outnumber fans of the home team, as happened again last night at Nationals Park. It's remarkable.

ONE ANECDOTE:

Emily Ross is one of Senator Elizabeth Warren's key aides. She emailed before the event to say how excited she was to hear Castiglione and O'Brien, that she had grown up listening to Joe, and that the nightly telecast on NESN of Sox games with Dave, were big in her life.

She asked if it would be okay to meet them? Absolutely, I answered, and that happened yesterday before the lunch.

After the two had dazzled the audience with their stories and insights, Ms. Ross was one of those who asked a question. Dave answered by saying, "Emily, that's a great question."

Later "Emily" emailed to say, "Hearing Dave O'Brien call out my name is the highlight of my life!"

I am indebted to Billy Tranghese of Congressman Richie Neal's staff and to Anthony DeMaio of the Massachusetts Society of DC, for their support, and to former Congressman Jim Moran and the law firm of McDermott Will & Emery, for providing their terrace overlooking the Capitol for the venue — and, always, to Tim Mitrovich who assisted in registering guests.

QUOTE OF THE DAY:

THE ANCESTORS:

Stoop-shouldered grandfather
Overalled, deep in the farm field,
The mule-pulled plow nicks an hour
For my father to dream of baseball.

And I am a consequence
Of that blade,
Of his steady grip,
Of that jubilant dream.

— Tim Peeler, Poet Laureate of the Carolinas

BASEBALL NOTES — MONDAY, JULY 9

SHOHEI OHTANI PINCH-HIT FOR THE ANGELS IN THEIR SUNDAY NIGHT ESPN GAME VS. THE DODGERS FROM ANAHEIM, and Ohtani won the game for LAA, as his deep drive to left center field, off a knee-high slider over the middle of the plate, was the margin of victory, 4-3.

Ohtani has been on a slightly downward curve, so maybe his big blast Sunday night will renew his offensive threat. It would be good for him, his teammates, and Angel fans, but even bigger for the game.

Of Shohei's HR, Alex Rodriquez, in the ESPN booth, said it reminded him of the dramatic HR Kirk Gibson hit for the Dodgers in the '88 World Series against the A's.

Not exactly.

With the victory, the Angels took the series from the Dodgers, two games to one.

MARK REYNOLDS OF THE NATIONALS HIT A PINCH HIT WALK-OFF HR FRIDAY NIGHT VS. MIAMI as Washington won, 3-2.

On Saturday night he started for DC and proceeded to have a 5-5 game, including two HRs and drove in 10 to set a team record, as Washington won big, 18-4; and that coupled with Trea Turner's eight RBIs in Thursday night's remarkable 14-12 comeback win, after being down 9-0, set an additional record for the Nationals, as no two players in team history had done that in a single week.

Those three wins helped ease the stain of the team's being swept by Boston in the beginning of the week; however, they faltered yesterday, losing to the Marlins, 10-2.

But you are reading this because in Sunday's *LA Times*, Houston Mitchell, who does a feature entitled, "Stat Corner," compiled a list of players from Baseball-Rererence.com, who had the least productive major league careers — think of it as the opposite of WAR (wins above replacement) — beginning with someone named Bill Bergen, who played from 1901-11.

Of current players, the list is topped by, yes, Mark Reynolds. The irony that Mitchell's listing of Reynolds appears in print the morning after Mark drove in 10 runs, and two days after he hit a walk-off HR, is too good not to mention.

But there will be no further references to LAP (losses against replacement), because I have lived 75-years as a baseball fan not knowing of such a stat, and would be happy to live another 75 in similar ignorance.

WEEKEND REVIEW:

THE PADRES WENT 16-INNINGS IN THE VALLEY OF THE SUN before winning over the D-Backs, thanks to Wil Meyers' HR off of Jeff Mathis, who was on the mound after catching for Arizona the previous 15-innings. It was Will's fourth HR in the last two games. Eighteen pitchers and one catcher were used in the game. The win earned SD a much needed split in the series.

THE RED SOX WON IN KC, 7-4, winning their sixth straight by sweeping the three game series, and giving Rick Porcello his 11th victory of '18 against only three losses. The Sox come home to face Texas and Toronto. Their record, 62-29, is the game's best, and has them on track to win 124 against only 38 losses. If that happens, it would mean two things: 1) a new MLB record, and 2), facing Luis Severino in a one game playoff at Fenway. Oh, my!

THE YANKEES & BLUE JAYS WENT 10-INNINGS AT THE ROGERS CENTRE, before Brent Gardner singled in the go-ahead run and NYY prevailed, 2-1.

THE AMAZING A's SHUTOUT THE INDIANS, 6-0, at Progressive in Cleveland, and are now 10 games over .500. Who saw this coming? Anyone? And, they're playing in the game's toughest division, the AL West, whose five teams are a combined, 254-201.

PABLO SANDOVAL, one of the Red Sox's biggest off-season signing blunders, is quietly resurrecting his career in SF with the Giants (not that any Sox fan would care), and Sunday hit a HR and drove in five as Bruce Bochy's team beat the Cardinals at AT&T, 13-8.

AUSTIN BIBENS-DIRKX, yes, that Austin Biben's-Dirks, pitched impressively for Texas as the Rangers won in Detroit City, 3-0.

DALLAS KEUCHEL PITCHED SEVEN STRONG INNINGS FOR HOUSTON and Jose Altuve homered as the Astros won a close one on Chicago's Southside, 2-1.

MORE FROM BASEBALL DIGEST, JULY/AUGUST ISSUE:

FROM 1918 THROUGH 2018, there are four players who four times in a season had five or more hits in a game — Ty Cobb (1922), Stan Musial (1948), Tony Gwynn (1993), and Ichiro Suzuki (2004).

Seventeen players had five or more on three occasions, the last being Ender Inciarte (2017), who hit .304 in 662 ABs for the Braves (I had no clue).

Since 1908, 81 players have had three doubles and a HR in a game, last accomplished by Mike Trout against the Yankees at the Stadium in May of '17,

DID YOU KNOW through Sunday's games Aaron Judge and Giancarlo Stanton of the Yankees have struck out 120 times, tying them for third in the majors; that Eduardo Escobar of the Twins has 35 doubles to lead in two baggers; that Yolmer Sanchez of the White Sox leads in triples with nine; that the leader in HRs among second basemen is the Braves' Ozzie Albies with 18, and the pitcher with the majors' best ERA is Kirby Yates of the Padres with 0.79.

QUOTE OF THE DAY:

CURT FLOOD REDUX:

He may have left us too soon,
But his post-assassination portrait
Of MLK still hangs in the King living room,

And athletes he helped transform
Into small corporations
Are rounding up their posses
And recalculating their worth,

Desperately unaware that
In 1969 the pundits said
90K had taken that Oakland boy
Beyond his raising,

That his artwork had become distraction
Enough to make him
Misjudge a fly ball in Game 7, '68,

That he was a radical
Because he could articulate his anger
When he said,

"A well-paid slave is nonetheless a slave."

BASEBALL NOTES — WEDNESDAY, JULY 11

"FOWLER KEEPS THE FAITH" is the title that leads Sports in the *San Diego Union-Tribune* today.

"Fowler" is Ron Fowler, chairman of Padres, and the timing and placement of the story couldn't have been better, because last night at Petco Park, his team beat the Dodgers, 4-1.

Mr. Fowler is a good man, whose philanthropy is legendary, but he is also a fan and his team frustrates him — a frustration shared by others who love his team.

The frustration was felt especially last night.

Yes, the Padres won, but manager Andy Green decided after eight and two-third innings to pull his starter, Eric Lauer, who had been brilliant, allowing the Investment Bankers from Chavez Ravine, but one run on four hits, striking out eight and issuing only two bases on balls.

Why did Green do that? Why didn't he trust his rookie to close out the win and complete the game? Yes, Lauer was within one out of becoming the first Padres rookie in 12-years to throw a shutout, when Max Muncy homered, a ball that barely cleared the left center field fence, but the kid needed only that last out and should have been permitted to stay in the game.

The Padres are not very good. Their wins of late have been few and far between, which is frustrating, so why compound the frustration by their manager denying fans the joy of watching rookie Lauer get his complete game victory?

I accept what I'm told, that Andy Green is very Baseball smart, but being smart about the game and understanding PR are not necessarily the same. Mr. Green being case in point.

THE O's OF BALTIMORE BEAT THE YANKEES OF NEW YORK AT CAMDEN, 6-5, as Manny Machado homered twice and Jonathan Shoop drove in the winning run in the bottom of the 9th with a two-out single.

With Andrew Cashner slated to start last night for the O's, I conceded the game to New York. I did so because I remember Cashner from his losing years with the Padres, and have no faith in his ability to win a game (he's 44-73 all time).

And, before 18,418, he was true to form, allowing NYY five runs through six and one-third innings, before Buck Showalter wisely pulled him from the game, thus giving Baltimore a chance to win.

Every time I see Cashner's name and remember that Anthony Rizzo was traded for the then Cubs' pitcher, my mood darkens considerably. The late Dick Enberg and I were against the trade — and we were right.

BUT, HEY, THE RED SOX APPRECIATE THE O's GIFT, as they move three and a half up on the Yankees in the AL East, winning their eighth straight by beating Texas at Fenway, 8-4.

The Sox had 12 hits, zero HRs, but banged out six doubles, and defensively benefited by fab plays by Jackie Bradley and Mookie Betts. The first on a line drive denying a single to center and the second from an above the right field wall HR-denying catch.

Today, in America's Game, the B-Boys, Benintendi, Bradley, and Betts, are baseball's best outfield — and maybe the best ever. To fully appreciate that claim, you need to see them every day. I do, and the level of their play is a marvel to behold.

Six Sox pitchers were used, with the win going to Matt Barnes, who pitched all of one inning, while the starter, Hector Velazquez, who went three, got nothing but his name in the box score.

If this is where we are, pitching by committee, then baseball needs to seriously change its rules on who gets the win, because it's absurd that it went to Barnes and Velazquez got nothing.

Big Time Stupid!

MENTIONING MATT BARNES, brings to mind an item in Notes from July 10 of '17, which I here repeat, because I had a truly unique idea:

Because Barnes has an ERA under 1.00 at Fenway and was 5.57 on the road, I suggested that then manager, John Farrell, leave Barnes at home and save fans the anxiety of having to watch him pitch away from 4 Yawkey Way (now Jersey Street).

To be fair, Barnes is having a good year, with his overall ERA at 2.27.

OTHER STUFF:

TAMPA MADE IT 13 OF 14 AT HOME, winning over Detroit, 5-2. The Rays' won/loss record at home bumped the crowd count all the way up to 13,478. Wow!

LAA BEAT SEATTLE ACROSS FROM DISNEYLAND, 9-3. Pujols and Calhoun homered for the Angels and Shohei Ohtani was 1-4 with an RBI.

CINCY MADE IT SEVEN OF TEN, Beating Cleveland at Progressive, 7-4. The Reds are still 10-games under .500, but their play recently has been remarkable, not least winning six of eight from the Cubs.

DANIEL MURPHY OF THE NATIONALS IS COMING BACK, as he went 4-4 last night vs. Pittsburgh, as DC won, 5-1.

QUOTE OF THE DAY:

The late Dick Enberg loved the poetry of Tim Peeler (discovered here in Notes), one of which, "Aunt Lucille," so touched Dick that he left instructions to have it read at his memorial service. It was:

As we get older we will shake the dust off our
Shoes and walk into the picture like
Ghosts from the corn field and you will hear the
Call of our boyish voices through
The open kitchen window where you watch
The pattern of the game beyond the clothesline
And the flap of grandpa's overalls in
The soft August wind. We will play by the
Rules of the land till our sweat turns gray in
The evening – you will think of us later
From a bed in a rest home as the light
Dims slowly and you are floating, floating
Back home to the farm.

When you realize Dick grew up on an apple farm in Michigan, the poem takes on added meaning.

POST ALL-STAR GAME NOTES — WEDNESDAY, JULY 18

BEFORE LAST NIGHT'S ALL-STAR GAME'S FIRST PITCH ON FOX SPORTS, the following graph was displayed:

	Wins	Ties	Runs	BA
American League	43	2	361	.246
National League	43	2	361	.244

Amazing!

THE 89TH ALL-STAR GAME IS HISTORY & THE AMERICAN LEAGUE HAS SEVEN STRAIGHT WINS, as the National League lost last night at Nationals Park, 8-6.

On Sunday eight HRs were hit in the Futures Game, a record for the minor league all-stars; but last night the major leaguers shattered their own record by hitting 10 — Bergman, Judge, Segura, Springer, and Trout, for the Junior Circuit; while Contreras, Gennett, Story, Votto, and Yelich, for the Senior Circuit (as both leagues were once known).

And, wholly consistent with this year's play, a season marked by strikeouts and HRs, 25 All-Stars struck out.

Since my idea of a great baseball game is Philly beating the Cubbies at Wrigley, 23-22, I am obviously pleased by the offensive show put on by this year's All-Stars.

MONDAY NIGHT'S HOME RUN DERBY & LAST NIGHT'S ALL-STAR GAME WERE GREAT FOR OUR NATION'S CAPITAL, still reeling from the shutout Putin threw at Trump in Helsinki Monday.

I seldom hand out bouquets to anything named Fox, but I enjoyed the telecast immensely. Joe Buck and John Smoltz did themselves proud, and I loved Bryce Harper, Charlie Blackmon, and Francisco Lindor, especially, being miked, exchanging quips and comments with Buck, while on the field of play.

Matt Kemp was also miked, but he kept ducking the tough question from Buck on whether he expects his pal, the O's Manny Machado, to end up with Dodgers. The frustrated Buck finally gave up, by suggesting that since the game was being played in Washington, where getting a straight answer from pols is always difficult, Kemp was in good form.

I RAN ACROSS THIS QUOTE ON THE ALL-STAR GAME BY THE WHITE SOX'S GREAT FRANK THOMAS, which surprised me.

"I got snubbed about eight times for the Mid-Summer Classic, and I know what type of career I had, and I know that I'm a true All-Star. The selection process is not very accurate."

I went to Baseball-Reference.com and looked at Thomas' 19-year career and his 162 game average, a notable feature of the Web site, which reports as follows:

Games, 162; ABs, 572; Runs, 104; Hits, 172; HRs, 35; RBIs, 119; BA, 301; OBP, 419, and SLG, .555.

So, what was Frank Thomas talking about, this great Hall of Fame player?

The fact that he, stunningly, was an All-Star only three times in 19-years, that's what he was talking about.

Why?

I have no idea.

Sorry.

QUOTE OF THE DAY:

ALL THAT I OWNED:

Are the edges of my life
The tractor shed's loose tin,
The pines snapped and left
In the double track by the wind.

Kneeling in the garden
I pat the wet soil around
The newly planted peppers,
Mud on my gray t shirt,
Under my fingernails,

My shovel foot throbbing,
I think of my father
Working his massive garden,

Dead now thirteen years;
How though he owned the middle

Of his life, all those things
I have given up,

He always taught me
When he caught me
In endless backyard games,

To work the edges;
With his worn mitt
Guiding me to the corners.

Today the joint grass
Creeps toward the heirlooms,

And I am here with the hoe.

— Tim Peeler

George and La Verle.

BASEBALL NOTES — THURSDAY, JULY 19

I WASN'T DOING NOTES TODAY, BUT THEN THE O's TRADED MANNY MACHADO and someone named Billy Witz wrote in *The New York Times* that Brian Cashman should trade Aaron Judge.

BUT FIRST, MANNY MACHADO COMING TO LA TO PLAY IN CHAVEZ RAVINE for an ownership that denies 70 percent of its fan base the chance to see their team on television, does not improve their standing with me.

While the trade may be in the Dodgers' best interest, it is not in the best interest of the game, and Commissioner Rob Manfred should have stopped it, but because he's Rob Manfred and not Bowie Kuhn, he didn't.

Remember what happened in the summer of '76, when Charlie Finley sold three of the Oakland A's three biggest stars to the Yankees and Red Sox?

Here, in part, is what Sports Illustrated's Ron Fimrite wrote about the deal stopped by Bowie:

"It was a week of surprise and outrage, the only unsurprising aspect being that the chief characters were those familiar antagonists, Bowie and Charlie. The circumspect former Wall Street lawyer and the megalomaniacal wheeler-dealer are the Flagg and Quirt of baseball, only much less amusing. Bowie is forever fining Charlie for assorted misdemeanors—like firing players in the middle of a World Series or offering incentive bonuses—and Charlie is constantly campaigning to depose Bowie and replace him with the jackass he employs as the A's mascot.

"The departure of the three stars would all but complete the demolition of a team that had won five consecutive division titles, four straight American League pennants and the World Series of 1972, '73 and '74. Reggie Jackson and Ken Holtzman had been dispatched to Baltimore earlier, and now only Sal Bando, Gene Tenace and Bert Campaneris remained of the players who had built this remarkable record. Never in baseball history had a championship team been dismantled so swiftly..."

So, the Dodgers get Machado, thus ending the race in the NL West, as LA will win the division going away, because the trade screws the Rockies, D-Backs, and Giants, who, until yesterday were still in competition, but that's over. As for the last place Padres, they were already out of it.

"Life isn't fair," President Kennedy famously said, but in case you forgot the president's truism, the Machado deal should remind you.

NEXT, HARD TO BELIEVE BUT NONETHELESS TRUE, one of the world's greatest newspapers' sports writers did write yesterday that the Yankees should trade Aaron Judge,

No, really, trade Aaron Judge.

I refuse to dignify this ludicrous idea beyond what I've written, other than to write that if it was Mr. Witz's intent to be provocative, he succeeded.

But if it was also his hope that while being provocative he avoided being thought stupid, he failed. True, I'm writing this as a Red Sox fan, but one who loves the Linden Legend, Aaron Judge, who, in addition to being a great player, is an inordinately decent human being.

Oh, the pretext of Mr. Witz's "reasoning" was the Yankees should trade for Machado. He was a tad late on that.

DID YOU KNOW THAT 250,993,000 AMERICANS DID NOT SEE THE OUTCOME OF TUESDAY'S ALL-STAR GAME because they were in bed asleep; that they missed the game's denouement, the 8-6 win by the AL; missed seeing the final HR total of 10, because Rob Manfred's and his minions didn't start the game until 8:35 pm Eastern time, and the game wasn't over until nine minutes past midnight.

If you are among the 74,706,315 of us who live in Mountain and Pacific time zones, a 4:35 or 5:35 pm start time is fine, but if you live where the other 250,993,000 live, starting the All-Star Game at 8:35 pm, is monumentally dumb.

If the commissioner won't change it, those advertisers who pick up the multi-million- dollar tab, should.

QUOTE OF THE DAY:

HENRY RIVER POEM 55:

I have existed before and after here.

Dragon, gargoyle, a hurled peach pit,
Starved rooster crowing,
Beneath the maple's antlered crown,
The doffer's ugly meniscus,
Pain tight as his bowels.

I have leaned against an oak
Beyond the mill hill ball field,
The sun making its squeeze play
Into the mountain's dime slot,

Orange and yellow, pagan gray
As the strike zone
Of my sniper eyes,
Pouring across the river,
Muddy and distant
As another time.

When I became a machine hum,
Or a brake squeaking
In the flat curve
Before the high bridge,
I filled up with everything
The clock could pump into me.

— Tim Peeler

Top row, left to right: Mark Mitrovich, Lisa Dashnaw, Lisa Mitrovich, Tim Mitrovich.
Middle row, Left to right: Carolyn Mitrovich, Jessi Mitrovich, Matthew Mitrovich (Carolyn's son), La Verle Mitrovich.
Bottom Row, Left to right: Juliette Mitrovich, Marissa Mitrovich, Rachel Mitrovich, Dan Mitrovich.

BASEBALL NOTES — FRIDAY, JULY 27

ON WEDNESDAY NIGHT THE RED SOX/O's WERE RAINED OUT. The Sox were not happy with the decision. They wanted to play on, because at 10:45 pm the skies above Camden Yard were clearing.

Boston had the lead over Baltimore, 5-0. Three Sox players had hit HRs — Andrew Benintendi, Mookie Betts, and J.D. Martinez. But Fielden Culbreath, the umpire in charge, decided to call the game.

But you're reading this, not because the game was called, but because Benintendi, Betts, and Martinez, lost their HRs.

I'm okay with a game being "official" when five innings are completed. I am totally not okay that a game called before that wipes out whatever happened before, i.e., three HRs.

I did not come to this view yesterday. For as long as I can remember, the idiocy of wiping off the books what has transpired before the completion of five innings, has struck me as, well, idiocy. That was my view at 18, and it is still my view two days away from turning 83. If you hit a HR in a major league game, you've hit a HR in a major league game — period!

It happens, that my great pal, Dick Flavin, disagrees. He tells me, if baseball says it didn't happen, it didn't happen.

Now, Flavin is a Boston icon, 22-years on television news, lifelong Red Sox fan, best-selling author, Poet Laureate of Red Sox Nation, a big hit in the new television documentary on Ted Williams, an unrivaled humorist, an acclaimed public speaker, who has graced the platforms of The City Club of San Diego, The Denver Forum, and stars at all Fenway Park Writers Series events.

So, I'm having a problem understanding how this otherwise sophisticated, intelligent, hugely accomplished human being, could be so illogical about wiping off the books whatever a major leaguer does — single, double, triple, HR, stolen base, strike out — because the game didn't go five innings.

Had he have voted for Donald Trump, I might understand his lack of reasoning, but he dislikes Trump almost as much as I do, so it's not that. I think it can only be explained by acknowledging that among the species Homo sapiens, you can't assume logic prevails.

Or, as a very smart chief of staff to a very powerful U.S. Senator, once told me, "You can't get people to agree on the color blue."

True, but taking away a HR because the game was called before five, no, that should be the exception.

And, if Tony Clark wants to prove he's an effective players union president, he should start by getting MLB to change this before five, it didn't happen, rule.

Plus, if that happens, Flavin, the Strict Constructionist, or Antonin Scalia of Baseball Rules, would have to agree that since baseball said it did happen, it did happen.

Your Honor, I rest my case.

A POTPOURRI OF THURSDAY'S PLAY:

THE RED SOX AND TWINS PLAYED THEIR FOURTH GAME OF '18, and the Twins won for the third time, 2-1, at Fenway last night, as Minnesota's Kyle Gibson threw eight strong innings..THE YANKEES, meanwhile, beat KC at the Stadium, 7-2, as Zach Britton, their new acquisition from the O's, threw a scoreless eight…OAKLAND BEAT TEXAS IN TEXAS, 7-6, and won the four game series…THE CUBS WERE ALSO WINNERS BY THAT SAME 7-6 SCORE over Arizona at Wrigley…MANNY MACHADO HIT HIS FIRST LAD HR, and his new team beat the Cobb County Braves, 8-2…THE NATIONALS WON OVER MIAMI, 10-3. The win got them back to .500, but as to where this leads, I have no clue — unless Scherzer's pitching…THE ANGELS TOPPED THE PALE HOSE, 12-8, as Justin Upton was 4-5, but my hero, Shohei Ohtani, was hitless in five ABs.

QUOTE OF THE DAY:

The bright memories help you climb across cracked rocks,
Fissured into curves that slash back south through red leaves,
Glistening like a third glass of wine on a quiet afternoon,
Memories of classic baseball,
Of the excited voices that brought it into cool autumns,
Gowdy calling Gibson and Lonborg –
While young men zipped in body bags
Were sent home just in time for the Series,
Red and yellow memories
Of when you were ten
And it all seemed to make some scary sense,
Like your bald headed dad who kept his confidence
In the pulpit in 1967.

— Tim Peeler, *Waiting for Godot's First Pitch: More Baseball Poems*, McFarland & Company, Inc., Publishers, Jefferson, North Carolina and London (2001).

BASEBALL NOTES — 8-2-18

THE O's WON THEIR FOURTH GAME OF THE LAST PLAYED, as they beat the Yankees in the Stadium across the Harlem River from Manhattan, 7-5.

Alex Cobb won for Baltimore, as he gave up one run through six, striking out eight and walking nary a batter. By his superior performance he lowered his ERA to 5.83. It was only his third win against 14 losses.

Where was the Mr. Cobb witnessed yesterday in defeating in the Bronx perennial power New York? Does even Buck Showalter know?

Rain fell on the House Babe Ruth did not build, and with their loss the lads in pin stripes fell one-half game farther back of the idle Red Sox, who await the coming of NYY tomorrow night at Fenway; four games loom, but the number one Sox will face the game's number three without Chris Sale — who is, with Max Scherzer, the majors' best pitcher.

The absence of Sale means that David Price will be on the mound against the team that owns him. It will be David's chance for redemption and to temper Dan Shaughnessy, and I believe he will pitch splendidly.

But the Yankees arrive absent Aaron Judge, which hurts NY more than Sale on the DL hurts the Sox. I'm a Red Sox fan, but no less a fan of the Linden Legend; for his talent, yes, but no less his character.

If the Hall of Fame had a special wing for transcendent character above talent, Judge and Mike Trout are already in.

OVERNIGHTS:

LAD BEAT THE BREWERS in the Ravine last night, 6-4, as Yasmani Grandal hit a two-run walk-off HR in the bottom of the 10th, and with their win slipped back into a tie for the NL West lead with idle Arizona, while the Rockies were losing, 6-3, to St. Louis, to fall a game back of the leaders…CARLOS CARRASCO GOT HIS 13TH WIN OF '18 and newcomer Brad Hand (ex-Padre) the save, as Cleveland beat Minnesota, 2-0, at Target…THE NATIONALS'

TOMMY MILONE was terrific through seven and won his first game in over a year, beating NYM, 5-3, despite Washington's run production being down by 25 (see below)...COLE HAMELS, BACK IN THE NL, won at PNC for the Cubs, 9-2. He gave up one run on five hits through five.

IN SCORING 25 RUNS IN TUESDAY'S GAME VS. NYM, the Nationals became the fifth highest scoring team in modern major league history, topped only by:

*Texas, 36-10 vs. O's, 2007

Red Sox, 35-19 vs. A's, 1939

Texas, 30-3 vs. O's, 2007

Cubs, 26 vs. Phillies, 1922

HERE'S HOW THEY SCORED (courtesy, Washington Post):

NATIONALS FIRST:

Turner singles. Turner steals second. Turner steals third. Rendon called out on strikes. Harper doubles. Turner scores. Zimmerman singles. Harper scores. Soto singles. Zimmerman to second. Murphy singles. Soto to third. Zimmerman scores. Taylor called out on strikes. Wieters is intentionally walked. Murphy to second. Roark doubles. Wieters scores. Murphy scores. Soto scores. Turner singles. Roark to third. Rendon singles. Turner to second. Roark scores. Harper flies out. Nationals 7, Mets 0

NATIONALS SECOND:

Zimmerman strikes out. Soto singles. Murphy homers. Soto scores. Taylor triples. Wieters singles. Taylor scores. Roark reaches on a fielder's choice. Wieters out at second. Turner reaches on a fielder's choice. Roark out at second. Nationals 10, Mets 0

NATIONALS THIRD:

Rendon singles. Harper walks. Rendon to second. Zimmerman strikes out. Soto grounds out. Harper to second. Rendon to third. Murphy homers. Harper scores. Rendon scores. Taylor singles. Wieters lines out. Nationals 13, Mets 0

NATIONALS FOURTH:

Roark grounds out. Turner strikes out. Rendon walks. Harper doubles. Rendon scores. Zimmerman homers. Harper scores. Soto flies out.

Nationals 16, Mets 0

NATIONALS FIFTH:

Murphy flies out. Taylor walks. Wieters lines out. Roark singles. Taylor to second. Turner walks. Roark to second. Taylor to third. Rendon doubles. Turner scores. Roark scores. Taylor scores. Harper flies out.

Nationals 19, Mets 0

NATIONALS EIGHTH:

Zimmerman flies out. Soto doubles. Adams homers. Soto scores. Taylor walks. Wieters walks. Taylor to second. Reynolds homers. Wieters scores. Taylor scores. Turner singles. Rendon flies out. Difo triples. Turner scores. Zimmerman hit by pitch. Soto flies out.

Nationals 25, Mets 4

*The run deferential +52 for the Rangers, who finished last in the AL West in '07, while thc O's, were fourth in thc AL East.

QUOTE OF THE DAY:

COOPERSTOWN 2006

On the first day
We met the owner of a breakfast grill,
The young female desk clerk
Who would fetch ice for Bill each day
Multiple times, the liquor store clerk,
The older gentleman at the Hall
Who let both of us in free
On the lifetime pass
They had sent me years ago.

On the second day
We found a tennis court
And played till I got the lead
And Bill's knee suddenly got gimpy.

We met another breakfast grill owner
And Bill was shocked to hear
About the high property taxes.

We took a second, more thorough
Free tour of the Hall
And were amazed to discover
That most of their holdings
Are kept underground
In five floors of refrigerated vaults.

We went to a farmer's museum
And took a leisurely drive
Out into the country.

Nearly everyone we met
Had moved from Long Island
To Cooperstown we noticed.

The third day we attended
The giant pumpkin festival
In the parking lot by Doubleday Field,
Attempted to play tennis again,
But were again thwarted
By my inexplicable success.

I ran about five miles
While Bill badgered the motel clerk
And may have possibly
Slipped in a marriage proposal
And an invitation to NC.

That night we finished the vodka
And Bill ate all the leftovers
The clerk had been fetching
Ice all weekend to maintain.

The next morning we took
One final look at the
Quaint village on the bank
Of the glacial Otsego Lake
And headed back to our lives.

BASEBALL NOTES — PART II, MONDAY, AUGUST 6

THE ROCKIES WON SUNDAY AT MILLER PARK IN MILWAUKEE, beating the Brewers, 4-3, in 11-innings, as Nolan Arenado, hit a towering HR for the win, number 29 to lead the NL.

"Towering," as in 150 ft. high, the equivalent of a 15 story building, but, off the bat, the Rockies play-by-play television announcer, Drew Goodman, wasn't sure it had the distance, saying, "This one may have a chance." The ball carried to the seventh row of the second deck in left field. I didn't think it was ever in doubt. Nor did Arenado.

When Ian Desmond made a great catch at the top of the wall in left-center, Jeff Hudson, the color analyst, likened it to a play a "Broncos' free safety" might make. Goodman said to his broadcast partner, "I loved your analogy."

Really?

If you are paid to broadcast baseball games, please spare us football analogies. If you cannot describe a great defensive play by an outfielder without referencing football, you should seek another line of work.

My man, Trevor Story, the Rockies' shortstop I said would be a major league star the first time I saw him play, holds to the promise, as he hit his 24th HR of the season, driving in three yesterday, as his RBI count rose to 79.

A big win for Buddy Black's team, as they had dropped five of six on the road, after sweeping the Giants at home, so Sunday's victory mattered, keeping Colorado only two games back in the NL West.

THE PADRES, WHO WERE 6-20 FOR JULY, BEGAN AUGUST WITH A SPLIT AT WRIGLEY WITH THE CUBS, winning 6-1 and 10-6, while dropping games two and three by the identical score of 5-4.

A hit here, a hit there, and a sweep, but that didn't happen.

And then, late Sunday, the Padres placed pitchers, Tyson Ross, and Jordan Lyles, on waivers. That was a surprise, but the future is now, and Ross and Lyles are gone to St. Louis and Milwaukee.

If this means, for instance, Brett Kennedy is called up from El Paso, where he's 10-2 on the season with an ERA of 2.72 in the hitter happy Pacific Coast League (PCL), then that justifies the release of Ross and Lyles.

In Yesterday's game, my man, Hunter Renfroe, hit his 9th HR, his 26th extra base hit among his 53 in 214 ABs.

Kevin Acee, who covers the Padres for the *San Diego Union-Tribune*, compared, in Sunday's newspaper, Renfroe's 2018 stats with last season, writing that they're down. Acee wrote that last season Renfroe hit 26 HRs in 445 ABs.

So, my math tells me that if you double his ABs this season you get 18 HRs, and add 35 more and he has 20, and if he plays every day until season's end, he would get approximately another 196 ABs, he would end with 32 HRs; and if he had played every day and been to bat 600 times in '18, his HR total would be 42 — or two more than my promised 40.

Oh, Acee didn't mention the three weeks Renfroe spent in El Paso last summer, where he hit over .500, before the Padres brought him back. Of all the inexplicable decisions the Padres' GM and manager have made, this remains to me the most inexplicable— and, sorry, annoying.

WEEKEND REVIEW:

SHOHEI OHTANI HAD A 4-5, TWO HR GAME VS. CLEVELAND FRIDAY NIGHT, as the Angels beat the Tribe, 7-4. It was the Halos first win at Progressive since '14...THE NATIONALS AT HOME TOOK THREE OF FOUR FROM CINCY, winning Sunday, 2-1, to move three games over .500 and only six back in the NL East. Is this the start of the anticipated turnaround? Yes...THE GIANTS WON OVER THE D-BACKS, 3-2, on an Evan Longoria HR, dropping Arizona into a first place tie with the Dodgers, who saved their series with Houston by winning in the Ravine, 3-2...THE PHILLIES MADE IT FIVE STRAIGHT, beating Miami, 5-3, completing a four game sweep at Citizens Bank Park, as 42,543 watched. The win enabled Philly to stay a game and a half up on the Braves, who beat NYM in 10...THE A's, OH MY, THE A's, won again, as they beat the Tigers, 6-0, at the Coliseum, to move 13 games above.500 and only four games back of the Astros in the majors' toughest division, the AL West...SEATTLE WON AT SAFECO, 6-2, over the Blue Jays, to move one game up and six back of Houston, as Kyle Seager hit two HRs to get to 18 on the year, while Nelson Cruz hit his 29th.

QUOTE OF THE DAY:

THE MESSENGER:

The news sat beside me in a fresh stack.
I rolled the news with one hand, in my lap,
Pitching it toward driveways, against porches.

I chucked the news into damp paper boxes
Feathering the brakes as the moonlight fell.

I carried the news down country roads,
Into quick gaps of darkness. I transported
The news for the sleepless, for the waking,
For the ones who'd smell smoke in
Their reading like a ghost in their coffee.

I carried the news to the mansions by
The river, then to the shacks at the edge
Of town, turning home past the factories,
By the high school ball field where I once
Hurled sliders instead of Charlotte Observers.

— Tim Peeler, Poet Laureate of the Carolinas

At the National Cathedral La Verle, Juliette, Jessica, Regina, Lisa.

BASEBALL NOTES — MONDAY, AUGUST 13

OMG! THE NATIONALS WERE UP OVER THE CUBS, 3-0, BOTTOM OF THE 9TH, BASES LOADED, TWO OUTS, and a rookie by the name of David Bote, pinch hits for Chicago, and bam, he hits a grand slam — and, a not in the basket grand slam to left or right, but a Bote grand slam bomb to dead center field.

I had turned away from the game when DC scored two in the top of the 9th. I had other things to do, and having already watched most of the Red Sox/O's game at Camden and the last five innings of Rockies/Dodgers from Coors, and a peek at Padres/Phillies, it was time to finish reading three newspapers, walk the dog, and fix dinner.

I only learned of Bote's heroics when I went to MLB highlights and saw the stunning results.

So, put this loss on the Nationals' manager, who, first, removes, after seven shutout innings, one of the game's two best pitchers, Max Scherzer, which was criminal enough, and, second, replaces him with Koda Glover, whose ERA is 0.00, then removes Glover after one solid inning with, wait for this, Ryan Madison, whose ERA is 5.19, who, in turn, gives up a single, hits two batters, and then the grand slam. What, Glover couldn't go one more inning?

Memo to the manager: Glover had only thrown 12 pitches — 12! He's 6'5. He weighs 215 pounds. His arm isn't falling off.

Memo to the GM: Until you replace your manager and hire Joe Girardi, your ball club isn't winning the NL East

RYAN McMAHON OF COLORADO hit a three run, walk-off HR against the Dodgers Saturday night, sending 47,633 deliriously happy Rockie fans spilling onto Blake Street in Denver's LoDo, no doubt in a let's-party-celebratory-mood over their team's 3-2 win. That would be the same Ryan McMahon, whose three run HR Friday night in the 7th won it for Bud Black's ball club, 5-4.

Yesterday, at Coors, with two outs and runners at second and third in the bottom of the 9th, and McMahon coming to bat, LAD's manager, Dave Roberts, decided he wasn't going to let the kid beat him three times, so McMahon was walked.

Which brought up Chris Innetta, who promptly walked, giving Colorado a walk-off, literally, victory and the series, three games to one.

THE RED SOX AND O's HAVE MET 16 TIMES THIS SEASON, Boston has won 14 of those meetings, winning yesterday at Camden, 4-1, sweeping the four games, as they scored 41 runs on 39 base hits, including nine HRs.

The great Chris Sale won his 12th game of '18, striking out 12 in five shutout innings, before he was removed from the game, after throwing only 69-pitches.

Why?

Sorry, you'll have to ask Alex Cora.

The Sox, at 85-35, departed H.L. Mencken's Baltimore on Amtrak's Acela Express to Philly, where they meet the NL East division leaders tomorrow night.

With a day off, maybe their manager will suggest a visit to Independence Hall and a tutorial on American history — as in U.S. history.

Oh, my man, Jackie Bradley, was 7-14 in the series, including two HRs, four RBI, and seven runs scored.

When Jackie was hitting .147, some wanted him benched, but Cora stayed with him. For two reasons: 1) he is the game's best outfielder, and 2) he has a history of coming back as a hitter. A very wise decision was made to keep him in the lineup. Some teams wouldn't do that. The Sox did. Perhaps another reason why they're in first place.

WEEKEND REVIEW:

SEATTLE PLAYED STRONG MOST OF THE SEASON, went into a slump, fell eight back of the Astros in the AL West, but then came this weekend at Minute Maid in Houston, and the Mariners won three of four from the World Champions, and are now just four games back, with 43 to play, while the ever-surprising A's have moved to within 2.5 of the lead.

CC SABATHIA PITCHED MAGNIFICENTLY FOR THE YANKEES SUNDAY, six innings of one-hit baseball to win his seventh game of '18, as the Yankees beat Texas, 7-2, at the Stadium. Didi Gregorius hit his 21st HR and Giancarlo Stanton, his 30th (look for Giancarlo to hit another 20 before season's end).

THE PADRES, 6-20 IN JULY, opened August with a split in four vs. the Cubs at Wrigley, took two of three from Milwaukee at Miller Park, came home to SD and won two of three from the Phillies, winning Sunday, 9-3. Freddy Galvis, the Padres' brilliant defensive shortstop, has, since June 1, led the team in RBI, upping his totals to 33, as yesterday he hit a grand slam.

QUOTE OF THE DAY:

DO YOU REMEMBER

How we child hooded
Before probable cause
And the neighbor's bull
Shouldered into the cherry trees?

I sold a gallon bag to the wife
Of the man who arranged
For Dad to attend college.

He was a principal,
A minor league baseball GM,
And a drunk —
We never knew him
Yet we were ghosted
Into his orbit—
His rawboned 1928
Third base pose
Hovering between
The parsonage trees.

Mom left home at 16,
Met Dad washing dishes
In the college cafeteria,
Married at 18 —
They couldn't wait for life
Like we did
And ours did —
It was not an option
For farm kids—
No time to play
They took the shortest line
Even if it ran
Through shoe stores
And drivers license offices
And taking ten classes,
So it started at third base,
Not because they hit a triple
But because someone

Who did not know them
Hit one for all of us,
Even if he paid
The star pitcher hush money
Behind the elementary school dumpster,
Or passed out in the little league
Parking lot drinking scotch
In his Cadillac.

He was there
In the wild blue sky
Where the oak trees
Almost touched,
The crackling record
Of the church chimes
In the brick tower
A hundred yards away,
Music to which,
Even without belief,
I still sway.

— Tim Peeler, Poet Laureate of the Carolinas

Tim, Juliette, and George at Fenway.

BASEBALL NOTES — TUESDAY, AUGUST 21

THE EAST & CENTRAL DIVISION LEADERS MET AT FENWAY LAST NIGHT, and the team with 17 fewer wins at game time, the team that had struggled to get above .500, even while leading its division, that team, the Cleveland Indians, beat the better team, the Boston Red Sox, 5-3.

They did this with three ABC HRs — Allen, Brantley and Cabrera. For Brantley it was his 16th. For Cabrera, his fifth (one day after hitting his first grand slam Sunday vs. the O's), while Allen, a .250 hitter, hit only his second of '18. The pitch he hit from Rick Porcello for his HR was one that hung over the middle of the plate, belt high, just demanding to be hit out, and it was.

Mr. Cabrera owns Mr. Porcello, as he is 16-29 lifetime against the Sox ace.

Porcello, who had two recent magnificent outings, against the Yankees and Phillies, also had two clunkers, one of which was last night. But the man still has 15 wins.

The Sox, who had only two hits against Tampa Sunday, had 13 last night, but lost nonetheless.

Oh well, still nine up on NYY with 36 to play.

THE A's CAME BACK FROM THEIR LOSS SUNDAY TO WIN BIG MONDAY, 9-0, against Texas, and with Houston's losing to the Mariners at Safeco in Seattle, 7-4, are tied for a second time with the Astros for the AL West lead.

Mike Fiers, in his second start since coming to Oakland from Detroit, pitched one-hit ball through seven innings, as the A's hit four HRs, two by someone named Ramon Laureano.

Khris Davis, maybe the game's least known best player, also homered, his 37th of the season to put him one behind the Red Sox's J.D. Martinez for the lead in the majors.

The game jersey worn by Davis bore the signatures of Make-A-Wish Foundation children.

OVERNIGHTS:

JEDD GYRKO AND MATT CARPENTER RUDELY WELCOMED BACK LAD's KENLEY JANSEN FROM THE DL, as they hit back-to-back HRs in the top of the 9th at Chavez Ravine to win, 5-3. It was Carpenter's 34th HR to lead the NL. St. Louis is 12 games over .500, two games better than the Dodgers on the season, but still trail the Cubs by three and a half.

THE BRAVES HELD ONTO THEIR ONE GAME LEAD IN THE NL EAST, as they beat the Pirates at PNC in Pittsburgh, 1-0.

THE PADRES FACE COLORADO AT COORS TONIGHT, the Rockies back home after sweeping the Braves. Buddy Black's ball club is a half-game back of Arizona in the NL West.

THE RAYS GOT THEIR SECOND STRAIGHT SHUTOUT, this time at home, as they won over KC, 1-0, to move three games above .500 — and they did it before 10,036. That's tickets sold, not fans under the dome at Tropicana.

STUFF:

I RAN AN ITEM ON INDIVIDUAL AND TEAM ACHIEVEMENTS OF THE A's (one team, three cities), but here's one on the Los Angeles Angels from the *LA Times*:

The Los Angeles Angels of Anaheim have won one World Series, one pennant, nine division titles, while winning 4,619 games, losing 4,607. They have had one season of 100 or more wins and zero with 100 or more losses.

In individual performance, Tim Salmon leads in HRs, 299; hits, Garrett Anderson, 2,368; RBIs, Garrett Anderson; wins, Chuck Finley, 165; strikeouts, Nolan Ryan, 2,416, and saves, Troy Percival, 316.

ON SUNDAY, WHEN THE RAYS SHUT OUT THE RED SOX ON TWO HITS AT FENWAY, 2-0, Nick Cafardo wrote that morning in the Globe:

"The Red Sox have been off the charts in rankings, which explains them starting the weekend 50 games over .500. Their strengths are plentiful. Their hitters lead the majors in average (.270), slugging (.463), and OPS (.802)..."

AND, THERE WAS THIS FROM CAFARDO'S BILL CHUCK FILE:

"Last year, MLB set a record with 117 players with 20-plus homers. Through Wednesday, there were 45 this season. At an approximate equivalent point last season, there were 54 20-homer hitters."...Also, "National League teams are hitting .248, their lowest batting average since they hit .248 in 1988 (which was the lowest since they hit .248 in 1972 and 1915)."

NEVER BEFORE IN BASEBALL HISTORY HAD TWO PLAYERS ON THE SAME TEAM HIT FOR THE CYCLE IN THE SAME GAME, but that is what happened April 7 and August 11, Tyler Kepner reported in Sunday's *New York Times.*

The most recent occasion was the August 11 game between Indianapolis and Lehigh Valley in the Triple A International League, when Jacob Stallings and Kevin Newman hit for the cycle in the Indians 12-7 win over the Iron Pigs (no, really they're called Iron Pigs).

The earlier occasion occurred in the Class A California League when Gio Brusa and Jalen Miller of the San Jose Giants became the first in pro ball to accomplish the feat.

So many years, so many leagues, so many teams, so many players, so many games, without it ever occurring, and then it happens, not once but twice.

Which is why:

WE LOVE AMERICA'S GAME!

BASEBALL NOTES — THURSDAY, AUGUST 26

BUSY DAY IN BOSTON, WITH COLORADO GOVERNOR JOHN HICKENLOOPER SPEAKING AT THE RED SOX WRITERS SERIES AT FENWAY PARK AT NOON, so Notes will be brief.

Notes is about America's Game, with an occasional dig at your president, but the coming of the Governor, who has provided great leadership to the Centennial State, raises a question. Since he is completing his second and final term as Governor, will he announce he's running for president?

I would love if he did that, as it would be a first for The Writers Series, and, actually for the Red Sox, since no one has ever done that before at Fenway Park.

The Sox have 116-years of baseball, hockey, football games, and concerts, one presidential address (Franklin D. Roosevelt, November 4, 1944), but nah, that's not happening. But, trust me, during Q & A, the question will come up. (The question did come up, as I asked it. The Governor said he and his wife are discussing it, and when a decision is made, I would be the first person he calls.)

One additional thought:

Were the Governor to run and win — my dream ticket is Hickenlooper and Joe Kennedy III — it would mean that once again a president would be invited to throw out a First Pitch on Opening Day.

ON TUESDAY IN PHILLY, A FIVE HOUR AND FIFTY-FIVE MINUTE GAME TOOK PLACE, finally won in the 16th inning, 7-4, on a walk-off HR by the Phillies' Trevor Plouffe.

Eighteen pitchers were used in the game, but the losing "pitcher" was Enrique Hernandez, a second baseman who came into the game as a relief pitcher, resulting in one base hit (Plouffe's HR), two bases on balls, 15 pitches thrown.

As Hernandez put afterwards, he lost the game and was 0-7 as a hitter.

It's probably a memory he would like to get past.

But that will be hard, as he became the first player ever to lose a game and go hitless in seven ABs.

Oh, my.

BUSTER OLNEY, WRTING FOR MLB.COM about the Padres seeking an established big league pitcher, like the Mets Noah Syndergaard, wrote:

"But then there is this: Rival evaluators report the Padres are searching for an experienced starter with a few years of team control remaining before free agency — someone like the Mets' Noah Syndergaard, Toronto's Marcus Stroman, or the Rays' Chris Archer, who will be working under a team-friendly contract for 3 ½ more seasons.

"Which makes no sense, for one of the many reasons the Padres' big-money signing of first baseman Eric Hosmer last winter made no sense to other teams — the timing is all wrong."

AS I'M ABOUT TO HEAD FOR LOGAN AIRPORT FOR MY RETURN FLIGHT HOME TO SAN DIEGO, and this has been, as noted above, a very busy day, this is it for Notes today, I'll do my best to get back to my norm, tomorrow.

QUOTE OF THE DAY:

RUNNING LAPS:

Today I put another one in,
bright March, windy; my shoes
tracked the powdery ground,
crunched the white wiry grass,
and I thought again of the games
as I ascended the drive
behind the old school gym,
how even now, with ruined knees
and shoulders that barely turn,
I am still working my way
off the coach's bench,
grinding out the hill
by the baseball field,
tight roping the edge
of Plateau Road where
Mecklenburg Yankees
have fled, horsey girls in tow,
never that Hatley boy again,
undersized second baseman
who hung out the window
of his robin egg blue Torino,
driving with his feet,
though I watch for him yet;
the coach is gone as well,
buried by the race track,
but I am still here
on the end of his bench
fighting my middling way
through splinters of sunlight.

— Tim Peeler

BASEBALL NOTES — FRIDAY, AUGUST 31

THE NEW YORK YANKEES LED THE DETROIT TIGERS, 7-5, going into the top of the 9th at the Stadium.

But the closer on the mound for NYY was Dellin Betances, not Zack Britton, because Britton had pitched a perfect eight and, on the theory he was exhausted from the 17 pitches he threw, manager Aaron Boone turned to Betances.

Well, Boys & Girls, that did not quite work out because Betances gave up back-to-back HRs to Victor Martinez and the immortal Niko Goodrum and a 7-5 Yankees' victory became an 8-7 Detroit win and New York loss — and with the greater Sox beating the lesser Sox in Chicago, NYY is now back to being eight and a half back in the AL East.

Oh, Mr. Stanton and Mr. Torres homered for the Bronx team, numbers 33 and 21 on the season.

SPEAKING OF THE GREATER & LESSER SOX, it was 4-0 for the Southsiders in the Windy City through six, when the Boston ball club scored four to tie and then five more in the top of the 9th to win, 9-5.

Mookie Betts hit his 29th HR in the 7th and J.D. Martinez his 39th in the 9th and thus did the Red Sox prevail, as Mookie now has five hits, including two HRs in his last eight ABs and his BA is back up to.342 and with it he again leads the MLB.

Rick Porcello, who threw a complete game one-hit masterpiece vs. the Yankees at Fenway, August 3, seems to have disappeared, as he could not get past the 5th inning last night, having given up eight hits and four runs, but the Sox bullpen, which has imploded with frightening frequency of late (Sox fans would say), was superb vs. the Pale Hose, as they surrendered but two hits and zero runs, with an equal number of bases on balls and five strikeouts.

OVERNIGHTS;

THE PADRES & ROCKIES WENT 13-INNINGS AT PETCO, TIED 2-2, but then Franmil Reyes, the big guy, hit a walk-off HR just beyond the leap of center fielder Charlie Blackmon (who may have leaped six inches higher and gloved the ball above the wall, except for his heavy beard). Robert Stock pitched the final three for SD, picking up the win and lowering his ERA to 2.22. Tough loss for Buddy Black's team, as they slip a game and a half back of the D-Backs, who beat LAD in the Ravine, 3-1, on David Peralta's 26th HR in the 5th inning.

THE CARDINALS WON THEIR 10th STRAIGHT SERIES, as they shutout the Pirates beneath the Arch, 5-0. Harrison Bauer and John Gant hit back-to-back HRs for the Red Birds, who stayed, however, four and half back of the Cubs, who beat the Cobb Country Braves in Georgia, 5-4.

THE ANGELS BEAT THE ASTROS AT MINUTE MAID, 5-2, as Andrew Heaney threw six scoreless innings (you do know, right? that six has become the new nine). Andrelton Simmons, LAA's brilliant shortstop, was 3-4 in the game and his BA is now .297. The young man is great but plays in virtual obscurity.

THE MARINERS BOUNCED BACK FROM TWO LOSSES TO THE PADRES, as they won at Oakland over the A's, 7-1, as Wade LeBlanc pitched seven scoreless innings for the win, his eighth of the year against three losses. Seattle needed the win to stay relevant in the AL West. This is a four game set with three to go. It may tell us whether the Mariners or A's stay close enough to Houston to pose a threat to their title.

CLEVELAND WON FOR THE 33RD TIME AGAINST THEIR AL CENTRAL RIVALS, as they beat the Twins at Progressive, 5-3, thanks to a Jason Kipnis three run HR in the 6th. The Tribe, 33-11 vs the other four teams in its division, are 43-46 against the rest of baseball.

WITH CLAUDIA WILLIAMS, TOM CLAVIN, DICK FLAVIN, AND BILL NOWLIN, as principal participants, the two day, Boston/San Diego tribute to Ted Williams is now history; closing it out yesterday in late afternoon at San Diego's quite magnificent Central Library, as Teddy Ballgame was remembered on his 100th birthday.

I'm grateful to Sam Kennedy of the Red Sox and Tom Seidler of the Padres for their support, and to Jerry Sanders of San Diego's Regional Chamber of Commerce, as well as San Diego County Supervisor Ron Roberts, City Librarian Misty Jones, and USMC Lt. Colonel William Walker, for helping make our remembrance of Theodore Samuel Williams complete.

QUOTE OF THE DAY:

PITCH COUNT:

How far do you go
Before you say I'm done,
How many pitches you got in you,
How many swings, how many words,
How many laps around the field,
Hikes up the mountain,
How many Ground Hog days listening to yourself
Talking to others,
How many trips down this same cement highway,
Past cheap motels and tire stores,
How many times returning,
The sun in your eyes, both ways,
How many lawnmower circuits,
How many trash can trips to the road,
What you got left,
What can you take,
How much light,
How much dark,
How many dreams,
Always waking
One more time than you sleep,
How far do you go
Before you say I'm done—
If you get to say.

— Tim Peeler

BASEBALL NOTES — FRIDAY, SEPTEMBER 7

ONLY FOUR GAMES IN THE MAJORS YESTERDAY, so I'm leading with the Padres, who had one of their better games of '18, as they beat the Reds in Cincy, 6-2.

Beat them on three HRs, including Francisco Mejia's first two big league hits, both HRs, accounting for four RBI. No, really, first game ever and in his first two ABs, he hits HRs.

Mejia came to SD from Cleveland in the trade that sent the team's closer, Brad Hand, to the Indians.

Then, there was my man, Hunter Renfroe, who a) hit his 20th HR, b) made a sensational running, diving, tumbling, rolling over catch, down the left field line with two outs and the bases loaded, saving three runs, and c) on a ball hit down the line in left, he scooped it up, turned and threw a laser, no hop strike to Luis Arias at 2nd base, who tagged out the Reds runner in what should have been a double, but wasn't.

And, to think, there are those who questioned Hunter's fielding ability.

I never did.

SPORTS ILLUSTRATED IN ITS BASEBALL ISSUE IN APRIL predicted the Washington Nationals would win the World Series.

Probably not.

They lost again yesterday, this time in 10 innings to the Cubs, 6-4, a team that might actually win the World Series, as Chicago's David Bote had a pinch hit, RBI double, and then scored the Cubs' final run.

The Nationals are now three games under .500 and have three more games in DC against the Cubs, so it's possible the home team will lose all three and go 0-4 for the series, unless they face Max Scherzer.

On the Tony Kornheiser Show yesterday, Tony and crew finally discussed why the Nationals' manager should go and Joe Girardi should be his replacement.

Some of you will recall, I've been saying that since mid-summer.

PAUL GOLDSCHMIDT, THE GREAT ARIZONA FIRST BASEMAN, hit a game tying HR in the bottom of the 9th with two out, but, alas, the Braves came back with a run in the 10th to win at Chase, 7-6.

IN THURSDAY'S OTHER GAME, the Indians won over Toronto at the Rogers Centre in Toronto, 9-4, as Shane, not Justin, Bieber, won his ninth game against only three reversals, and Francisco Lindor hit two HRs, his 31st and 32nd of the year, including his seventh lead off HR to tie a club record.

Lindor, the Indians' shortstop, like the Rockies' Trevor Story, is one of the game's best, but who knows that beyond their respective fans?

If he's playing in New York, the media capital of the world, Lindor is known and hailed, but he's playing in Cleveland. What else can I tell you?

TGIF AS BIG THREE SERIES BEGIN TONIGHT, with the Astros visiting Fenway to play baseball's best team, the 97-44 Red Sox, and the Dodgers coming to LoDo in Denver to play NL West leading Colorado, while NYY is in Seattle at Safeco to face the Mariners.

I am a serious person, which no friend of mine doubts, but I am also a serious sports fan, of baseball, first, and then college football, so a big weekend looms, but I welcome it, as I find, amid the daily insanity that has become Trump's Washington, a diversion necessary to one's mental health.

So, Boys & Girls, Ladies & Gentlemen, have a wonderful weekend!

QUOTE OF THE DAY:

EIGHTH GRADE:

My catcher trudged, slow motion
Overweight son of a well digger,
To the chicken wire backstop
Behind Wittenberg School,
In the luscious apple orchard
Cow pasture part of Alexander County,
To retrieve my curve ball that had
Evaded both the batter's swing
And his butterfly mitt.

After he'd waddled back,
I looked over my glove
Into the afternoon sun.
He was flashing the upside down
Peace sign again.
A couple home team parents
Sat behind the backstop
In old aluminum lawn chairs.

I could hear them laughing
As I held the ball behind my back,
Placing the left knuckle down
Across the wide seam,
Came to the stretch and waited,
Listening to cows bawl
For their afternoon feed,
Aiming for the batter's shoulder
Reciting the apostle's creed.

— Tim Peeler

BASEBALL NOTES — THURSDAY, SEPTEMBER 20

THE ROCKIES FELL TWO AND A HALF BACK OF THE DODGERS, losing last night on a pinch-hit, three-run HR off the bat of Yasiel Puig in the bottom of the 7th at Dodger Stadium.

Buddy Black's ball club has lost five of six on this nine game road trip and in the process their NL West lead, with Arizona ahead in the desert this weekend.

I hate the Rockies are losing, especially to LAD, but two things account for it: 1) losing Trevor Story, losing his 32 HRs and 102 RBI, and 2) the Dodgers at long last are playing to their skill level.

While Colorado has lost its lead, it has also fallen behind the Cardinals in the NL Wild Card race by one and a half games.

The Rockies now get the D-Backs for three at Chase, the Dodgers the Padres for three in the Ravine.

Timing is everything, it's said, and timing appears not to favor the Rockies.

But we play on to the denouement of September 30.

OVERNIGHTS:

SEATTLE WON OVER HOUSTON, 9-0, and did it by committee, using seven pitchers — Festa, Lawrence, Warren, Armstrong, Duke, Grimm, and Elias — only one of whom pitched more than one inning, that would be Lawrence, who went three and got the win, his first of '18.

If this is the way forward, this Tampa innovation, then the rules committee must change the method by which wins and losses by pitchers are determined. The five inning rule is already unfair, but failure to address it this off-season would be manifestly ridiculous.

WHILE SEATTLE WAS WINNING BY NINE, OAKLAND WAS WINNING BY 10, beating LAA in the Coliseum, as Stephen Piscotty homered and drove in five. Anderson, Dull, Montas, and Brooks, held the Angels to four hits for the shutout win. The A's are now four back of Houston in the game's toughest division, the AL West.

THE YANKEE STADIUM CELEBRATION FOR THE S0X WINNING A THIRD STRAIGHT AL EAST TITLE REMAINS ON HOLD, as Boston lost big to NYY, 10-1. Luke Voit hit two HRs off David Price, who, despite brilliant pitching of late, seems lost in the Bronx. How lost? This lost: In his 15 previous starts, Dave O'Brien pointed out in the NESN booth, Price had walked 13 batters. Last night, he walked four in the first two innings. Is it mental? Maybe.

THE GRAND SLAM PHENOMENON CONTINUED LAST NIGHT, as Jason Kipnis hit a one-out bases loaded HR in the bottom of the 9th at Progressive and with that dramatic blast the Indians won over the Pale House, 4-1. It was the Tribe's 10th grand slam of the year and their fifth walk-off win. Oh, my.

THE D-BACKS HAD A BIG NIGHT AT CHASE IN PHOENIX, as they beat the Cubs, 9-0, while the Brewers were winning 7-0 over the Reds, so Chicago's NL Central lead is back to two and a half games.

THE BRAVES HELD TO THEIR FIVE AND HALF NL EAST LEAD, as they beat St. Louis, 7-3, with Freddie Freeman hitting a two-run HR and the immortal Touki Toussant pitching into the sixth inning.

THE PHILLIES STAYED IN CONTENTION WITH THE BRAVES, as they won over the Metropolitans, 4-0, with Rhys Hoskins becoming the seventh-fastest player to reach 50 HRs. Zach Eflin had his second consecutive strong start, winning his 11th game against seven losses.

THE PADRES PUT TOGETHER A 10-HIT NIGHT AT PETCO and defeated the Giants, 8-4. The 4th, 5th, 6th, and 7th hitters — Hosmer, Reyes, Spangenberg, and Galvis — were 8-14 in the game that drew 31,933 on a Wednesday night, while winning teams were drawing 19,085 (Phillies), 25,715 (Arizona), 13,073 (Pittsburgh), 18,263 (Cleveland), 25,195 (Atlanta), and 16,425 (Oakland). As I've noted, the Padres' sales team is superb. And maybe next season the team on the field might be as good as the team in sales.

PLAYOFF NOTES — FRIDAY, OCTOBER 5

FOR THE TWENTIETH TIME THIS SEASON, THE RED SOX AND YANKEES WILL PLAY ONE ANOTHER; this time in the American League Division Series (ALDS).

Of the nineteen games played the Red Sox have won ten, but that was then and this is now and neither their edge in the season series nor their record setting 108 wins are relevant tonight at Fenway Park.

The game on Fenway's Sacred Green features A.J. Happ for New York and Chris Sale for Boston. Happ is 17-6 on the season Sale, 12-4, but was often on the DL. He is considered one of the two or three best pitchers in the game, but Happ is also a major talent.

The concern within the Red Sox clubhouse is whether Sale is whole. We shall see.

THE OTHER ALDS MATCHUP IS CLEVELAND VS. HOUSTON AT MINUTE MAID, and I've already written the Indians prevail in four games.

The pitching matchup today is Corey Kluber for Cleveland and Justin Verlander for Houston.

The enduring mystery about the Tribe's record this year is why it took them so long to get untracked? As of May 26 they were 24-25, but they would beat Houston that day to reach .500 and would slowly play at the level expected of them before the season began and would end, 91-71.

They're a formidable ball club, with some of the game's best players, but largely unknown beyond the boundaries of Cuyahoga County.

GOING INTO THE 9TH INNING YESTERDAY AT MILLER PARK IN MILWAUKEE, the Colorado Rockies had scored only two runs in the previous 21-innings. True, both were critical because they enabled the Rockies to beat the Cubs in the NL Wild Card game Tuesday at Wrigley, but they were then scoreless until they pushed across two in the 9th to tie the Brewers, 2-2.

However, they would have scored more in that 9th and won the game, save for a quarter-inch that separated what would have been a ringing double for Charlies Blackmon, but became instead just a line drive foul down the right field line — a quarter of an inch to the left and Blackmon's ball would have kicked up white chalk; but, alas, the only thing it kicked up was brown dust.

I'm not dwelling on this game, except to say with the bases loaded and two outs in the 9th, Trevor Story came to bat, one of baseball's most dangerous hitters.

He swung at three pitches and missed all three and all three misses were breaking balls eight inches off the plate and in the dirt.

Story hit some of the longest HRs in the game this year, but they were not hit off breaking balls outside and low. Mostly they were hit off fastballs.

So, my question is: If you're the manager opposite, why would you ever throw him another fast-ball? Since Story's one of my favorite players, I'm not picking on him, because the same question can be asked of other great hitters, including Mookie Betts, the major league's leading hitter in '18.

THE DODGERS WON OVER THE BRAVES IN THE RAVINE, 6-0, as South Korea's Hyun-Jin Ryu pitched brilliantly through seven and Max Muncy, LA's greatest addition in the off-season, hit another HR.

QUOTE OF THE DAY:

IN HIS MUSINGS THIS WEEK, DICK FLAVIN PUT TOGETHER HIS ALL-TIME RED SOX TEAM, with certain conditions.

"You must have seen the [Red Sox] players in action, either in person or on television. Plus one other ground rule: a player must have spent at least three years in a Boston uniform.

"That said, this is my all-time Red Sox team:

"Right-handed pitcher – Pedro Martinez. He is the best pitcher I have ever seen. Period.

"Left-handed pitcher – Mel Parnell, the winningest left-hander in Red Sox history, having led the team in victories every year from 1949 through 1953.

"Catcher – Carlton Fisk. An easy choice. He was great when he played here, and he was great for more than another decade after he left. Letting him get away was one of the most colossal blunders in Red Sox history.

"First base – Carl Yastrzemski. Huh?! He's remembered, and rightly so, as a great left-fielder, but people tend to forget that he moved to first base to make room for Jim Rice in 1975 and that he played the position masterfully.

"Second base – Bobby Doerr. I love Dustin Pedroia, his fielding, his hitting, and his attitude, but I'm a Bobby Doerr guy.

"Third base – Wade Boggs. A hitting machine who made himself, through constant work, into a Gold Glove defender.

"Shortstop – Nomar Garciaparra. What a wonderful player he was. The way he would sling the ball across the diamond was unforgettable. Until his bat slowed down because of a wrist injury, he was perhaps the best hitter in the game.

"Left field – Ted Williams. Surprise! No one who saw him play will ever forget the beauty of his swing. He was not only the best hitter I ever saw, but also the most charismatic player.

"Center field – Dom DiMaggio. The most underrated great player of my lifetime. He retired from the game more than sixty-five years ago, but still holds the record for most putouts per game by an outfielder over the course of his career.

"Right field – Mookie Betts. Mookie is the perfect player. He excels in every aspect of the game, hitting, hitting with power, running, fielding, and throwing. In addition, he has great instincts.

"Designated hitter – David Ortiz. It's been only forty-five years since the American League adopted the DH rule. But it could be much longer than that before anyone tops Ortiz's record.

"Manager – Terry Francona. He broke the curse of the Bambino. He won two World Series."

BASEBALL PLAYOFF NOTES — THURSDAY, OCTOBER 18

I WORKED ON NOTES TUESDAY NIGHT UNTIL 12:30 AM. I'm not doing that with today's Notes. That said, I begin here with the Dodgers beating Milwaukee, 5-2, in the early game. They lead the NLCS three games to two. The series goes back to Milwaukee Friday night.

NOW, IN THE TIME I HAVE LEFT ON THIS WEDNESDAY, I will focus on a very great baseball game at Minute Maid last night; a game that had just about everything you would ever hope to see in one game — including two heart stopping moments in the 9th inning.

I should tell you Boston won, 8-6, that they now lead the ALCS three games to one, with a chance to close it out today, but first they'll have to beat the great Justin Verlander, who's only lost once while pitching post-season.

Chris Sale, every bit Verlander's equal, would be expected to pitch for the Sox, but he developed stomach issues after his start Saturday and ended up at Mass General overnight, and it's unclear whether he's good to go.

The Sox beat the Astros despite Craig Kimbrel, the $13 million closer who is anything but. He's been one disaster after another when he enters a game and last night was no exception; indeed, he was pathetic.

Matt Barnes closed out the bottom of the 7th by striking out Tyler White. And then, inexplicably, he was gone and Kimbrel was brought in to pitch the bottom of 8th, with Boston up, 8-5.

The first batter he faced Tony Kemp lined a ball down the right field line and attempted to stretch it into a double, but Mookie Betts made a dazzling pickup of the ball, spun and threw a laser to second, where Sox shortstop Xander Bogearts applied the no-hop throw to Kemp's batting helmet as he slid into the bag. One out. That was a bad decision on Kemp's part but a fantastic play by Betts.

Kimbrel hit the next batter, Alex Bregman, the great 3rd baseman, putting him on first with one out, but, save for Kemp's mistake, there would have been two on and no outs. George Springer came up against Kimbrel and promptly wacked a double to right field, putting Bregman on 3rd, who then scored Houston's sixth run on Jose Altuve's ground out to short. Kimbrel followed that by doing what he's supposed to do, by actually striking out the next Astro, Marwin Gonzalez, and, mercifully, thanks to Mookie, Kimbrel and Boston were out of the inning, still leading by two.

In the top of the 9th, the Red Sox again loaded the bases as Steve Pearce walked, Brock Holt singled, and Jackie Bradley Jr., who had earlier hit a two-run HR putting the Sox up, 8-5, was hit by Colin McHugh. That brought up Mookie who lined a rocket to right center field, which Josh Reddick raced to catch and somehow, miraculously, gloved the ball with a totally stretched out dive and roll over for the third out, absent which Boston's lead would have likely been, 11-5, rather than, 8-6.

That brought us to the bottom of the 9th and for reasons only Alex Cora understands, he stayed with Kimbrel.

No, seriously, Kimbrel was still in the game and heart rates were rising wherever Sox fans had gathered to watch their team, from Halifax to Hawaii.

The Astros' first batter, popped out. Alright, Craig. The second and third batters, Josh Reddick and Carlos Correa, however, walked. Brian McCann then flied out to JBJ in deep center field. The TBS broadcast crew opined that McCann just got under the pitch a tad, otherwise, they said, the ball is gone and Houston wins, 9-8. Tony Kemp then becomes the third Houston batter Kimbrel walks.

So, it comes down to this: Bases loaded, two out, and the very dangerous Alex Bregman coming to bat.

OMG, what will Craig Kimbrel do now? He doesn't have a choice. He must pitch to Bregman.

He does and Bregman hits a line drive to left field. Two runs will score and the game will be tied, I thought, my disdain for Kimbrel mounting with each mph the ball was traveling, but Andrew Benintendi left field was closing in fast on the line drive and, not unlike Reddick for Houston in the top of the 9th, Benintendi dove with a dramatic slide and, miraculously, also gloved the ball, and with that astounding catch, the game ended — Boston had won, 8-6.

I'm told that this is Craig Kimbrel's out year in his contract. Good.

DAN SHAUGHNESSY WROTE YESTERDAY IN THE GLOBE OF THE SOX WINNING GAME THREE:

"In this season of whopping success, JBJ (Jackie Bradley Jr.) has been a controversial topic across Red Sox Nation. He is, without question, one of the best defensive center fielders in baseball today, and there are veteran Sox watchers who say he is the best they have ever seen — better than Jimmy Piersall or Freddie Lynn."

Oh, that will not please Dick Flavin, Red Sox Nation Poet Laureate, who says the Sox's best ever center fielder was Dominick DiMaggio, and has the evidence to support his claim.

But Flavin as a young man saw Dominick play; Shaughnessy, doubtful. And Flavin, all grown up became Dom's friend, as you would know if you read Dave Halberstam's best selling book, "The Teammates," which is about DiMaggio, Johnny Pesky, Bobby Doerr, and Ted Williams, but Flavin is prominent in Halberstam's masterpiece.

And then Shaughnessy quoted Sox manager Alex Cora saying after his team's 8-2 win,

"'As soon as he hit it, we knew that ball was gone,' said Cora. 'It was a good feeling. It makes it easier to manage with a six-run lead...'"

You think?

QUOTE OF THE DAY:

"Launch angle. A 2018 baseball innovation? Here's what Ted Williams wrote in 'The Science of Hitting' in 1971 (page 13): 'The ideal swing is not level and it's not down,' and (pages 62-63): 'If you get the ball into the air with power, you have the gift to produce the most important hit in baseball — the home run. More important is that you hit consistently with authority. For those purposes I advocate a slight upswing (from level to about 10 degrees), and there is another good reason for this — the biggest reason: Say the average pitcher is 6 foot 2. He's standing on a mound 10 inches high. He's pitching overhand, or three-quarter arm. He releases the ball about ear level . . . The flight of the ball is down, about 5 degrees.'" — Dan Shaughnessy, Boston Globe, Sunday, April 7.

BASEBALL WORLD SERIES NOTES — FRIDAY, OCTOBER 26

THIS IS AN ITEM FROM PETER ABRAHAM OF THE BOSTON GLOBE AND STAFF YESTERDAY:

"The Red Sox were not scheduled to travel to Los Angeles immediately after Wednesday's game, deciding instead to spend the night in their own beds and leave early Thursday afternoon.

"The Sox also will not use their workout time at Dodger Stadium on the off day other than to have a few pitchers stay on their throwing programs."

AS ITEMS GO, NOT QUITE, STOP THE PRESSES, but it is interesting to me because I've never quite understood why a team travels overnight if it has the next day off, as the Sox did yesterday.

Consider, by the time the game ended Wednesday night, it was almost midnight. Players did media interviews, showered, dressed, would have boarded then the bus to the airport, while the truly heavy lifting was being done by the clubhouse attendants — the unsung heroes on any team.

At the airport, the manager, coaches and players board the plane, the clubhouse attendants load large trunks in the belly of the jet — bats, balls, uniforms, hats, jackets, spikes, medical stuff, etc. — and finally the plane is airborne at, say, three or four am.

It's a six-hour flight to LA, so you arrive at six or seven that morning, then the reverse process takes place, everybody and everything that went on the plane comes off the plane, you board another bus and make your way to a hotel, say downtown LA, and it's rush hour traffic, so, barring any overturned semi that closes down the freeway (it happens), you arrive at your hotel, check in, and get to your room around ten or eleven, and sleep the day away.

By not flying the night of the game, the Sox avoided all of that, slept at home in their own beds (as noted above), made their way to clubhouse and airport around noon Thursday, flew to LA, arriving mid-afternoon, boarded their bus to downtown on freeways already backing up, finally arriving at their hotel, checked in, found some time to relax and have a nice dinner, got to bed around ten or eleven (one or two am, Boston time), rose mid-morning, will board the bus yet again, this time to Chavez Ravine and Dodger Stadium — ready for game three.

All of this happens because of a gentleman named Jack McCormick. He is the Red Sox traveling secretary, and to clubhouse attendants, players, coaches and managers, there may not be a more important individual in their professional life than Gentleman Jack.

Jack does a great job — and the Sox are lucky to have him.

ON THE ISSUE OF TIME & BASEBALL, I add to the thinking of Roger Angell, Tom Boswell, and John Freeman, this email from Steve Peace, the former California State Assemblyman, State Senator, and State Finance Director (and a teammate of mine on the Marston Mets, San Diego Adult Baseball League).

George with Jeff Marston and Jay Jeffcoat, throwing out first pitch at a Padres game.

These are the Honorable Steve Peace's suggestions as to how to avoid three and four hour games:

1. Automate the strike zone. Stabilizing a consistent strike zone helps hitters.
2. Eliminate video appeals. Install technology at fences to determine home run with certainty.
3. Take the black away from the pitcher. Making strikes a hittable pitch will speed games.
4. Reverse roster rules changes to force teams to play with 25 man rosters.
5. Put a clock on the pitcher on each pitch. Automate it.
6. After second strike, 4 fouls and you're out.

QUOTE OF THE DAY:

THIS IS FROM DYLAN HERNANDEZ IN THE LA TIMES YESTERDAY. His column appeared under this headline:

"Roberts tanks another move."

As you read his critical comments about Dave Roberts, pay attention to his last sentence and why Pedro Baez wasn't brought into games at more critical times:

"BOSTON — Let's preface this with a reminder that [Dodger manager] Dave Roberts' decision-making process remains a mystery.

"What's known is that Roberts receives input from Andrew Friedman's analytically inclined front office before games on the situations he might encounter and how he should respond. Less certain is the degree to which Roberts is expected to follow the blueprint.

"Roberts says he has autonomy, but transparency is not a trademark of the Dodgers' organization.

"The point is that Roberts might not be entirely responsible for the choices he has made in this World Series, which the Dodgers trail two games to none. Maybe Friedman, general manager Farhan Zaidi and the army of number crunchers employed by the Dodgers are equally at fault.

"Except the details have become insignificant. Regardless of how the decisions are being made, they're not working.

"The single-most important at-bat of the 4-2 defeat to the Boston Red Sox in Game 2 on Wednesday night was in the fifth inning, when starter Hyun-Jin Ryu departed with two outs and the bases loaded. The Dodgers had a 2-1 advantage at the time.

"With Steve Pearce batting for the Red Sox, Roberts called on Ryan Madson, the team's designated fireman.

"That was the difference in the game right there," Roberts said.

"Of the previous six runners Madson inherited, four of them scored, including the two who were on base when he replaced Clayton Kershaw in the Dodgers' Game 1 loss. The 38-year-old right-hander also had shouldered a considerable workload this month, appearing in eight of the team's previous 12 games this postseason.

"And in Pedro Baez, the Dodgers had another hard-throwing right-hander, albeit one who wasn't as tested with men on base. Baez has become the team's best reliever, giving up only one earned run in 71/3 inning."

THIS IS JACKIE ROBINSON, who played football, basketball, and baseball at UCLA, and once held the NCAA long jump championship. The man who broke the color barrier in the major leagues when he signed to play for the Brooklyn Dodgers, and who is remembered on his birthday every year on January 31 by the Boston Red Sox, the team that also started the process to get him the Congressional Gold Medal, which culminated at the Capitol of the United States in March of 2005, when President George W. Bush presented the Gold medal to Rachel Robinson, Jackie' widow.

That might have been the Dodgers, but it wasn't. It was the Red Sox.

A NOTE ON BASEBALL NOTES:

WORLD SERIES GAME THREE IS IN THE 14th INNING and the Dodgers just scored on an error in the bottom of the 13th to tie the game at 2-2.

It's been an extraordinary baseball game, definitely one for the books. Until Kinsler's error in the bottom of the 13th, the game had been virtually flawless, save for two runners being picked off first — Bradley of the Red Sox and Bellinger of the Dodgers.

Being in San Diego, I will stay with the game for a while, but I am emailing Notes now, 11:00 pm, and if you read Notes in other time zones, I suggest you check in with ESPN Saturday morning to see how it ended. And if you TiVoed it, set aside the time so you can watch an amazing example of America's Game — in all its anxiety ridden splendor.

That said, since this is Edition Six of Notes this week and more than 5,000 words, I am signing off, and giving you the Musings of Dick Flavin, my pal and Poet Laureate of Red Sox Nation.

http://www.dickflavin.com/blog/2018/10/musings-hats-off-to-baseball-caps

Musings: Hats Off To Baseball Caps

October 23, 2018

By Dick Flavin

Boston Red Sox Poet Laureate

and New York Times Best Selling Author

HATS OFF TO BASEBALL CAPS

I got to thinking about baseball caps the other night. That'll give you an idea of what an exciting life I lead – I spend my evenings thinking about baseball caps. I was watching a playoff game between the Milwaukee Brewers and the Los Angeles Dodgers (the Red Sox and the Astros were off) and the Brewers were wearing caps with an old team logo from forty years ago on them - the one that shows a baseball in a glove. I'll never forget the eureka moment that I had years ago when I suddenly realized that the logo was not just a baseball in a glove, but that the fingers on the glove formed the letter 'M' and the thumb and the leather around the ball was a lower case 'b'. It wasn't just a baseball in a glove after all; it was a Milwaukee Brewers' baseball in a glove. Ever since then I've thought it was the coolest logo in all sports. I'll never understand why the Brewers changed it. Baseball caps have always featured team logos or the letters of the cities they represent.

The classic old English 'B' on the Red Sox caps has doubled as the team's logo for as long as I can remember. For a while a few years ago the Red Sox, a night or two a week, used a cap with their alternate logo, hanging socks, on them; it wasn't long before they gave up the practice - although it is not uncommon to see fans at the ballpark and around town wearing their hanging socks caps. The hanging socks are also on the left sleeve of the road uniforms.

The New York Yankees have always used the distinctive intertwined 'N' and 'Y' on their caps and home uniforms. The logo has stood the test of time for a good reason; it was designed by Louis Tiffany. One of Jacob Rupert's partners had been New York City police commissioner, and he had the design crafted by Tiffany for a police medal. He liked it so much that he brought it with him when he joined forces with Rupert to buy the Yankees and the logo has been in use since 1909. The only difference in the letters is that they have become somewhat larger on Yankee caps over the years.

Teams representing other cities with multiple words in their names (Los Angeles, St. Louis, et al) have long since used interconnected letters on their caps.

Since 1947 the Cleveland Indians have from time to time used Chief Wahoo, their infamous cartoon character/logo on their caps. The Chief has been derided for years by many as demeaning to native Americans. Indians management finally gave in to their critics this year, and, once the Indians were swept by the Astros in the ALDS, he was retired, if not summarily executed; but he went out in style, plastered all over the team's caps and uniforms in those final games.

That's not the end of cartoon figures on caps, though. One of the caps worn by the Baltimore Orioles features a cartoon of an oriole. After the year Baltimore had, 115 losses and only 47 wins, one would think they'd be well advised to avoid putting cartoons on their caps. There are other major league caps that feature a variety of birds; some have fish; there is a rattlesnake, a halo, a compass, and a star.

The Oakland Athletics' baseball cap is the only one that has an apostrophe; it says, "A's". The team also wears a logo on its sleeve that depicts an elephant standing on a huge baseball and wielding a bat in its trunk. It doesn't make any sense until one looks up its history. In 1902, when the Philadelphia Athletics joined the American League, John McGraw of the New York Giants dismissed the new team as, "a white elephant." The manager, none other than Connie Mack, defiantly decided to use a white elephant as the team's mascot, and thus the logo. The Philadelphia A's moved to Kansas City in 1955; then fifty years ago the Kansas City A's moved to Oakland, which in turn, has been looking for a new home for years; but still the elephant mascot lives on, at least on the sleeves of the uniforms.

Some teams, the Red Sox, Yankees, and Dodgers are examples, use only their classic caps during games although even they might use alternative versions in pre-game activities. Many of the others vary the design and colors of their caps. It's not done to win games; it's done to sell hats. It's all about the marketing, of course. The selling of team caps, uniforms, jackets, and the like is a big business. Who would have thought that the lowly baseball cap, whose original purpose was to simply shade the eyes of players from the glaring summer sun, would become such a marketing behemoth?

Everyone sells them now, not just baseball teams. Football teams, whose players wear helmets, sell baseball caps with the team logos on them. Hockey teams do the same. Basketball players play bareheaded, but their teams sell baseball hats. Businesses of all types and sizes use them as marketing tools, and so do charities. The president of the United States sells them, for cryin' out loud.

Is there anyone anyplace who doesn't own at least one of them? I'd be willing to bet that, somewhere in the vast wardrobe of Queen Elizabeth, a wardrobe that includes ermine capes and gold-braided gowns, there are a couple of baseball caps. Same thing with the Pope. Doesn't he strike you as the kind of guy who'd wear a baseball cap, maybe a white one, while puttering around the yard? My fervent hope is that, when the expiration date of my time on the planet expires and I appear before Saint Peter at the Pearly Gates to explain and defend my actions while on earth, he'll be wearing a Red Sox cap.

WORLD SERIES NOTES — MONDAY, OCTOBER 29

ON THE SIX THOUSANDTH, FIVE HUNDREDTH AND THIRD DAY OF THE 21ST CENTURY, THE BOSTON RED SOX WON THEIR FOURTH WORLD SERIES CHAMPIONSHIP BY DEFEATING THE LOS ANGELES DODGERS, FIVE RUNS TO ONE!

This is The Priceless Gift the Era of John Henry, Tom Werner, Larry Lucchino, and Sam Kennedy, have given to Red Sox Nation, where, in the previous 86-years there had been none — id est quartus mundum vicit in seriem pilae Boston Red Sox in XVI annis, et non est prior vicit in LXXXVI.

In either English or Latin, it's a Very Big Deal!

And to the names of Henry, Werner, Lucchino, and Kennedy, I would add: Theo Epstein, Ben Cherington, Dave Dombrowski, Terry Francona, John Farrell, and Alex Cora, for these are the gentlemen who created the teams that won these four World Series.

I WAS PRESENT LAST NIGHT TO WITNESS THE DENOUEMENT OF THE 2018 WORLD SERIES, as I was present in 2004, 2007, and 2013. Indeed, when a Mitrovich — Tim, Matthew, Jessica, and the composer of Notes — has been present for a World Series game, the Red Sox have never lost, wining all 10 of the games we were privileged to watch.

Of the game itself, I will write sparingly, as among the scribblers of baseball, especially in Boston, led by Dan Shaughnessy, whose lead story on the Red Sox' 2018 World Series victory leads the front page of today's Globe, while inside he's joined by Nick Cafardo, Peter Abraham, Tara Sullivan, Chad Finn, Alex Speier, and Owen Pence, I would direct you to their stories on what transpired in Chavez Ravine last night; and to those in the *Boston Herald* by Steve Buckley, Jason Mastrodonato, and Michael Silverman, or to any other newspaper in our country —because the World Series is when baseball, America's Game, gets America's attention.

THE PAST IS PROLOGUE, BUT IN FRIDAY NIGHT/SATURDAY MORNING'S 18-INNING GAME, EDUARDO NUNEZ, was involved in three ass-over-tea-kettle plays, the first of which I have never seen before in any baseball game I've ever witnessed — ever.

In the top of the 13th inning, Nunez was at bat when Brock Holt, who had walked, attempted to steal second base. The pitch from the Dodgers' Scott Alexander was low and bounced in the dirt, caroming off catcher Matt Barnes' chest protector, the ball rolling between Nunez's legs. Barnes, inexplicably, tried to reach for the ball between the Sox batter's legs, and in the process flipped Nunez upside down, so that he landed hard on his back beside home plate, while Brock's steal of second was successful.

Whether his teammate at the plate would be able to continue playing, was in doubt, as Nunez was prone on his back in the batter's box. Finally, after being spoken to by his manager and team trainer, Nunez got up, walked around, and said he was good to go. This was rather significant, since the Sox were out of position players, and it was uncertain who among the pitching staff, would play third base — or if they had ever played third base in their careers.

Nunez, back in the batter's box, then hit a soft roller toward second base, Alexander came over to field the ball, slightly fumbled the pickup, and then threw to first, as Nunez slid hard into the bag, but Alexander's throw was off the mark and escaped Max Muncy, his first baseman, permitting Brock to score the go ahead run, but Nunez was still down on the ground. Out came his manager and trainer, again. After a couple of moments, Nunez was back on his feet, ready to go. What was left of the Red Sox pitching staff, were breathing easier.

In the bottom of the 13th, Muncy led off with a walk. Cody Bellinger, next up, popped up down the third base line. In the shift for the left-hand hitting Bellinger, Nunez was now playing in the shortstop's position, as Xander Bogearts moved behind second base.

When Bellinger popped up, Nunez raced for the ball near the third base box seats, he was able to glove the pop up, but his momentum was so great that he hit the wall in front of the box seats and flipped over it, landing hard in what had been someone's box seat. In the meanwhile, Muncy, smartly, tagged up at first and moved to second, which became a critical play, as he then scored on Yasiel Puig's infield single and throwing error by second baseman Ian Kinsler.

So, there you have it. Eduardo Nunez, one Red Sox player, one, involved in three tumultuous, ass-over-tea-kettle plays, all within four outs on the field of play.

As noted, I have not seen it before. Do not expect to see it again.

God, I love baseball!

BILL NOWLIN, THE TED WILLIAMS SCHOLAR AND SABR MEMBER, writing about a Facebook posting by Marty Appel concerning Friday/Saturday's 18-inning affair in Game Three of the World Series, wrote that it lasted more than the entire 1939 World Series.

"Naturally, I believed him, but my curiosity got the better of me, so I looked it up.

"This year's game – it was officially 3:29 in the morning on the East Coast when it ended – lasted 7 hours, 20 minutes. In other words, 440 minutes.

"I looked up the 1939 games and here are the times:

Game One – 1:33

Game Two – 1:27

Game Three – 2:01

Game Four – 2:04

"That's a total of 425 minutes.

"And Game Four lasted so long because it went into extra innings!"

QUOTE OF THE DAY:

THIS IS TOM BOSWELL IN TODAY'S WASHINGTON POST, writing about the 2018 Red Sox and asking, is this the greatest of all Red Sox teams?

"That will be the question that baseball history tries to answer and that towns all over New England will debate joyously all winter and for years. Just 15 years ago, those winter baseball conversations were muted and depressed as Red Sox fans in six states were, more likely, deciding where their team's latest choke job stood in their pantheon of pathetic.

"That is so buried, so sad-old-twentieth century now.

"Now Red Sox fans, their shoulders unburdened, freed by their Series winners in 2004, 2007 and

2013, can travel the country, anticipating glory. On Sunday night, they almost took over Dodger Stadium in their moments of maximum joy.

"And there were plenty.

"As is appropriate for appointments with destiny, for nights when a team can leave its lasting image burned in our memories, the Red Sox bludgeoned the Dodgers with four monstrous home runs, three of them off Clayton Kershaw, to stamp a final, decisive victory into every baseball mind."

SO, THE SUMMER GAME IS OVER, and now we will do what Rogers Hornsby suggested, we will sit by the window and wait for spring.

BASEBALL NOTES — WEDNESDAY, DECEMBER 19

YOU ARE SEEING THIS BECAUSE TIM PEELER, THE POET LAUREATE OF THE CAROLINAS, sent me his latest ode and I want to share it as a gift for the holidays.

Baseball Notes has featured Tim's poetry since the time he came to Boston and spoke to the Red Sox Fenway Park Writers Series on one of his books of poetry, *Waiting for Godot's First Pitch.*

We became friends and he has shared his talent ever since.

BASEBALL POEMS:

Poems like plastic cleats,
Like metal bats, like batting tees,
Sweeping curveball poems,
Psychological submarine poems,
Poems that clack in cement dugouts,
Poems that tightrope sewage pipes,
Poems that lay flat on railroad tracks,
Baseball clown poems,
Cheap broccoli poems,
Wholly bucolic indigestion poems,
Poems lost in the tall grass
Beyond the outfield wall or
Bouncing down Bedford Avenue,
Poems thrown from a catcher's crouch,
Poems waiting for the rolled tarp,
Day-night doubleheader poems,
Used car night at the stadium poems,
The hero always out beyond himself poems,
Poems of home run etiquette,
Left-handed batting practice poems,
Just one more autograph poems,
Smokey Burgess and Rube Walker poems,
Yankee Stadium poems with your favorite uncle,
Roseboro, Campanella, Elston Howard poems,
Gun metal gray-eyed pitcher poems,
The fact you got to see a Henry Aaron home run poem,
Poems that knock in other poems,
Poems that lean over the plate,
Poems that take crazy leads,

Poems that give a rookie a chance,
Caught in a pickle poems,
Overpaid stoic first baseman poems,
Spoiled, ungrateful fan poems,
Love your momma, love your brother poems,
Poems that steal bases, home runs, and hearts,
Poems that never end, once they start.

2019

BASEBALL NOTES — WEDNESDAY, APRIL 3

ONE OF THE GAME'S MEGA STARS RETURNED TO WASHINGTON LAST NIGHT and delivered three base hits, including a long HR, as the Phillies beat the Nationals, 8-2 — winning over the great Max Scherzer.

Bryce Harper, unlike last year when he played for Washington, the Las Vegas Kid is off to a great start for Philly, as he has hit three HRs and is batting .429 for the undefeated NL East leaders.

He will cool off and go into a prolonged slump, and the fans in Philly, who have booed Santa Claus (no, really), will boo Harper, but he'll recover and lead Philadelphia to a division championship.

Oh, 35,920, a very big crowd for the Nationals for a Tuesday night, were on hand to see the prodigal's home coming (sorry, but it was Sunday's Scripture lesson for Lent).

THE RED SOX'S CHRIS SALE WAS BACK TO BEING CHRIS SALE, but it wasn't sufficient, as he yielded one run on three hits through six, while the pitcher opposite for the A's, Mike Fiers, threw six shutout innings and Oakland won, 1-0.

Boston is now, 1-5, for the new season. A year ago they didn't lose their fifth game until they had won 17.

What does it mean? I have no idea. Other than, it's called baseball, and it's why we play the game.

MY MAN, HUNTER RENFROE OF THE PADRES HIT TWO HRs for the Padres at Petco Park last night. The second was a line shot to left that caromed off the Western Metal Supply Building boxes and took all of three seconds to exit the ballpark.

Alas, for Padre fans, the D-Back also got two HRs, both coming off the bat of Zack Greinke.

Zack Greinke? Yup, Zack Greinke.

He also pitched six innings, the new nine, to pick up the win, as Arizona won, 8-5, as 12 of the runs came off HRs — five by the D-Backs and three by the Padres.

SHORT HOPS:

TAMPA BAY WON ITS FIFTH STRAIGHT, beating Colorado, 4-0, as Blake Snell, one of the game's best pitchers, went seven strong innings, giving up but two hits. Bud Black's Rockies are 2-4 on the nascent season.

THE METROPOLITANS SCORED FIVE IN THE FIRST, added one more and beat Miami, 6-5, before 5,943 at Marlins Park. Derek Jeter was one of the Yankees all-time greats, but he may be something less than that as a major league executive.

SEATTLE WON ITS SEVENTH GAME OF '19, beating LAA at T-Mobile, 2-1. Only 13,567 watched, as Marco Gonzales won his third game. Weather is never a factor with M's at home, so why the pathetic attendance?

THE TIGERS WON OVER THE YANKEES AND AROLDIS CHAPMAN AT THE STADIUM, 3-1, scoring twice in the top of the 9th for the win.

I SPOKE TO A FRIEND YESTERDAY and asked whether she read Baseball Notes? She said she didn't because she's not interested in baseball. I asked, "Is your husband a fan?" She said he is. So beginning today he will receive Notes.

If you have family or friends who are fans of America's Game, share their email addresses, and I will see they're added to the list of the more than 500 readers of Notes.

What prompted this conversation with my friend, was a Tim Peeler poem I wanted to read to her (you'll find it below, "Summer of Love"), which I did, and its ending made her laugh.

Tim is a friend. He's been a guest of The Great Fenway Park Writers Series, where he recited poems from his book, "Waiting for Godot's First Pitch." He's also appeared in Quote of the Day more than any other writer.

The late Dick Enberg was a regular reader of Notes, and more than any other reader I often heard from him. He would text or call to say how much an item or two had appealed to him.

One day, he called to tell me how greatly touched he had been by Tim's poem, "Aunt Lucille."

So touched, he said, that he had copied it and placed in a folder with instructions, "Aunt Lucille" was to be read at his memorial service, which it was by his son, Ted.

Here's Tim's "Love Story" as,

QUOTE OF THE DAY:

My brother was a whole handful even then,
Stopping to dock his bat at the dugout entrance,
Saying "Didn't give me no time to get ready, Daddy"

In a mournful southern voice that cracked
As his father stood, white legged in Bermuda shorts
In the first base coach's box, watching the pitcher.
"Didn't give me no time to get ready, Daddy,"

He said it louder, nearly deaf, autistic, close to meltdown.
"That's enough, son," he said, straight at him,
Where he knew he could read his lips, "Enough."

But Lutheran minister Dad held hope,
Why hadn't the boy hit five home runs last year,
One unbeknownst off future NASCAR great Dale Jarrett,
"The Lord's will, the Lord's will, Lord's will" he chanted to himself.

'Then it started, another boy, who would one day
Hit 420-foot home runs for the Legion team,
"Didn't give me no time to get ready, Daddy,"

Then another one joined in the taunt
Till down near the end of the bench,
Scorebook in my lap, future English teacher,
My face reddened with shame and hatred
For everything in my life.

"Any time, you dumbasses," I said.

BASEBALL NOTES — WEDNESDAY, APRIL 24, 2019

YESTERDAY, APRIL 23, THE SAN DIEGO PADRES BECAME THE FIRST EXPANSION TEAM TO PLAY 8,000 GAMES.

The *San Diego Union Tribune* informed its readers today with a bold black headline that led sports.

The Padres, through Monday, had won 3,895 games, while losing 4,308, for a percentage of .461.

Three of its managers, Jack McKeon, Dick Williams, and Greg Riddoch, had winning percentages, led by McKeon at .541, Williams, .520, and Greg Riddoch, .508.

Its longest serving manager, Bruce Bochy, won 951 games before he was fired and went to San Francisco, where he has won three World Championships.

The U-T also chronicles the fate of three other expansion teams — Washington, Kansas City, and Milwaukee. Those three teams have better winning percentages than the Padres, as the Nationals have won .488 of their games (3,895-4,091), with KC following at .482 (3,849-4,136) and Milwaukee winning .480 percent of the time (3,837-4,156).

Oh, the Padres won last night, beating Seattle at Petco, 6-3. Two SD players hit HRs, Franmil Reyes, who hit two (the man is big, as in 6'5, 275), and Austin Hedges, who hit his fourth.

Hedges' HR was a long drive to the center field fence that Alex Mallex caught up with, as the ball landed squarely in the pocket of his glove, but then bounced out and landed on the other side of the fence.

It wasn't quite like the ball that hit Jose Canseco squarely on top of his head in Cleveland's ancient Municipal Stadium, with the ball bouncing high over the fence for a HR. (You can watch the Canseco replay on YouTube, as 417,000 have.)

THE RED SOX SWEPT THE RAYS IN TAMPA, CAME HOME TO BOSTON AND DROPPED A DOUBLEHEADER TO DETROIT.

OMG!

Really?

Yes.

Twenty-four games into 2018 the Sox were 19-5, but this is 2019 and the Sox are 9-15, but this is now and that was then and never shall the twain meet.

The only good news coming out of the doubleheader loss was the performance of Chris Sale, who through five innings gave up five hits and two runs, while walking two and striking out 10, a notable improvement.

THE CUBS AT WRIGLEY BEAT THE DODGERS, 7-2, as Jose Quintana won his third straight game with a strong performance, as Javier Báez hit his 7th HR and is now batting .315. Mike Rizzo also homered, his fourth, but his BA is only .200, but Rizzo is a notoriously slow starter.

THE CARDINALS WON AGAIN AT BUSCH OVER THE BREWERS, 4-3, as Paul DeJong hit a leadoff HR in the bottom of the 8th, and Yadier Molina had three hits and two RBIs. Ponce de Leon pitched five strong innings for St. Louis, but the win went to Andrew Miller, who threw one shutout inning.

PABLO SANDOVAL, REMEMBER HIM? IS BACK IN SF and last night at the Rogers Centre in Toronto, he had three hits, including his first HR of '19, as the Giants beat the Jays, 7-6. Three other Giants also homered to give them their season high of four.

THE O's BEAT THE PALE HOSE AT CAMDEN, 9-1, as 8,953 watched Ivan Nova, Chicago's starting pitcher surrender four HRs, including one to Chris Davis, in what was for Nova a terrible game, as he gave up all nine of Baltimore's runs in only four innings, while the White Sox's bullpen was perfect through five innings, as in no-hitting the O's batters. Weird.

THE YANKEES WON AGAIN OVER THE ANGELS IN ANAHEIM, 7-5, as Luke Voit hit two HRs, his sixth and seventh of the new season. New York's starter, Domingo German, won his fourth game against one loss, going 6.2 innings and yielding one run on four hits, while lowering his ERA to 1.76.

OKAY, IT'S STEPHEN PISCOTTY OF THE A's AND PATRICK CORBIN OF THE NATIONALS, and we move on.

Oh, Piscotty was 4-5 in Oakland's 11-6 win over Texas, while Corbin, Patrick, won his second game of '19, beating Colorado at Coors, 6-3, but he wasn't that impressive, as he gave all of the Rockies' runs through six, but the Nationals' bullpen saved him — which doesn't happen that often.

BASEBALL NOTES — THURSDAY, MAY 9, 2019

TODAY WOULD HAVE BEEN TONY GWYNN'S 59TH BIRTHDAY, He was a very, very, great player, but even a better human being.

Those of us who are privileged to have known him, miss him, and extend to his family this day our thoughts.

I'M IN WASHINGTON FOR TONIGHT'S WORLD SERIES TROPHY RECEPTION HOSTED BY CONGRESSMAN RICHIE NEAL, chairman of the House Ways & Means Committee, for members and staff of the New England delegation.

George with Jeff Kornhaas and the 2013 trophy.

Chairman Tom Werner and President Sam Kennedy of the Red Sox will represent the team, and I will be in the room.

THE RED SOX WON IN 12 INNINGS AT CAMDEN LAST NIGHT, 2-1.

They won for three reasons:

1. Chris Sale
2. Andrew Benintendi
3. Jackie Bradley Jr.

First, Sale was magnificent through eight innings, giving up but one run on three hits, walking none and striking out 14. In the 7th, he struck out the side on nine pitches!

Second, Benintendi's game winning HR in the top of the 12th.

Third, Bradley Jr. made another catch for the ages, when he raced to left-center field to the wall, jumped high, extended his left arm four feet above the eight-foot-high wall, and pulled down what would have been a walk-off HR off the bat of Trey Mancini.

The play was so spectacular that all Mancini could do was watch in astonishment, and then tip his batting helmet to JB.

But absent Bradley Jr.'s play, Sale's performance would have been for naught and Bentendi's HR would not have happened.

Was it, The Catch, Bradley Jr.'s best?

The one he made at Fenway, when running flat-out to the corner of the triangle in right center, he again went high, miraculously gloved the ball, and tumbled over the wall into the Red Sox's bullpen.

Twenty-two O's struck out in the game last night, as Boston evened its season record to 19-19.

Oh, the loveliest part of the evening, was the presence of Jackie's father.

FOR THE SECOND NIGHT IN SUCCESSION, the Cubs won on a walk-off HR. Tuesday night it was Kris Bryant, and last night, Jason Heyward.

But let MLB's Jordan Bastian describe what happened:

"Jason Heyward knew the baseball had a shot at finding the bleachers, but then it began to tail more toward the left-field line. One quirk of Wrigley Field's dimensions is that the wall in left is deeper down the lines in comparison to the gaps. The more a ball in flight turns, the more the chances of it leaving the Friendly Confines diminish.

"'When I saw the ball going left a little bit, I'm like, 'You've got to be kidding,'" "Heyward said. "'You know it's deeper as it gets closer to the corner. Thank God for the basket.'"

"Yes, the ball dropped into the ballpark's famous basket that juts out from the top of the wall, giving the Cubs a 3-2 walk-off victory over the Marlins in 11 innings on Wednesday night. As soon as the baseball met the metal above the bricks and ivy, the crowd's gasp turned into an eruption of cheers, high fives and hugs in the stands. On the field, Chicago's players stormed to the plate for an on-field party for a second straight night."

THE REAL DEAL PADRES WON OVER THE METROPOLITANS AT PETCO, 3-2.

San Diego won because *my man, Hunter Renfroe, hit another game winning HR, his fourth of the early season. True, it lacked the drama of Sunday's grand slam walkoff against the Dodgers, but the team will take it.

Matt Strahm pitched well though six, and for the first time in five games, actually walked a batter.

The Padres are now 21-17, which may not seem that impressive, but it's their best start since, 2010, Kevin Acee tells us in his *San Diego Union-Tribune* game story.

*It's is well known to management of the Padres that "my man" is Renfroe. I have lobbied for him to be in the everyday lineup since he came up to the majors. I have said, if he plays every day he will hit 40 HRs.

But we will never know that, unless he plays every day — and so far that hasn't happened.

Yes, the Padres have five outfielders who could play every day, but the rules only allow for three. I understand the challenge, but my choice is Hunter's name on the lineup card manager Andy Green turns in before every game.

THE NATIONALS WENT DOWN AGAIN, losing to Milwaukee, 7-3, as the great Christian Yelich hit his MLB leading 16th HR.

Reading Boswell in the *Washington Post* today, I rather think that if the team doesn't hold together for the Dodger series in LA, Dave Martinez may not be on the flight home.

If that happens, then they should do what I suggested they do last year, hire Buck Showalter.

BLOWOUT GAMES YESTERDAY WERE Seattle over the Yankees, 10-1, Minnesota's beat down of Toronto, 9-1, Detroit winning over LAA, 10-3, and Houston beating KC, 9-0. Run deferential in those four games, 38-5. Oh, my!

QUOTE OF THE DAY:

Gravity 136

With the face and lips
of an old drunk he bows into
a left handed crouch that
keeps the sunflower seed
puff in his ruddy right cheek
pointed toward the pitcher.
Two on two out he's forgotten
the count, but he's licked
the caffeine nausea hangover
and he stares at the lamb chopped
fat boy closer, who looks like
an Eastwood cowboy villain,
with a star's bloodshot disdain
and when he swings it's as if
memory and injury become one
with imagination and he stands
at the gate of the ages waving
to the ringing in his head.

— Tim Peeler, Poet Laureate of the Carolinas

BASEBALL NOTES — FRIDAY, MAY 24, 2019

THE MINNESOTA TWINS HIT EIGHT HRs AS THEY BEAT LAA, 16-7. Thus joining the 2005 Texas Rangers in becoming the second team in MLB history to have multiple games in a season with eight or more HRs.

In hitting eight or more they also swept the Angels and did it on the road across I- 5 from Disneyland.

C.J. Cron was 5-6 with a HR, his 13th HR of the season, while Eddie Rosario hit his 14th to go with 39 RBI, placing him eighth among all major leaguers.

It was the Twins 8-2 after three and 16-2 going into the bottom of the 9th, but Tommy La Stella hit a grand slam to save some dignity for the Angels.

At 33-16 the Twins have the game's best record and lead the AL Central by eight games, the biggest margin of the six divisions — and all of it achieved under first-year manager Rocky Badelli, who as a player was one of my favorites.

I WATCHED THE END OF THE TIGERS/MARLINS GAME and witnessed a two-out grand slam off the bat of Garrett Cooper that gave Miami a 5-2 win, as the Tigers suffered their ninth loss in succession, and did it under the cruelest of circumstance, as all of the Marlins runs were unearned.

The losing pitcher was Shane Green, who came into the game as one of the best closers in the majors, only to have the indignity of the grand slam written into his record, which, despite the ending, is a superb 1.29.

SHORT HOPS:

THE YANKEES WON AT CAMDEN to sweep the four game series, 6-5, and are now 10-2 on the season with Baltimore; which, Tom Clavin reminds me, approximates the Red Sox 15-3 dominance of the O's last season…THE RED SOX WON AT THE ROGERS CENTRE OVER THE JAYS, 8-2, as somebody named Ryan Weber pitched six innings to win his first career start…THE WHITE SOX BEAT HOUSTON AT MINUTE MAID to earned a split in the four game series, 4-0, as Lucas Giolito pitched his first major league shutout…JON LESTER OF THE CUBS, despite an ERA of 2.68, is only 3-3 for '19, as he lost yesterday to the Phillies, 9-7…THE ROCKIES SCORED SIX RUNS, but the Pirates scored 14. Josh Bell hit his 16th HR of the season and has driven in 47 runs to lead the majors — and his .339 BA places him third in the majors…TAMPA BAY BEAT CLEVELAND AT PROGRESSIVE, 7-2, to stay two back of the Yankees in the AL East.

IT TOOK TOM BOSWELL OF THE WASHINGTON POST a year to follow my lead on Dave Martinez, manager of the Nationals, but Boz finally got it, suggesting Martinez be fired. Thus he reasoned in his column yesterday, writing:

"But with the Nats nine games behind the Phillies, if the double whammy of lame fundamentals and a poor (and poorly managed) bullpen keeps dogging the Nats, then I will understand if the team loses patience and decides that someone — maybe anyone — would be a better match for this team than Dave Martinez. He's a fine role model for many. Just not, it seems, a very good big league manager.

"For weeks, I have reluctantly worked my way back from 'Have Patience' to 'Wait Till Midseason' to 'It Will Get Better' as the roster gets healthy and relievers pitch like the backs of their s'mi-decent baseball cards. But every brutal loss changes the picture. When you're just one more bad skid from a dozen-game deficit and a 90 percent chance of 'wait till next year,' then it's probably time to get Joe Girardi, Buck Showalter, Mike Scioscia or 'other' on the horn.

"Watching bad things happen to nice people is sad. But so is watching these Nats under Martinez."

AND TO BOZ'S POINT, THE NATIONALS LOST AGAIN, as they were swept by the Metropolitans at Citi Field, losing yesterday, 6-4.

Stephen Strasburg was fine through seven, but Steven Matz was better, giving up one run to Strasburg's three.

I am fundamentally an agnostic about the fate of Washington's team, except when the great Max Scherzer pitches, but even he has had some tough outings, but otherwise when he has been superb, his ball club has not compensated for his excellence.

Buck Showalter awaits GM Mike Rizzo's call.

QUOTE OF THE DAY:

Another of Tim Peeler's poems, which he provides to Notes as the Poet Laureate of the Carolinas:

Gravity 107

On the left of Main Street

that runs straight and flat

from Landis right into Kannapolis,

Corriher Field, town kept for Legion games
a quarter mile from the massive mill
now mostly filled with overall-ed ghosts,
a simple dirt infield, dragged smooth
where seventy-five years ago
Glenn "Razz" "Preacher" Miller
stretched line drive doubles
into unholy triples, and rumor
had it that old man Corriher,
dissatisfied with their hitting,
called his ringers out at practice
one day, and they said, "You think
you can do better," so he laid
his hat on the wooden bench,
draped his suit jacket over the fence,
stepped up to the plate and
lined the first pitch into center,
then looked at every last flannel-
suited badass character in the bunch
and said "That's how you do it, boys."

BASEBALL NOTES — FRIDAY, JUNE 7, 2019

THIS IS FOR TONY, MICHAEL, GARY, CHRIS AND NIGEL, the final score of the Nationals/Padres game, saw San Diego win, 5-4.

Kornheiser is a notorious early to bed and early to rise, so there's no chance he's staying up until 1:36 am eastern to hear the final score. (How do I know the sleeping habits of Kornheiser? I listen to the podcast.)

Twenty-one Nationals hitters in a row went down to close out the game.

Hunter Renfroe hit his 18th HR and is on course to top 40, which is the number I have consistently said here in Notes he would hit.

And, the return of Fernando Tatis Jr. to the starting lineup after an absence of 28-games, was a big plus.

THE ROCKIES BEAT THE CUBS, 3-1, AS THEY WON BEHIND PETER LAMBERT, a kid making his first start in the majors.

He was quite splendid, Lambert was, pitching all of seven innings, giving up four hits and one run, walking one and striking out nine.

He is a kid out of San Dimas, CA, and if his introduction to the Big Show holds, then he will stay the course.

THE RED S0X EMPLOYED THE PITCHING BY COMMITTEE APPROACH and it worked, resulting in a 7-5 win over KC and a series sweep.

I'm still unsure how they decide the winning pitcher in such a deal — Colten Brewer was the lucky winner among the seven — but the "official scorer" makes the decision.

The Sox were outhit, 14-9, as six of KC's hits were for extra bases — three doubles and three HRs.

CHRISTIAN YELICH HIT HIS MAJOR LEAGUE LEADING 23RD HR and Mike Moustakas added two, to give him 18, as Milwaukee beat Miami, 5-1.

Freddy Peralta pitched six strong innings, giving up one run on four hits to record his third victory of'19.

THE YANKEES ENDED THE ABERRATION OF LOSING TWO TO THE JAYS, as A.J. Happ pitched seven strong innings for the win, 6-2.

The two teams were even in hits, eight, but New York hit two HRs off the bats of Hicks and Urshela accounting for four runs.

SHORT HOPS:

MIKE KEPLER HIT THREE HRs for Minnesota, as Jose Barrios won his eighth game, 5-4... ST. LOUIS BEAT THE REDS, 3-1, as Paul DeJong homered for the first time since May 18... ATLANTA LOST TO THE PIRATES, 6-1, as Moran and Polanco hit back-to-back HRs... THE RAYS OF TAMPA beat the Tigers of Detroit City, 6-1, as Travis d'Arnaud homered for the first time in over 14 months and did it twice...THE ASTROS WON AGAINST SEATTLE IN 14 INNINGS, 8-7, as the Mariners botched a bases loaded, one out situation in the bottom of the 11th...THE A's BEAT LAA, 7-4, as Stephen Piscotty was 2-4 with a HR and Ramon Laureano drove in four.

THE POET'S CORNER WITH TIM PEELER:

Back in 2007 when Barry Bonds was chasing Hank Aaron's record, Tim Peeler, the gentle North Carolinian, wrote the following:

HAMMERED – 1952

He said it was a sound
he'd never forget.
The team had swung north
from Winston, stopping
in Richmond and then
on to Washington where
they filled the stadium
for an afternoon double header,
were taken to a DC diner for dinner
where they ate quietly
in the wide-eyed customer glare,
wiped their tired faces and rested
while the kitchen workers cursed
and crashed dishes into metal
containers rather than reuse
what colored hands had touched,
and he knew that if they
had fed stray dogs with those plates
they would have washed them.

Just a skinny black kid
a long way from Mobile,
he folded and refolded his napkin
as cheap china smashed the silence
and he kept his eyes down on
the checkered tablecloth.

BASEBALL NOTES — MONDAY, JUNE 24, 2019

IT WAS AN EMOTIONAL WEEKEND IN ST. LOUIS WITH THE RETURN OF ALBERT PUJOLS. Every time he was introduced he received a long standing ovation. It was a tribute to the career he had with the Cardinals — a gentleman of class in a city of class.

The Angels won the last game, 6-4, but the first two went to the Cards.

THE ROCKIES LOST THREE IN WALK-OFFS HRs TO THE DODGERS, 4-2, 5-4, and 6-3. Will Smith, upon his return to the majors, did the honors this time with a three-run walk-off.

Oh, my! as the late Dick Enberg would have said had the occasion been his.

With 12 straight losses in a row to LAD, over two seasons, Colorado must now play for a Wild Card in the NL, as it is too obvious the class of the Senior Circuit is the damnable Dodgers.

And to think they stick it to 70 percent of the fan base by denying them the right to watch them on television.

THE PADRES PLAYED MISERABLY AND WERE SWEPT BY THE PIRATES AT PNC IN PITTSBURGH, 2-1, 6-3, and 11-10.

Two of the losses were directly attributed to Manny Machado, the $300,000,000 plus third baseman, who in games one and three erred on routine ground balls that slipped under his glove.

He can be a brilliant, but he can also create the impression that he is too casual in his play, as he did Friday night and Sunday afternoon. Had he fielded those two ground balls, the Padres would have walked away with two wins — not three losses.

The irony is that the three game sweep at the hands of the Pirates, came after a three game Padres sweep of the vaunted Brewers.

And, no small thing — the relief pitchers stunk up PNC, which is hard to do, as it was a beautiful day in a beautiful ball park at PNC in Pittsburgh.

HOUSTON'S LOSSES HIT SEVEN IN A ROW until they slammed on the brakes at the Stadium Sunday, winning 9-4 over the Yankees. The losses included a 12-0 defeat to Toronto, three straight to Cincy and three to New York.

It was the 26th consecutive game the Bronx Bombers have hit HRs; a new MLB record.

Prior to Sunday's game the Astros were 48-23. They are now 49-30.

The leading teams In the AL are Minnesota with 50 wins, New York and Houston at 49.

SHORT HOPS:

THE RED SOX WERE ON A ROLL, winning eight of nine before blowing two games to the Jays, especially the game on Saturday, thanks to Matt Barnes…THE MARLINS BEAT THE PHILLIES, 6-4, as they added to Philadelphia's losing streak of six straight…THE INDIANS WON OVER DETROIT, 8-3…THE BRAVES TOPPED THE NATIONALS, 4-3…THE BREW CREW defeated the Reds, 7-5, but the NL Central is tightening up, as five and one-half games separate the division leaders…THE CUBS WON OVER THE METROPOLITANS, 5-3, at Wrigley, to even the series, 2-2…THE RANGERS BEAT THE WHITE SOX, 7-4… THE RAYS REBOUNDED AGAINST THE Q'S, 8-2…THE D-BACKS TRIMMED THE GIANTS, 3-2…THE MARINERS WALLOPED THE O's, 13-3, including a 4-4 day for J.P. Crawford, including a HR.

QUOTE OF THE DAY — 1:

'How low has it gotten for the 2019 Toronto Blue Jays? They are now being upstaged by a baseball team that has neither a stadium nor a team.

"The Montreal Expos are coming back. Maybe. To share a club with Tampa Bay.
It'll be halfsies. Florida gets the first three months of the season; Quebec gets the last three. It's like Montreal and Tampa Bay used to live together, decided to call it quits, but want to keep things civil for the kids, of whom there are several thousand.

"Baseball has some good ideas, a lot of bad ideas, a few shockingly stupid ideas and then it has whatever this idea is.

"This is an idea so ridiculous you know in your bones someone in a boardroom said, "'That's just crazy enough to work,' "and, a dozen terrible decisions later, we ended up here. With an indefensible idea.

"'Here's Jays general manager Ross Atkins on Montreal's as-yet theoretical resurrection model: "Really cool idea.'

"Atkins would say that. As long as people are talking about an imaginary baseball team in Montreal, they aren't talking about his team. That's a PR win (the only sort the Toronto Blue Jays can hope for any more)." —Tom Szcerbowki, Toronto Globe & Mail

QUOTE OF THE DAY — 2:

Outlaw Ballplayer

I was fifteen, pitching JV,
A game behind what they now call
The Old Rock School in Valdese,
A small foothills town
Built by conservative Italian Protestants,
Escaping persecution
In their mountain home.
We had won by ten runs,
And I had pitched well,
Striking out twelve,
Even adding two hits myself.

Throughout the game
Their fans had put the needles in me,
Chanting, jeering, lobbing casual
Redneck insults, and this on the field
Where the great outlaw ballplayer
Edwin "Alabama" Pitts had coached
The high school team the year before
He was stabbed to death
In a tavern at the edge of town
When he tried to cut in
On some 2 AM dancers.

I didn't know this as I walked
Toward our waiting bus,
Or that 5000 people came
From all over the country
To view his body,
Or that there was a huge manhunt
For Newland LeFevers,
The assailant whose knife
Severed Pitts' artery.
How could I have known this
As I mounted steps and turned
Toward their exiting fans
And yelled, Everybody from
Valdese can go to hell,
My mild-mannered coach

Grabbing my shoulder
And shoving me
Back through the aisle
As the door closed
And the first chunks of gravel
Pelted our bus.

We fled quickly
The way Pitts did,
Left down Main Street
Pointed toward
That country Methodist church
Where they chipped his name
Wrong, Edwins instead of Edwin,
In the gravestone that would
Mark him forever.

BASEBALL NOTES — WEDNESDAY, JUNE 26, 2019

AT THE BREAK THE LEAGUE LEADERS ARE — The NL East, Atlanta; NL Central, Chicago; NL West, Los Angeles.

The AL East, New York; AL Central, Minnesota; AL West, Houston.

IT WASN'T QUITE THE HOMECOMING FOR MANNY MACHADO THAT ALBERT PUJOLS RECEIVED AT BUSCH STADIUM, but even though there were 26,355 empty seats at Camden Yards, the fans exulted in their adoration.

Manny had returned home, where it all began. Seven years ago and the O's chose wisely. He was splendid and he quickly established as a world class third baseman. Then he was gone to the Dodgers to help them win the NL championship and, surprise of surprises, signed with the Padres.

On his return to Camden, he singled and homered and led the way to an 8-3 victory.

Logan Allen won his second straight, as Fernando Tatis Jr. and Manuel Margot hit HRs.

IN THE STADIUM THE YANKEES RIPPED-OFF FOUR HRs TO SET THE ALL-TIME MLB RECORD FOR CONSECUTIVE GAMES AT 27, but there is no indication they will even slow down.

The Big Boppers were LaMahieu, Judge, Torres, and Encarnacion for the New Yorkers.

Nestor Cortes Jr. was the winning pitcher, as he relieved
Chad Green, who threw all of one inning.

THE RED SOX WON THEIR 20th GAME AT FENWAY PARK and by that act moved one game ahead of .500 at home.

One must believe that topping parity is a must and the Sox engaged the Pale Hose, 6-3, on a rainy Tuesday and miserable night.

However, the brilliant shortstop, Bogearts, made up for two miscues in the field by launching a power stroke into the night, that carried all the way out of the ancient oval.

SHORT HOPS:

THE NATIONALS DEFEATED THE MARLINS behind the brilliant pitching of the great Max Scherzer, 6-1, as he threw eight innings of five-hit ball and struck out his customary 10… TEXAS BEAT DETROIT 5-3…THE INDIANS WERE BEATEN BY THE ROYALS AT PROGRESSIVE, 8-6…THE BRAVES DEFEATED THE CUBS at lovely Wrigley Field, 3-2…THE TWINS BEAT THE JAYS, 9-4, as Eddie Rosario was four for five…HOUSTON BEAT PITTSBURGH, 5-1…SEATTLE DEFEATED THE BREWERS, 8-3, as Vogelback hit his 19th HR…COLORADO LOST TO SF AT T-MOBILE, 4-2…THE A's DEFEATED THE CARDINALS at Busch, 7-3…THE PHILLIES BEAT THE METROPOLITANS for the second night in a row, 7-5…THE ANGELS BEAT CINCY, 5-1…AND DODGERS HELD ON TO WIN AT ARIZONA, 3-2.

QUOTE OF THE DAY:

When I Talked to Junior:

He didn't trust me,
Looked at me like
My father-in-law's farmer friends
Who respected me on the one hand,
Thinking that I knew something,
But also suspected that what
A college boy knew
Might not be worth that much.

But when I told him
That I was doing a book
About local baseball
He brought out pictures
And scorebooks, programs,
And newspaper articles.

When I read through it all later
I found out he was one of the top
Pitchers and shortstops
In the early 50s
For the best mill league team
In the area, a squad that
One old timer after another
Informed me was better
Than the local minor league teams.

Junior had gray slicked back hair
And dark suspicious eyes.
He told me he was a preacher now
But turning to a picture on the wall,
Asked me, "do you know who that is?"

And I looked at what had to be
A picture of Charlie Daniels,
I mean a dead ringer,
But something kept me from saying, "I know
That is Charlie Daniels" before Junior announced,
"Why that's me, before I found the Lord."

He shook my hand when we were through
And I was about to cart a box of his stuff out the door.
"Now where'd you say you live?" he asked,
Squeezing hard with his old man's pitching grip,
And I waited for a moment,
There in his sanctuary,
For all the ways
He had to release me.

— Tim Peeler, Poet Laureate of the Carolinas

BASEBALL NOTES — FRIDAY, JUNE 28, 2019

WELL, WELL, WELL, TEXAS TAKES DOWN MIGHTY DETROIT CITY, 5-3, 4-1, AND 3-1.

Talmage Boston reminds us that Texas seems intent on winning and has put together a plus winning streak over .500.

"Rangers' last 3 runs come on 3 consecutive home runs in the 6th inning. Mike Minor gets his second complete game win of the year—ERA now below 2.50. Rangers 8 games over .500 for the first time this year, and have now won 4 in a row."

So, there you are. Houston beware.

CUBS DEFEATED THE BRAVES AT WRIGLEY, 9-7, and obviously took it to the Atlanta team, who had led 6-1 until the change in the game.

Craig Kimbrel threw for the first time since his hire, and he was successful in that he saved the game — although Freddie Freeman scorched a ground ball toward first, but Rizzo smothered the ball and raced Freeman to the bag and the Cubs won.

I think the deal shows signs of falling apart, with Kimbrel a loser.

THE PHILLIES TOPPED THE METROPOLITANS IN A WIN, and did it in the most unusual fashion, 6-3.

Here's the description of MLB beat writer, Anthony DiComo:

"A nightmarish 11-game road swing came crashing to an end for the Mets on Thursday, when Edwin Diaz blew another save in a 6-3 walk-off loss to the Phillies. That was the final act of a four-game sweep at Citizens Bank Park, capping a 3-8 trip that saw them dismiss their pitching coach and bullpen coach, and become embroiled in a clubhouse altercation in Chicago.

"Unlike in their previous four losses, the Mets did not hold an early lead. Instead, they waited until the ninth to record four of their five hits, going ahead for the first time on Todd Frazier's two-run homer off closer Hector Neris. Amed Rosario added an insurance run with an RBI groundout, giving Diaz a two-run cushion in the ninth…"

ALYSON FOOTER WROTE ABOUT THE PIRATES WIN OVER HOUSTON, 10-0:

"He made a mental note months ago, memorizing when the Pirates would be playing in Houston. He inwardly hoped his turn in the rotation would come up during the three days that his current team would be playing his former team, in the very ballpark where he experienced one of his greatest career triumphs.

"It did, and Musgrove capitalized on it, shutting out the Astros over six innings, as the Pirates rolled to a 10-0 win to capture the series and hand the Astros their first series loss of the season at home.

"It's fair to say Musgrove, the pitcher of record of the Astros' epic Game 5 World Series win over the Dodgers in 2017, was extra fired up for this outing. While he couldn't have known his offense would steamroll Astros pitching for a second game in a row, his approach, with or without the run support, was clearly a sound one."

Houston has fallen hard and goes into tonight's game with a mere four and one-half game lead — it was once a double-digit lead.

THE DODGERS MADE IT CLEAR OVER THE ROCKIES, as they won at Coors Field, 12-8.

Home runs were hit by Bellinger, Hernandez, Turner, Taylor, Verdugo, and two were hit by Muncy.

It was as though the three games lost via walk-offs to rookies when they last played Colorado at Chavez Ravine, was mere foretelling of events.

They may have to consider whether they will win no games against LAD this year — a better pill to swallow.

THE PADRES COME HOME TO FACE THE CARDINALS in a three game series beginning tonight at Petco.

SHORT HOPS:

THE D-BACKS BEAT THE GIANTS AT T-MOBILE, 5-1...OHTANI WENT DEEP FOR LAA, as they whipped the A's, 8-3...STRASBURG DEFEATED THE MARLINS, 8-5, to give them a sweep in the series...THE BREWERS BEAT THE M's, 4-2...THE TAMPA TEAM did the honors as they turned back the Twins, 5-2.

QUOTE OF THE DAY:

Hickory Spinners Park:

It looked so solid in the black and white past,
Concrete grandstand, packed dirt infield,
The angel faced players warming up
Along the sidelines where summer grass
Sprigged through red sand beyond
The butt polished bench that was the dugout,
So we set out to find it someplace along
Where First Avenue becomes old 70
And all the neighborhoods are mill houses,
Haphazardly slapped beside potholed streets.
We looked and looked for something so real
Where games were played, championships won,
Bets made, and love pledged in on-field weddings
That were popular then, the couples promenading
Under raised bats at home plate. Up and down
Every street behind the great brick fortress
They called Hickory Spinners 1 where a procession
Of lintheads labored 75 years to spin
Enough yarn to shell this planet.

More Atlantis than Atlanta now,
Nothing left like that piece of fence
Where Aaron hit his homer,
No cornfield ghosts,
No sign of home plate,
Left field, or second base,
No invisible world
Beyond a hidden gate,
Waiting for those boys to reappear
In their proud flannel,
Shoe shined cleats,
Blue caps with white cursive H's.

BASEBALL NOTES — MONDAY, JULY 1, 2019

THE GREAT MAX SCHERZER THREW ANOTHER IMPOSSIBLE GAME, eight innings of one-run ball, striking out 14 batters and walking none.

Ridiculous!

He came into the game with a broken nose and he did not back down against the Tigers. Pitching for the world to see his luminescent; to behold his superiority as a hurler — the finest in the game of baseball.

And, yes, the Nationals won on a HR from Anthony Rendon in the top of the 8th.

All's well that ends well.

IN THE WORLD OF THE UNIMAGINABLE the Rockies split a four game series with LAD at Coors Fields, winning Friday and Saturday nights, 13-9 and 5-3.

They broke their 12 game losing streak Friday when they won and added to it the following game.

Roland Arenado was 6-16 in the four game set, including a HR.

THE PADRES DID NOT WIN SUNDAY, losing in 11, 5-3. They did win four in a row over the O's and Cards.

They're a supposing team. One of two NL teams with three sluggers on the ball club, as defined by 20 HRs — Renfroe, Reyes, and Machado.

And, in Fernando Tatis Jr., they may have the Rookie of the Year. There is nothing he cannot do.

The Padres play against Giants at
Petco.

SHORT HOPS:

THE NL/AL schedule calls for six games — KC vs Toronto (won by the Jays 7); Cubs vs Pittsburgh; LAA vs Texas; Milwaukee vs Cincy; Baltimore vs Tampa, and Padres vs SF.

QUOTE OF THE DAY:

Moor Park, Mooresville, NC:

Can't say I know what it looked like then,
When Jim Poole who played for Connie Mack
And coached for fifty years and, big Norman Small,
Who hit 336 minor league homers
Haunted these base paths.
Places have a way of growing bigger
Or getting tiny, depending on
Where you've been.
Picnic tables on concrete
Behind home plate,
Set of aluminum bleachers
On each baseline,
Perfectly manicured turf,
The kind of Piedmont, NC, red dirt
One remembers from childhood,
If it were here,
And if it was Hoyt Wilhelm
On the mound just after the war,
Honing his famous butterflies.

Now like most such venues,
It's college wood bat baseball,
It's players' girlfriends
And parents in slouch chairs
Drinking craft beer,
Eating hotdogs,
And a smattering of old guys wearing throwback Moor caps,
Who never stop chatting about the good old days,
And think that if they sit here long enough,
They can wish their way back,
And I'm with them.

— Tim Peeler, Poet Laureate of the Carolinas

BASEBALL NOTES — SATURDAY, JULY 6, 2019

HUNTER RENFROE WAS A SULTAN OF SWAT LAST NIGHT AND HIS HR IN THE 8TH DELIVERED A 3-2 PADRES VICTORY AT CHAVEZ RAVINE.

Hunter's my guy. Plain and simple. He's been my guy since he first came up.

He may hit 50 HRs. He may drive in 100. He's become a superb outfielder, one of the best.

But, the way in which the Padres have dealt with him strains credulity.

Two years ago they sent him to El Paso in August. All he hit was .500 plus and earned a return to the bigs.

A day-in-and-day-out of the lineup was frustrating in the extreme, but he, at last, has proven he belongs.

I've made two profound picks in my career.

One, was Steph Curry, when I saw him against Oklahoma in Norman and knew he would be an NBA all-star, and Trevor Hunter, the kid from Mississippi.

Let the good times roll.

QUOTE OF THE DAY:

The Minister was an Outlaw:

Glenn "Razz" "Preacher" Miller played

On Lenoir-Rhyne's College Field

Seven years before Pinkie

James, the town's Jim Thorpe convinced

The school to move the football

Lights so night baseball was born

In my hometown—the coach had

Found Razz in his daddy's field,

Muddy and ready to do

What it took to leave the farm,

And he roamed the dark outfield

’26 to ’29,

Trained to teach, then trained to preach,

The caption printed underneath

His photo in the yearbook

Said, “To study little,

To worry less

Is my idea

Of happiness.”

— Tim Peeler, Poet Laureate of the Carolinas

BASEBALL NOTES — SUNDAY, JULY 7, 2019

OH, YEA! WE DONE DID IT. THE PADRES TOP LAD, 3-1.

Hunter and Margot hit HRs and scores less was Fitzpatrick through five and a two-thirds.

The second night in a row the Padres beat the Dodgers thanks to number 27 off the bat of Hunter and they have a chance to win the four game set.

And, get back to .500.

THE RED SOX WON AT DETROIT CITY, 10-6, as outfielder Benintendi had four base hits in his slump.

It was a game arranged against a four oh five pm start but did not get under way until much later.

A night game.

Yes, a night game.

THE MAJOR LEAGUE LEADERS IN MVP ARE THE ANGELS' MIKE TROUT AND THE BREWERS' CHRISTIAN YELICH, so says the LA Times Andy Mccullough.

QUOTE OF THE DAY

THE SECOND ROUND OF OPENING DAYS IS AHEAD, which means the chosen few will have the high honor of throwing out the First Pitch.

Every president save Donald Trump has had that honor, led by FDR, who did it eight times, followed by Harry Truman, seven times, and Calvin Coolidge, on six occasions.

But the president who may have been the most knowledgeable about America's Game, other than George W. Bush, was Richard Nixon.

Three items about that:

"I don't know a lot about politics, but I do know a lot about baseball."

"I never leave a game before the last pitch, because in baseball, as in life and especially politics, you never know what will happen." – Richard Nixon on America's Game

"This isn't a guy [President Nixon] that shows up at season openers to take bows and get his picture in the paper and has to have his secretary of state tell him where first base is. This man knows baseball." - Dick Young, New York Daily News
Baseball Notes — Monday, July 8, 2019

One.

Two.

Three.

Three of four took the Padres from the Dodgers since 2004 at Chavez Ravine.

Holy cow. Way to go Padres.

And as sensational as even, in the field and at bat, was a 20-year old wiz kid named Leonard Titis Jr., who merely hit two HRs.

The Padres, in winning three straight, restored .500 ball at the break and are likely to end up winning 93 games.

THE RED SOX WON ALL THREE FROM THE HORRIBLE TIGERS AT DETROIT CITY and go into the break at 49 wins and 40 losses.

Rafael Devers hit 4-15 and was 1-11 for his last ABs.

THE YANKEES LOST TWO IN A ROW TO MIGHTY TAMPA and went to the break at 57 wins and 31 losses.

The Rays have four starters in the rotation with ERA all under 3.00, led by Charlie Morton, who heads the way with 10.

THE NATIONALS WHO WON AGAIN FOR THE 47th TIME AGAINST 43 LOSSES AND CLAIMED CREDIT FOR THE NL'S THIRD BEST THIRD MARK, despite the start — and who made it by a 5-2 victory.

QUOTE OF THE DAY:

"In 1933 CINCINNATI REDS an outfielder Chick Hafey blooped a single to center field for the first hit in an All-Star Game…" — Baseball Digest

This is the final entry of George's Baseball Notes.

As a closing word, this blog entry from Dick Flavin's MUSING, dated July 4, 2021,
And Mr. Flavin's Elegy for George

By Dick Flavin
Boston Red Sox Poet Laureate
and New York Times Best Selling Author

GEORGE MITROVICH'S MAN HUNTER RENFROE

Last December, when the Red Sox signed free agent Hunter Renfroe to a modest $3.1 million dollar contract (if 3.1 million bucks can be deemed "modest," and in baseball terms that's just what it is), I didn't pay much attention. The deal is only for one year and Renfroe is under Red Sox control for three years. It seemed at the time to be just a minor part of a major remake. After all, General Manager Chaim Bloom was busy wheeling and dealing and trying to rebuild the team that nosedived into the cellar of the American League East in 2020, and picking up a guy who'd hit only .156 in 2020 for Tampa Bay didn't seem to be the answer. Sure enough, for the first month of this season Renfroe wallowed well below the Mendoza Line, but for the two months since then he has hit above .300 with good power and a knack for coming through when the chips are down. In addition, he's turned out to be a terrific outfielder with a strong, accurate throwing arm. Did I mention that he's fast and a really good baserunner? Anyhow, he's the real deal, at least he is so far. Tampa Bay gave up on him after his lousy year in 2020. But there were extenuating circumstances in 2020. It was a lousy year for a lot of people – and not just ballplayers.

Renfroe would not even have been on my radar scale had it not been for my late, lamented pal, George Mitrovich. A man of boundless energy, George ran the City Club of San Diego, the Denver Forum, and the Great Fenway Park Writers Series and also found time to write a blog called "Baseball Notes" which appeared daily during the season except when he was on the road to or from somewhere, which was not uncommon. George passed away two years ago this month and I still miss him and his "Notes." They were a round-up of the day's events in baseball, complete with his comments, including the late games played on the West Coast. A facile writer, he'd type out his "Notes" after the games in the West were over, so those of us back East would find them on our e-mails first thing in the morning. The schedule didn't leave time for much (or any!) proof reading, and sometimes he'd get a score or a fact wrong, but that never seemed to bother him too much – he was on to the next day's project.

Anyhow, it was through "Baseball Notes" that I first became aware of, as George referred to him, "my man Hunter Renfroe." He (Renfroe, not George) broke in with the San Diego Padres in 2016, and for a while he shuttled back and forth between the big league club and its minor league affiliate in El Paso. Sending him back to the minors was something George, a lifelong Padres fan (dating back to its days in the Pacific Coast League) couldn't understand. He was convinced that Renfroe was big league material and made no bones about it in "Baseball Notes."

When George first started writing about Renfroe, I thought he must have had him confused with Hunter Renfrow, the wide receiver for the Las Vegas Raiders of the NFL. It's not a common name, after all, and how many Hunter Renfroes can there be who are also elite athletes? It turns out there are at least two, though they are not related and the football guy's surname ends with a 'w' and the baseball guy's with an 'e.' There is one other way to tell the difference between them: the baseball guy is built like football player (6' 1" 230 lbs. and very muscular), while the football player looks better suited for baseball (5'10" 185 lbs.), he's more a Mookie Betts body type.

Incidentally, have you been following Mookie since he signed his 12 year, $365 million contract with the LA Dodgers? The last time I checked, his batting average was under .250 with 10 home runs and 29 RBIs, well behind Renfroe's line of .272, 12 homers, and 43 RBI. This is not to say that Renfroe is the better player – at least not yet. But he's a whole lot better than 1% of the player Mookie is, which is all the Red Sox have invested in him so far.

Something seems to happen to players once they hit pay dirt with the big contract. It's not that they consciously let their foot off the gas pedal a bit, it's just that the pressure is off. Financially, their future is secure. If Mookie, perish the thought, should suffer a career ending injury, those paychecks with lots of zeroes and commas in them will keep on coming. The drive that pushed him to the very top is no longer there. He has already arrived there.

Will Mookie Betts ever have another year like the one he had in 2018, when he batted .346 with 32 homers, 129 runs scored and won the MVP? Possibly, but he sure as the dickens won't have a dozen of 'em, and that's what his pay scale calls for.

Overpaying ballplayers for extended periods is a fact of life with which teams must deal. Even Dustin Pedroia, who signed a contract extension back in 2013 calling for him to be paid an average of $13 million a year for the next eight seasons, thought at the time to be a bargain for the Red Sox, saw it become a burden when he couldn't play for its final four years due to his chronically-injured knee.

Will the Red Sox be faced with a repeat of the public relations disaster they confronted when Betts was traded in early 2020, when Rafael Devers reaches free agency? The moment of truth is only two and a half seasons away. Some team, desperate for a power hitter, will certainly be willing to overpay him. What will the Sox do? Sign him to a long term deal before free agency hits? Trade him while they can still get some value? Let him walk?

The decision is complicated by the fact that George Mitrovich's man Hunter Renfroe will be a free agent after the 2023 season, the same year that Devers is.

SO LONG, GEORGE

How did you and George first meet?
Did he greet you on the street?
Perhaps you waited on his table,
Or had a friend within his stable.
Or was it at a speakers' forum
Which he led with such decorum?
Did you read his Baseball Notes,
Or Facebook blogs, with all those quotes?
Whatever way your lives did blend
This is a fact - you had a friend.
He loved us all with his great heart.
He raised friendship into an art.
He cared for everything, you see -
Well, maybe not the GOP.
This much is certain, among men,
We shall not see his like again.
So let us bid him fond adieu;
So long, George. We love you, too.

—Dick Flavin, Poet Laurette and Senior Ambassador, Boston Red Sox.

ABOUT THE EDITOR:

Tim Peeler is a retired educator from Western North Carolina. He is the author of twenty books which include three volumes of baseball poetry and three regional baseball histories.

www.ingramcontent.com/pod-product-compliance
Lightning Source LLC
Chambersburg PA
CBHW081147090426
42736CB00017B/3224

* 9 7 8 1 9 5 2 4 8 5 8 4 8 *